Regulation and Inequality at Work

This book examines how the law has limitations to the extent that it can combat repression, isolation, and inequality. The main point the book explores is that isolation and inequality cannot be solved by driving up wages and having better working conditions. The true divide between management and workers is the inability of management to see the workers as people, and not just numbers. As the Swiss novelist Max Frisch remarked once, "We imported workers and got men instead." This encapsulates the dilemma of management— how to distance oneself enough from workers to command respect, yet not too distant as to be seen as inhumane. How can isolation and inequality within the workplace be overcome?

Regulation and Inequality at Work shows how workers can have an increased voice by using tools outside of the typical legal ones. Without state protection, the rights can be viewed as less stringent. Working outside the system allows for greater malleability and flexibility to be able to cater to individual workers in individual workplaces. Workers' rights are about better working conditions, hourly wages, and benefits, but are also about being treated in a more civilized manner where one's humanity is recognized. Only through all of these parts working together will a true version of workers' rights emerge—one where workers are not viewed as mere tools, but within and of the system itself. It shows the latest state of knowledge on the topic, and it will be of interest both to students at an advanced level, academics, and reflective practitioners in the fields of business and company law, labour law, and employment law.

Vanisha H. Sukdeo is a PhD Candidate at Osgoode Hall Law School in Toronto, Ontario, Canada. Vanisha currently works as a course instructor at Osgoode Hall Law School. Vanisha was called to the Ontario Bar in 2007 after completing her articles with Ryder Wright Blair & Holmes LLP, and the Ontario Public Service Employees Union (OPSEU). She received her LL.M. from Osgoode, LL.B. from Queen's University, and her Bachelor of Arts from York University where she majored in political science. Vanisha taught at Osgoode Hall as a Course Director for five years before becoming an adjunct professor at Western Law. In 2012, Vanisha was a nominee for the Ian Greene Award for Teaching Excellence, which is a University-wide teaching award.

Vanisha's first book contract was with UBC Press for a book titled *Best Interests of the Corporation': Whose Interests Matter?* that focuses on how the BCE (*BCE Inc. v. 1976 Debentureholders*) decision from 2008 has changed corporate governance in Canada. She looks at the movement from shareholder primacy model to stakeholder theory actualized. Her email address is VanishaSukdeo@osgoode.yorku.ca

Routledge Research in Corporate Law

Available titles in this series include:

Legal Approaches and Corporate Social Responsibility
Towards a Llewellyn's law-jobs approach
Adaeze Okoye

Disqualification of Company Directors
A Comparative Analysis of the Law in the UK, Australia, South Africa, the US and Germany
Jean Jacques du Plessis and Jeanne Nel de Koker

Beyond Shareholder Wealth Maximisation
Towards a More Suitable Corporate Objective for Chinese Companies
Min Yan

Corporate Law and Financial Instability
Andreas Kokkinis

Behavioural Risks in Corporate Governance
Regulatory Intervention as a Risk Management Mechanism
Ngozi Vivian Okoye

Indonesian Company Law
Soonpeel Edgar Chang

Regulation and Inequality at Work
Isolation and Inequality Beyond the Regulation of Labour
Vanisha Sukdeo

Regulation and the Credit Rating Agencies
Restraining Ancillary Services
Daniel Cash

For a full list of titles in this series, please visit www.routledge.com

Regulation and Inequality at Work

Isolation and Inequality beyond
the Regulation of Labour

Vanisha H. Sukdeo

Routledge
Taylor & Francis Group

LONDON AND NEW YORK

First published 2019
by Routledge
2 Park Square, Milton Park, Abingdon, Oxon OX14 4RN

and by Routledge
52 Vanderbilt Avenue, New York, NY 10017

First issued in paperback 2020

Routledge is an imprint of the Taylor & Francis Group, an informa business

British Library Cataloguing-in-Publication Data
A catalogue record for this book is available from the British Library

Library of Congress Cataloging-in-Publication Data
A catalog record for this book has been requested

ISBN 13: 978-0-367-58875-5 (pbk)
ISBN 13: 978-1-138-32342-1 (hbk)

Typeset in Galliard
by Apex CoVantage, LLC

This is dedicated to my mother and my sister who have always encouraged and supported me. Their love and endorsement have existed since I can remember, and I am grateful that it continues to thrive.

Contents

Acknowledgements   xiii
Overview of the book   xiv

1   **Historical Background**   1
North America 1
The Divergent Paths of Corporate Law and Labour Law 1
Brief Historical Background of the Corporation 2
Winnipeg General Strike 5
  Labour Strikes 5
  Background to the General Strike 6
  Socialist Sympathy as a Cause of the Strike 7
  Growing Communist and Socialist Sympathy 7
  Communist and Socialist Literature 8
  The Role of the SPC 8
  The One Big Union 9
  Another Cause—Soldiers Without Jobs 9
  Sedition 10
  Trial of Russell 11
  Trial of the Other Strike Leaders 11
  Trial of Dixon 11
  Release From Prison 11
  Andrews and the Committee of 1000 12
  Criminalization of Workers Struggles 12
  The Role of the Police in the Strike 12
  Sympathy Strikes 12
  Aftermath, CCF 13
Workers in Developing Countries: Is an
  Obligation Implied or Imposed? 13
The Specter of the Specter of Marx 13

Workers' Plight 15
   1800s 18
   1900s 19
   2000s 21
   Nike 23
   Arm's Length Exploitation 24
On the Factory Floor 25
Neoliberalism and Ontario Laws in the 1990s 27
Canadian Legislation—The Ontario
   Government Under Harris 28
   Bill 7 (1995) 28
   Bill 31 (1998) 31
   Bill 139 (2000) 31
Bibliography for Chapter 1 37

**2   Current Structure of Labour and
Employment Law**   **41**
Canada 41
   Right to Strike 41
   Background 42
   Where does the Right to Strike Get its Legality? 42
   Section 2(d) of the Charter 43
   The Labour Trilogy 43
   B.C. Health Services 43
   Natural Justice 44
   The Right to Strike—How Important is It? 45
   Recognition Strikes 45
   Collective Bargaining and the Charter *45*
   Framework of Fairness Agreement 46
The Framework of Fairness Agreement 46
Criticism of the FFA 49
   Sam Gindin's Critique of the FFA 49
   Other Critics 50
Works Councils and the German Model 51
   The German Model 51
Factory Occupations 52
The United States 52
   Precarious Work 53
Independent Workers? 53
Employees, Workers, or Something Else Entirely? 59
Everyone's a Critic—Yet No One Is in Charge 60

Let Me Talk to Your Manager—Wait,
   You Don't Have One? 60
No Manager? Who Trained You? 61
   Who Is Immune? 62
Wavering Work 63
   Gigging the Economy: What's Old Is New Again 64
Platform Capitalism and the New Economy 65
Labour Platforms 66
Uber and Seattle 68
Uber Loses Its License in London 68
Capital Platforms 70
Workplaces and Work Spaces 71
   Open Offices 72
   No Workplace and Just Space 72
   Technology and the Ever-Lengthening Chain 72
Bibliography for Chapter 2 79

3   How Can the Law Be Changed   82

Legislative Framework 82
Fiduciary Duty to Workers 83
   Fiduciary Duties 83
      How Traditional Corporate Governance
         Has Failed Workers 85
      Corporations as Citizens 86
'Good Corporate Citizen' versus
   'Good Samaritan Corporation' 87
   Good Samaritan Corporation 88
   Layering Governance 89
Employer Free Speech 89
Increasing Labour Standards on a Worldwide Level 93
   International Labor Organization 93
Transportable Law/Portable Law 95
Collective Agreement as Certification Scheme 96
   Consumer Autonomy 97
Unifor and Community Chapters 97
Worker Voice 98
Governance Models 98
Codes of Conduct as Tools to Increase Workers' Rights 100
Codes of Conduct 102
Codes Versus Certifications 106
Codes as Corporate Reformation 107

Governance 107
Ethics Codes 108
   The Gig Economy or the Rig Economy? 110
Isolation and Inequality 110
Bibliography for Chapter 3 115

4   Transnational Labour Regulation   119
Marxism 120
Marxism and the Law 120
Marx's Theory of Alienation 123
Beyond Marx 124
Distancing 124
Compassion Fatigue 125
Enlightened Self-Interest 125
Dignity and Respect 125
Kindness and Empathy 125
   Pro-Friendly 126
Collectivity 126
My Model Code of Conduct 127
Model Code of Conduct 130
   1. Forced Labour 131
   2. Child Labour 131
   3. Wages and Benefits 131
   4. Overtime 131
   5. Working Hours 131
   6. Working Conditions 131
   7. Health and Safety 132
   8. Harassment 132
   9. Discrimination 132
   10. Environment 132
   11. Freedom of Association 132
   12. Monitoring 133
   13. Access to Facilities 133
Monitoring Agencies 133
   Worker Rights Consortium 134
   Fair Labor Association 135
Bibliography for Chapter 4 139

5   Conclusion   141
Codes of Conduct 142
   Disruptor and Disruption 143
Reserve Army of Labour 143

Emotional Labour 144
Organizational Justice 144
There Are Limits to the Law 145
Expansion of Fiduciary Duties 146
Not OK Computer: Automization and the Worker 147
Luddism 147
Not Just Numbers, They Are Men (and Women) 148
Bibliography for Chapter 5 149

Index   151

Acknowledgements

I would like to thank Brianna Ascher and Routledge staff for accepting my book. Brianna's help and support in getting my work to completion has been greatly appreciated. The support and guidance I have received from Routledge has been more than expected. I truly value the time and effort of everyone who is a part of bringing my book to production.

I would also like to thank my friends who have endured me talking about the gig economy as well as isolation and inequality.

Thank you to my former students who make me proud of their accomplishments and their ongoing thirst for knowledge.

Thank you to the reviewers of the book proposal who enabled me to create a better product than I envisioned at the early stages. I have embraced 'Marxian light' in every incarnation.

What moved me to write this book was my desire to help workers in every form of work to create better working conditions. From the lowest wage earner to the highest income bracket, every *worker* is fighting for the same thing—to be treated humanely and fairly while at work. To have one's voice not merely heard but acknowledged and included. As well as the possibility of having one's life work align with one's life passion. To wage slaves everywhere, I hope this book helps to further the discussion about work at its very core as well as how to increase the rights of workers for individual workplaces, work spaces, and the broader society. For those who toil, suffer, and strain, my work attempts to enable you to gain better working conditions, while also helping one's humanity thrive. Workers have to come together to create a better world. I know such a world is possible:

> *And the little screaming fact that sounds through all history: repression works only to strengthen and knit the repressed.*
>
> —*The Grapes of Wrath*[1]

Note

1 John Steinbeck, *The Grapes of Wrath* (New York: Penguin Books, 1976), 249.

Overview of the book

This book is about the regulation of labour, but also about the limits to the law regarding how work is governed. This book examines how the law has limitations to the extent that it can combat repression, isolation, and inequality. The law can be used as a tool to help in the fight towards social justice; however, society and culture more broadly must be changed so true transformation could be actualized. The law does not exist in a vacuum and is often a mirror of society rather than the reverse. The main point that I explore is that isolation and inequality cannot be solved by driving up wages and having better working conditions. The true divide between management and workers is the inability of management to see the workers as people and not just numbers. "The Swiss novelist Max Frisch remarked at the time, 'We imported workers and got men instead.'"[1] This encapsulates the dilemma of management—how to distance oneself enough from workers to command respect, yet not too distant as to be seen as inhumane. How can isolation and inequality within the workplace be overcome?

Note

1 Jagdish Bhagwati, *In Defense of Globalization* (New York: Oxford University Press, 2007), 208.

1 Historical Background

North America

Current North American labour and employment law originated from the *Master and Servant Act* in Britain in the 1800s. This was a compilation of laws that governed the relationship between employers and employees. As the name alludes, the employee or servant was to be loyal and obedient to their employer with severe consequences for not doing so, such as jail sentences of hard labour. It was used to stifle unionization until 1871, when the *Trade Union Act* was implemented in Great Britain and recognized the legal status of unions. In Canada, the "Trade Unions Acts of 1872 widely celebrated by contemporaries and later historians as marking the decriminalisation of labour unions."[1]

The Divergent Paths of Corporate Law and Labour Law

The underlying theories behind Corporate Law and workers' rights are divergent. The competing theories about Corporate Law explore whether the corporation is 'a nexus of contracts,' whether the corporation serves the public or its shareholders, the role of agency and whether directors and officers are merely agents of the shareholders.[2] The competing theories about workers' rights are as extreme as those promulgated by Professors Bakan and McNally to the less radical theories put forward by Professors Fung, O'Rourke, and Sabel. These scholars explore the extent to which workers are the main vehicle in society and how much protection they deserve due to the corresponding role—if they are major vehicles then perhaps they are more worthy of protection and may be worthy of a greater level of protection than other groups.

The Salomon Principle is derived from the UK case *Salomon v Salomon & Co Ltd.*,[3] which states that the corporation is a separate legal entity from its shareholders, directors, and officers. This gave rise to the term 'the corporate veil' that allows for shareholders, directors, and officers to gain protection from liability by being separate from the corporation itself. The legal distinction between the corporation and its directors and officers is important because without that separation, the directors and officers could be personally liable for the debts and expenses of the corporation. There is a provision in the *Canada Business*

Corporations Act (CBCA) that directors may be held liable for unpaid employee wages up to a certain amount.[4] While it may be said that in Canada directors and officers have fiduciary duties to the corporation, the duties to other stakeholders may be duties, but not fiduciary duties. To elevate all duties to the level of fiduciary duty will be to dilute all duties. Rather than elevate the corporate obligations towards workers to that of fiduciary, it is better to implement standards through other mechanisms available including legislation, caselaw that sets a higher standard, as well as soft law mechanisms that can be enforced by a third party. These are possible ways forward to allow for workers to have greater autonomy and influence over their place of work.

As noted by Ewan McGaughey, "[Marx] invented the language of the separation of ownership and control, which was later adopted by Berle and Means."[5] So perhaps there is not just a wide gap between corporate law and labour and employment law. The same separation that upset workers being alienated from their work product also lays the foundation for corporate governance theory about the separation of ownership by the shareholders and management by directors and officers.

Brief Historical Background of the Corporation

As noted by Professor Fenner Stewart at the University of Calgary Faculty of Law, the earliest Canadian corporations such as the Hudson's Bay Company were not corporations in the modern sense but instead can be thought of as British Royal Charters.[6] They did not contain the same distance between modern corporations and the government as these former 'corporations' were very much intertwined with the government that they worked for. This allowed the government to control the corporation's operations and determine where and how a corporation would be run. "A Royal Charter was an exercise of the Royal prerogative, delegating the Crown's power to those in the Sovereign's favor."[7] These British Royal Charters were essentially branches of the British Empire or the King or Queen themselves. Because these corporations could be made at the Crown's pleasure, the Crown had both the ability to grant a corporation a Charter to operate and rescind a Charter for whatever reason.

In the late 1800s, there were no standardized statutes on how to incorporate a business in Canada.[8] This means that there was no uniformity or predictability in how to start a corporation. The system lacked consistency, which may have been the intention: to make sure that the conditions surrounding incorporation are vague so that they can be implemented in a haphazard way and that those who were most loyal to the Crown would be able to have corporations. Also, the corporations were to remit profits and benefits back to the government, so there was no detachment between the corporation and the government of the day.

The corporation in the 1800s evolved to a creation that was more akin to the modern-day partnership. As noted by Professor Flannigan, at the College of Law, University of Saskatchewan, "[j]oint stock companies, unless they were formally incorporate, were general partnerships."[9] He harkens back to the notion that there is a division in the corporation between the owners (the shareholders) and the governance of the corporation (through the board of directors).[10] This remains true today. This separation of ownership and governance is essential in corporate governance as that it gives way to agency theory, which is the theory that the board is merely acting as agent for the shareholders as owners. Agency theory is contrasted with the 'nexus of contracts' theory, which ascribes to the model that the corporation is simply made up of various contracts flowing from one party within the corporation to another, which all meet through the corporation as an entity—that employees have an employment contract at common law and statutorily, bondholders have a legally binding contract, etc.

Canadian law is very much influenced by UK law, and Flannigan asserts that the UK Act in 1844 changed the very structure of corporate governance. "In the years following the 1844 introduction of the Joint Stock Companies Act there was a failure on the part of some judges to comprehend the transformation in fiduciary accountability that occurred when a partnership converted itself into a corporation."[11] The distinction between a partnership and corporation is quite considerable. In a general partnership, liability is spread across all partners with the limited liability partnership sheltering some blame from the partners directly. The corporation acts as a shield or veil for all members of the corporation—be it executives, employees, etc. The decision to move from partnership to corporation is a significant move, and the responsibilities and duties that flow from such a decision are vast.

Patrick Lupa, of Osler Hoskin & Harcourt, notes that "In *Dodge*, shareholders' [sic] complained directors had breached their fiduciary duty when they decided to allocate corporate profits to lowering the costs of cars and increasing employment opportunities within the community rather than paying out dividends."[12] *Dodge* is an American case that stands for the proposition that the Board of a corporation will run afoul of its duty to maximize wealth for shareholders if they choose to give money to the community for betterment projects. This was the beginning of the discussion about whether corporate philanthropy (a corporation giving money to charities and the community) is against agency theory and against the duty to maximize shareholder wealth. If directors are merely agents for shareholders and if shareholders only care about profits and dividends, then the decision to give money to charity or the community would not be in the best interests of shareholders as it would result in an instant loss for shareholders. This discounts the difference between short-term and long-term gains as although shareholders may lose that money at the time, it may result in increased goodwill and better branding, which may result in more consumers, higher profits in the long term.

The premise that spending money on causes that benefit society rather than constantly worrying about how to make shareholders richer was thought to be too progressive in the late 1900s, but in 2018, these values have shifted within society and the role that the corporation once played has grown to such an enormous size that the reach and strength of the corporation must be critiqued and examined. If corporations are to continue growing in size and power, then that same power must be checked. To allow corporations to grow to sizes that rival nation-states is not a service to all of humanity. The reason to study where the corporation began to how it currently exists to how it should exist is to examine where corporate law currently stands and how it should evolve to keep pace with modern society. The law should reflect the changing values and beliefs of a society, and the law should not be stagnant and unchanging. Cases like *BCE* has allowed courts to keep progressing and making corporate law more about equality among stakeholders and moving away from privileging shareholders. This movement will result in a more democratic corporation.

The link between corporate law and labour and employment law is not well explored as these connections are often left untouched. There seems to be a mistaken belief that these two areas of law are separate and distinct. Workers are a fundamental component of any corporation, and to leave these two areas divided and distanced is not wise. The congruence between the two is greater than the divergent. A happy worker is a productive worker and a productive worker helps create greater wealth for the corporation. These two divided areas should not remain divided. Hopefully future researchers keep studying the many linkages between corporate and labour and employment law.

Corporate law begins with the assumption that the corporation is a legal person and that it is able to enjoy similar rights and privileges as a natural person—perhaps including the right to life, liberty, and freedom of expression. Shareholders are thought to be the true owners of the corporation as their investment in the corporation allows for the corporation to function. Without that investment the corporation would standstill. The role of other stakeholder groups such as other investors like creditors and bondholders became more important in the early 2000s in Canadian law with the *Peoples* and *BCE* decisions from the Supreme Court of Canada.[13] These decisions, along with the increasing fight for greater corporate social responsibility (CSR), have changed corporate governance and the corporation itself. Now there are responsibilities for directors and officers to consider other interests beyond merely shareholders when making corporate decisions. This has helped create space for workers as another stakeholder group whose interests should be considered in the boardroom and beyond.

Workers have a very significant role to play in regards to corporate governance. At its very foundation, the corporation is driven by workers, and workers are able to shine light on bad corporate behaviour as well as give praise for good corporate behaviour (see Starbucks and its plan to pay for tuition for its workers who attend certain colleges). These ways of gaining goodwill from workers, but also positive media attention, means that workers are able to shape change by using media and getting their voices heard. This also raises certain issues: Whose voice gets heard? Which worker is given the microphone, and which is not? And who exactly is a 'worker'? This last question will be explored later in this book and is central to the discussion.

The discussion of Canadian labour history begins in 1919 at the beginning of the Winnipeg General Strike. From there, the study of the right to strike is explored as well as captive audience speeches. These Canadian topics are then followed by the worldwide experience of the gig economy. The phenomenon of isolation and inequality is explored, and solutions are offered to help workers gain improved working conditions, as well as greater recognition and respect for their humanity.

Winnipeg General Strike

This section will examine the Winnipeg General Strike ('the Strike') and its role in Canadian legal history. It will demonstrate that the Strike was an attempted revolution, which was a result of the ability of workers to unite and form an insurmountable force against management, however the effort could not be sustained. The use of sedition charges against strike leaders to stifle unionization and curtail the rights of workers will also be examined.

The strike is a tool that workers have used in the past to solidify their rights. Without the right to strike, workers would have to devise other methods of enforcing their rights. The recognition strikes in the early 1900s were groundbreaking for the workers' rights movement. The Winnipeg General Strike was a monumental event in Canadian legal history as it is the culmination of various events being brought together to the point of eruption. The return of Canadian soldiers from World War I and the accompanying short supply of jobs upon their return helped to create tumultuous times. The suspected increase of communist sympathies among workers of the world was feared by the Canadian government and law enforcement officials alike. To quell the increase of socialists and communists, the government implemented new measures and started to enforce existing measures more stringently. This resulted in a criminalization of union activity and the decline of the labour movement as a result. The control of a city by the workers is an act of rebellion and one that prompted Sam Blumenberg to state at the Columbia Theatre in Winnipeg "[w]e are going to run this city."[14] I will argue that the Strike was revolutionary and was not simply another labour strike.

Labour Strikes

The power of the strike, especially in the manufacturing industry, was critical. The ability to withdraw one's labour was detrimental to management who relied on the workers to produce goods. The ability of the strike to stop production was a financial penalty to management. The power of the strike used in the context of recognition strikes is truly important. The Strike started out as a recognition strike as the refusal of management to recognize the bargaining agent voted on by workers sparked the momentum that would culminate the Strike.

> The specific and immediate cause of the general strike was the refusal by the employers in the Iron Contract shops to recognize the demands of the workers for agreement by those employers on the method of collective bargaining indicated by the Metal Trades Council on behalf of the employees.[15]

The reason that workers were striking in the early 1900s was to get the employer to recognize the union, the right to have a union, not a specific template of workers' rights. "While employers could refuse to recognize and bargain with unions, workers had recourse to an economic weapon: the powerful tool of calling a strike to force an employer to recognize a union and bargain collectively with it."[16] The strike and the threat to strike are beneficial to workers who feel that their demands are not being met by management.

Background to the General Strike

The Strike lasted from May 14 to June 25, 1919. It was evident that there was a link to the strike and the return of soldiers from World War I. "When, on November 11, 1918, the Great War was finally over, the Canadian people, like people of all the other warring powers, faced the task of reconstruction."[17] The Strike occurred in a particular place and particular time: Winnipeg, 1919. Why was this? What were the actual causes of the Strike, and what was the original intention of the alleged strike leaders?[18] It is important to examine the events leading up to the Strike. The growth of socialism and the increased membership in the Socialist Party of Canada (SPC) and the International Workers of the World (IWW) were seen as attempts to overturn capitalism and replace it with a Soviet-style system. "In February 1919, about sixty thousand workers joined together in Seattle, Washington to spawn the first general strike in North America, described by Mayor Ole Hanson as a 'weapon of revolution.'"[19] The exact form that this alternative to capitalism would take is not clear as some of the alleged strike leaders were from different political parties and had different views and desired outcomes.

On May 14, 1919, at 11 a.m. the Strike commenced.

> Over 22,000 workers answered the strike call within the first twenty-four hours. The atmosphere was almost festive, the belief in ultimate victory strong. Few among them believed that they were starting on a long hard road because, after all, how long could the employers stand up to the united power of the working class?[20]

Ninety-four of 96 unions voted to strike. Only the typographers and police unions did not participate, as this was decided that they were needed to keep working in order for information to be put forth and in order to avoid martial law. "A general strike is an attempt to effect a massive and permanent shift in economic power from capital to labour. Once labour has attained this economic power, political power must follow."[21]

Not to get into a debate about semantics, but it is important to note that the Strike was not an actual revolution because it was not successful in that workers did not achieve a Socialist paradise. A revolution[22] would indicate a successful overthrow, while the Strike was more akin to a rebellion. A rebellion is defined as "1: opposition to one in authority or dominance; 2 a: open, armed, and usually unsuccessful defiance of or resistance to an established government, b: an instance of such defiance or resistance."[23] In Pritchard's speech to the jury, he stated that " 'Revolution' he said was used much more casually by labour men and usually meant nothing more than change, not violence and bloodshed."[24] It is interesting to note their own definition and what revolution meant to them. Three is also the term 'revolt,' which gets used in the discussion about whether the Strike was a revolution or not. "While a revolt is not necessarily a revolution, it is implicitly and overtly a challenge to the structures of bourgeois power and the forms of workers' subordination."[25] The author notes that Pritchard's definition is apt in that when people speak about a workers' revolution, they are not often speaking about the Russian Revolution, but instead a paradigm shift or something more subtle. The workers in Winnipeg did not want to shed blood. They wanted to strengthen the rights of workers by unionization or increasing knowledge about socialism, but not in a violent manner.

With the streets becoming chaotic, the scene was becoming a battlefield. The end of the Strike was nigh.

Socialist Sympathy as a Cause of the Strike

Ten men were eventually charged with seditious conspiracy, seditious libel, and common nuisance: Frederick John Dixon, William Ivens, William Arthur Pritchard, Robert Boyd Russell, George Armstrong, Roger Bray, Richard Johns, James Shaver Woodsworth, Abraham Albert Heaps, and John Queen. The commonalities between the men may have been not astounding, but they were likely more than the differences in that all of the men were left leaning. The SPC meeting on December 22, 1918, at Walker Theatre may have helped to shape the design of the Strike in that many of the men later charged were present and active at the meeting.

Growing Communist and Socialist Sympathy

The Canadian government feared a rise in socialism and communism. This was not merely a problem for the Canadian governments, but one that governments worldwide were dealing with, especially the American government, which would lead the charge against communism and the celebration of capitalism. Canada's close proximity to America brings with it positives and negatives, in the case of the Strike the proximity brought home the 'Red Scare'—the fear that the communists would invade or that the populous would turn to communism. The fall of capitalism was so feared and thought to be so in need of protection that the government began to criminalize behaviour that was deemed to be repressing capitalism, that is unionization. The thought that workers joining unions and fighting to increase their rights is akin to communism seems rather absurd today, but those past characters that we study remain just that: products of their time. The fear of the Bolsheviks was thought to be real at the time, and the actions to stop the spread of communism, while harsh, were thought to be necessary at the time. This is not to justify the behaviour, but rather to explain it and situate it in the times of the Strike.

Communist and Socialist Literature

Much literature and other written works were lead as evidence in the numerous trials that resulted from the Strike. This evidence was to support the Crown's position that there was a conspiracy and that the socialist and communist work that was being read by the men on trial would provide their guilt. When police came to raid Armstrong's house, his wife, Helen, gave in. Many newspapers and newsletters were put into evidence. Even personal correspondence by Russell was entered into evidence. This salutation obviously indicated that Russell was true to the cause and echoes of modern-day salutations of 'In Solidarity' that can be found on union letters.

> One remarkable feature of the trial now proceeding against the eight men arrested during the Winnipeg general Strike, and charged with seditious conspiracy; one which the labour movement would do well to take cognizance of, as being indicative of the nature of the prosecution throughout, is the production, as evidence, of leaflets, pamphlets, standard works, etc.[26]

At Pritchard's trial, his address to the jury on March 23 and 24, 1920 echoed of his socialist values. This statement while believed to be true may have helped to further the jury's finding of guilt. Not only did the men read this literature, but they believed in its truth.

> The dominance of the Communist party in the UAW at this time was supreme. In fact, so influential was the party that the international headquarters in Detroit would ship the weekly edition of *The United Automobile Worker* to Communist party headquarters on Adelaide Street in Toronto to be distributed to the various UAW locals in southern Ontario.[27]

The literature that one owned was thought to prove that if one read such material one must not only believe it, but seek to make its preachings come to life. Not only must one be a Marxist by reading *The Communist Manifesto,* but one must be secretly striving to create a socialist and onward toward communist utopia. This was all that was needed to convict.

The Role of the SPC

The SPC was gaining members in the early 1900s, and it was causing an uneasiness among those who owned and controlled the means of production. If workers banded together and united to form unions, then the fall of capitalism must surely come next. This was the way in which people seemed have thought in the time of the Strike. Perhaps, they cannot be blamed for that way of thinking with the success of the Russian Revolution very new in everyone's minds. The 'Red Scare' was thought to be real. Pritchard, who joined the SPC on May 23, 1911,[28] felt that teaching the ways of the SPC and studying the work of Marx among others would lead the workers towards salvation. Without socialists to lead the way, the workers would be driving towards nothing. There is no point in having a plan without a goal. The SPC gave workers a plan, something that the Strike could be aimed towards and something that would be lasting. However, this would become reality when strike leaders would go on into politics after their release from prison.

> Methods had been suggested by many theoreticians, among whom three of the most prominent were Lenin, Bernstein, and Sorel. Each had advocated the destruction of the capitalist system, the first by violence, the second by parliamentary means and the third by the use of the general strike.[29]
>
> The radicalism of the IWW was different from that of its contemporaries, the Socialist Party and the Socialist Labor Party. . . . The Wobblies' critique, however, went beyond the socialists' concern for a more equitable distribution of wealth. It was a broader attack on power and privilege as well. Their view, known as syndicalism, held that workers' control was the essential element of socialism, and that the state was as much the enemy as capitalism, for the two were inseparable allies.[30]

The One Big Union

The preachings of the SPC were linked to the discussion of the One Big Union (OBU). The SPC first preached the idea of the OBU. Even the move from craft unions to industry unions was gaining headway, the success of the OBU could have been furthered. "The OBU was planned as the first large-scale Canadian experiment in 'industrial' unionism. Workers would henceforth be organized into one organization, rather than many restricted crafts."[31] The goal of the OBU was to unite workers from various fields into one union, the metal workers would be in the same union as the carpenters, etc. "The SPC did not regard the general strike as the ultimate weapon in the class struggle. They never discussed sabotage. They sought, instead, to build an inclusive united working class movement, the One Big Union, simply as the next stage in the class struggle."[32] The exact design of the OBU is debatable. The membership of the SPC, while growing, was still rather exclusive. The strength and sense of optimism felt by those in the SPC and OBU could not be underscored enough as they felt they were working towards a just and fair end, whatever the means may be. However their hopes were dashed as the Strike grew to an end.

Another Cause—Soldiers Without Jobs

The reasons behind that time and place must be examined. Canadian soldiers were just returning from war.

> And surely the 60,000 Canadians who had died in the mud of Flanders had not sacrificed themselves in vain. Out of the ashes of war, most Canadians

believed, would emerge a just society. To many workers, the triumph of the Soviets marked the beginning of the end of the exploitation of their class.[33]

While class struggles may have been thought to subside, the reality was a shortage of jobs due to the return of the soldiers from war.

Sedition

The sedition trials were used to stifle workers' rights by intimidating workers with threats (or the actual) laying of criminal charges arising from labour disputes. One effective, albeit unjust, way to curb unionization and the labour movement is to make criminal what is essential to the movement—the rising up of workers against management to increase their rights. "Charged with offences ranging from seditious conspiracy and inciting to riot down to common nuisance. . . . All were socialists of various shadings, or liberal social reformers."[34] Once this behaviour becomes criminal, it may lead to a decrease in occurrences. "No law was passed ordering workers back to work or prohibiting them from striking in the future. Strike leaders, however, were arrested and charged with seditious conspiracy, raising the question of whether a general strike was lawful."[35] The effectiveness of making certain offences criminal indicates to the perpetrator and society at large that the offence is severe. "Labeling misconduct as 'criminal' attaches to the offence a greater stigma than labelling it as a 'regulatory' offence. It sends a symbolic message to the wrongdoer, other potential wrongdoers, and society at large that the misconduct is most egregious."[36] Although the quotation is taken from the Securities law realm it is relevant as it portrays the severity that attaches to criminal offences.

> Most of the confusion in this area of law is attributable to the fact that sedition has two distinct meanings, one ancient and one modern, based on differing views of the proper relationship between the governors of society and the governed. The development from the one to the other has been succinctly summarized by Mr. Justice Rand of the Supreme Court in the leading Canadian case on seditious libel, *R. v. Boucher*.[37]

The definition of sedition had been left vague purposely so that government would have an unfettered ability to charge people with the offence without making it clear.

The current version of the *Criminal Code* still contains a section on sedition. The section 59(1) of the *Criminal Code* states:

59 (1) Seditious words are words that express a seditious intention.
And section 59 (4) states:
Without limiting the generality of the meaning of the expression 'seditious intention,' every one shall be presumed to have a seditious intention who

(a) teaches or advocates, or

(b) publishes or circulates any writing that advocates,

the use, without the authority of law, of force as a means of accomplishing a governmental change within Canada.[38]

This use of the *Criminal Code* as a way to punish those who speak against the status quo is a way of 'othering' the labour movement and its participants. To say that those who were fighting for the rights of workers in the Strike were basically committing acts against their country makes them seem unpatriotic and villainous.

Trial of Russell

The Court of Appeal upheld the decision[39], and his appeal to the Privy Council was denied. At Russell's trial evidence was lead that his actions at the Walker Theatre meeting helped to build on the outrage already felt by many. The sedition trials were used to curb unionization and the threat of communism. The fact that criminal charges were laid against former strikers indicates that the police and/or government saw the movement as a true threat.

Trial of the Other Strike Leaders

The other seven would face trial together. Bray, being a returned soldier, was only convicted of common nuisance. His sentence being shorter than his co-accused. The legacy of the Strike will be that the actions of its heroic leaders were eventually brought to face criminal charges. But the fight continued as criminal courts and the legal system will not be able to stifle the drive for workers to increase their rights.

Trial of Dixon

Dixon was tried separately from Woodsworth as Russell was tried separately from the other seven. Dixon was able to ground many of his arguments in free speech and freedom of the press. His arguments seemed more grounded or accepted by the jury than the arguments put forward by Russell and the group of seven others.

Release From Prison

When the six were released from prison, their notoriety increased. While in prison, many of them had been elected to political office. Also, unlike Russell, they had not filed for parole because by doing so would be admitting guilt. The legacy of the strike leaders would live on, whether they were thought to be revolutionaries or not.

Andrews and the Committee of 1000

The lawyer who would eventually act for the Crown at the trial, Andrews, was also an elite businessman and formed a group to help combat the Strike. The Committee of 1000 were formed to help end the Strike. The manner in which Andrews conducted the trial seemed rather loose or rather that he appeared to have untrammeled powers.

Criminalization of Workers Struggles

An effective way to curtail workers fight for rights is to criminalize behaviour that once expressed in regard to the labour movement becomes criminal—sedition charges against union organizers.

The Role of the Police in the Strike

The formation of the RCMP as result of the Strike was interesting because it really ties back to the link of labour strikes to criminal behaviour in that the strikers were thought to be criminals or maybe quasi-criminals.[40] After the police union voted to strike but were told to keep performing their duties to avoid chaos, they were eventually asked to sign a no-strike clause. When they refused, they were replaced with strikebreakers (in common vernacular, scabs).

When one looks to cases such as *Baron Metals* in modern-day society, it may often be that management uses criminal means to oppress, threaten or scare workers.

> In *Baron Metals*, the Board found that two days before the union applied for certification, the employer hired two "employees" well known within the Sri Lankan community as Tamil gang members with violent, criminal backgrounds. . . . They threatened employees of Sri Lankan descent with physical harm, even death, for supporting the union. The employees who were threatened, believed the threats and were quite frightened.[41]

While this may not be a common occurrence, the fact that it still does occur in society makes one aware that violence during labour disputes or simply in the workplace may flow from either side: union or management.

Sympathy Strikes

Sympathy strikes are strikes that occur because of a display of solidarity with another union who is on strike. The sympathy strikers are not actually in an industrial dispute but showing support for their fellow union members. The Strike was actually a sympathy strike. This is to be noted because it displays solidarity.

Aftermath, CCF

After the Strike was long over and the prisoners released, the Strike had a lasting effect. Some of the effects were very positive, as many of the strike leaders were elected to political office. In the 1920 Manitoba provincial election, 11 labour candidates won seats. Four of them were strike leaders. The impact of not just the Strike, but the legal implications and conclusions that can be drawn from the trials of the Strike leaders, is indelible.

Workers in Developing Countries: Is an Obligation Implied or Imposed?

Workers in certain countries face horrendous working conditions including being subjected to micromanagement about bathroom breaks, constant drug testing, and working in unsafe buildings. There are also studies that document women working in sweatshops being forced to take pregnancy tests and are fired when they test positive.[42]

In April 2013, 1,100 workers died in the disaster at Rana Plaza in Bangladesh. This incident brought to light the unsafe working conditions that many workers around the world face—the individual workplace may be hazardous in the form of dangerous machinery, but the building itself may be unsafe.[43] In some situations where workers are overworked to the point of fatigue they may become depressed and sometimes suicidal. In the case of the Taiwanese-owned factory in China where there were many suicides rather than address the underlying problems of overwork the owners installed safety nets for workers when they jumped.[44] Incidents like this should not be tolerated, and the fundamental problems about overwork and worker exhaustion should be dealt with before things become dire rather than waiting for workers to turn to self-harm.

Workers are denied basic rights such as limits to working hours, but also more advanced rights such as organizing and collective bargaining.[45] Wage increases and greater workplace safety legislation alone would not help workers escape from isolation and inequality. For critical theorists such as Marx, the legal system aids alienation as it sets up employers and employees as opposites when maybe the fact that they are people who should bridge some gap helps to foster alienation because it helps to distance two people in certain relationships. Both the employer and employee suffer as a result. Workers should have their voices heard in the governance of their workplaces to feel a sense of fulfillment that cannot be achieved through simply increasing wages and having better working hours. To help these workers whilst being in another country the best way to help them is to attach liability at the site of the corporation rather than changes to domestic law from people beyond the borders.

The Specter of the Specter of Marx[46]

Looking at workers' rights in a Marxist context allows for the fundamentals of workplace governance to be explored. If the basic contract of work is unfair then everything that flows from it must also be unfair. Similar to Locke and Rousseau and their theories about social contract, there is Marx's theory of the wage contract. The wage contract sets out that trading one's labour for wages is necessary and inevitable. So in certain ways the gig economy has allowed for the freeing of work and its constraints to a particular workplace and particular working hours. However at the same time workers have been forced to do without certain basics such as a set workplace, predictable working hours, health benefits, and perhaps job security itself. This duality cannot be simplified to state that all gig economy workers are being abused or misused, but rather that it is a spectrum where some workers choose such 'freedom' and others are forced into the gig economy due to lack of options.

The treatment of workers by management is important as a topic of study, but also worthy of study is the treatment of workers by those they work for beyond the employment relationship—customers, the public, citizens, students, etc. While your boss is the person who you report you to, who you work for is not a constant in the same manner. Someone who works in the retail industry has the direct supervisor, the corporation for which they work, and customers they serve. Someone who is a teacher works for the government, but also the public more broadly, and the students they teach are the people they work for. These are not static boundaries, but it is important to notice the flow of power and how energy gets distributed.

While employee Y has to listen to his or her supervisor, he or she has to serve the customers. This unit is not constant as customers will vary every day.

Those who choose to work within that system pursue it for a variety of reasons. It cannot be said that there is one truth that works for all gig economy participants. The statistics about those who work in the gig economy suggest that it is often the young, racialized, and other typically undervalued workers. So, to act like the gig economy is about freedom to surf during the day and drive Uber at

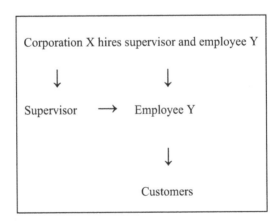

Figure 1.1 Chain of instruction and accountability

night is a false promise of freedom. What does that mean for the job prospects for those who are gig workers? Does being out of the typical workplace for too long mean that one is shut out forever?

> The gig economy is the collection of markets that match providers to consumers on a gig (or job) basis in support of on-demand commerce. In the basic model, gig workers enter into formal agreements with on-demand companies to provide services to the company's clients.[47]

So, if the workers who drive your Uber or you rent your AirBnB from are left out of the typical economy, should you as a consumer be blamed? Can the demand for Uber be attributed to bad cab services? Or to people wanting a viable alternative and perhaps cheaper alternative? Did the gig economy sprout out of the desire for richer individuals to be catered to? Or the less wealthy being forced to perform jobs that are on the outside? Can the poor be blamed for their plight? Or does the blame lie elsewhere? "As Prime Minister Indira Gandhi once remarked tellingly, it is hard to lift oneself up by one's bootstraps when one is too poor to be wearing boots."[48]

To move from unawareness about working conditions and the difficulties that underprivileged people face worldwide towards greater understanding, there needs to be more information available and shown to those in positions of power to make changes. By informing directors and officers about potential problems along the supply chain and who at the end of the chain is actually making the product and the conditions that individuals deal with at work will enable those privileged people to make better-informed decisions. That knowledge alone might not change their decisions, but at least they will be speaking from a place of knowledge rather than an uninformed one. If one knows about the suffering of workers and chooses not to act, then that is a different position than being unaware. This would allow for directors and officers to make better decisions because they decisions would be better informed and reasoned.

Workers' Plight

Workers have struggled for their rights against management since the advent of the wage contract. Workers have been forced to fight for every single advance in their rights as none have been given to them. The struggle is ongoing. From the fictional depictions of workhouses in *Bleak House*, Welsh coal miners in *How Green Was My Valley*, and American Oakies in *The Grapes of Wrath*, workers in fiction have been portrayed as being mistreated and sometimes abused at work. These fictional depictions are based on real-life experiences of workers in those time periods. While seeing children working in the garment factories of England and the farms of California may have gone away, those same working conditions still remain for some workers. Workers in coal mines still face harsh working conditions due to the very nature of the work itself. Farm workers are still exploited

in rural areas of Central America to make sure that the best fruit are able to deco-
rate North American kitchen tables. Workers are literally sweating in hot factories
in Honduras lacking proper ventilation to make sure that your t-shirt from the
mall is only $5.

The differing critiques of workers' rights vary from the right-wing argument
that wages should be driven by supply and demand, and when a worker is willing to work for a low wage, that is simply the workings of the marketplace.
Right-wing critics also argue against the 'Fight for 15' arguing that increasing
the minimum wage will drive away business. The critique from the left would
be that within a capitalist system, workers are forced to sell their labour to make
sure that they can get the needed money to buy the goods and services they need
from food and shelter and so on. Marx also comments that capitalism creates
alienation, which is the distance between workers and management. I will elabo-
rate on this later in the chapter. The underlying political issues behind workers'
rights and the societal issues that keep back workers are important, but the focus
of this book is on the legal mechanisms and extralegal ones that can be utilized
to help increase the rights of workers. I suggest both hard law mechanisms and
soft-law mechanisms that can be used to increase protection for workers and
allow them to have more input in corporate decisions through the use of stakeholder theory models that allow for greater participation for stakeholders, which
includes employees.

Workers are not a homogeneous group, and they can be divided into groups
along the lines of unionized workers versus non-unionized workers, public sector
workers versus private sector workers, and white-collar versus blue-collar workers. Workers in these various settings have different interests and needs. Workers in factories may place a priority on ensuring that the machinery they use to
work is safe and that their health is not being compromised, whilst office workers may place emphasis on guaranteeing more advanced rights such as paid sick
leave. Workers in factories are also concerned about proper ventilation and having enough washroom breaks. These differing problems can be as advanced and
mundane as compassionate leave to care for an elderly parent to workers being
forced to take pregnancy tests in a factory and face termination if they are found
to be pregnant. These different worlds of work expose diverse problems for each
subset of workers across the landscape, while offering few solutions. While workers in faraway lands may still be fighting for protection against long hours without
breaks, the more advanced rights for workers in Ontario are different: "Precarious work has increased by 50% in the Greater Toronto/Hamilton Area over
the past 20 years, and less than half of workers hold a permanent, full-time job
with benefits."[49] Canada and Ontario more specifically are not immune from the
changing nature of work. This decrease in full-time employment and the loss of
stable unionized jobs is not only occurring in the factories in developing countries, but in Canada as well. The decline of the auto industry in Southern Ontario
has lasting impacts on the Canadian economy. Marx coined the term "reserve
army of labour" to describe how Capitalism needs a certain percentage of workers
to be unemployed to keep wages down. If there is always a reserve army of labour

waiting to work for lower wages, then the market is able to flourish. If everyone was employed, then maybe workers could argue that they should be better paid for providing labour, but if that same worker sees someone over their shoulder waiting to work that job for less money than that keeps workers happy to have a job, while also keeping them compliant.

The rise of the gig economy and precarious work more broadly has led to full-time positions becoming part-time as well as lower benefits for workers. Work that was once well-paid and full-time has now become part-time and piecemeal, and stagnant wages are forced on to workers because they fear losing their jobs to outsourcing. The decline of manufacturing and in particular the auto industry has meant that those workers in those positions must find new work and their children who thought they could grow up to get their jobs must start anew.

The true divide between management and workers is the inability of management to see the workers as people and not just numbers. "The Swiss novelist Max Frisch remarked at the time, 'We imported workers and got men instead.' "[50] This encapsulates the dilemma of management—how to distance one's self enough from workers to command respect yet not too distant as to be seen as inhumane. How can isolation and inequality within the workplace be overcome?

After Rana Plaza, there were two competing governance models put forward to help secure workers from experiencing such a tragedy again. These competing models are both soft law instruments and the true strength comes from the enforcement mechanisms. The agreements themselves are merely reporting mechanisms if they lack strong enforcement structures and punishment those who breach the agreement. They should make sure that these agreements are not merely PR stunts to help protect Joe Fresh, Loblaws, etc. Workers need rules about proper safety equipment, hours of work, wages, and so on. These need to be codified in a tool that can be enforced targeting the corporation rather than rely on the laws of the nation where the factory operates. Making the corporation, the target is necessary, and forcing liability to attach to the corporation is the purpose of the code of conduct.

Migrant workers who come from other countries to work in Canada for seasonal work such farming are in a very vulnerable position as they are only able to stay in Canada while they are working. The working conditions that they face can be long hours performing manual labour, isolated from their family and friends. They also often live on the farm, so they are geographically isolated from others as well—almost plantation style. And because they are usually far away from family and friends, thus they are both socially isolated and geographically isolated.

I will look at the historical background of workers' rights in North America, as well as briefly touch on important historical incidents such as the Winnipeg General Strike and the Labour Trilogy from the Supreme Court of Canada (SCC) in 1987. I will also discuss *BC Health Services*, a SCC case from 2007. The Strike and caselaw are used as milestones in the fight for increased workers' rights from the criminalization of union activities in the past to the denial of rights for workers under the *Charter* in the 1980s. I then discuss the labour and employment legislation enacted by the Ontario government under Mike Harris, who became the Premier of Ontario in 1995. These Bills set back workers' rights in Ontario. I also explain what a Marxist critique of the labour law system would entail. I then discuss the rise of the gig economy which is a threat to both Canadian workers and workers in other nations. These are current issues of contention for Canadian workers.

Workers in Canada have a higher level of protection from hazardous or dangerous work including the right to refuse such work compared to workers in developing countries. However, they should not be complacent. Their rights could be further protected as there is room for improvement, and there are certain issues that impact workers' rights worldwide such as the distance between management and workers. This 'inequality and isolation' can be alleviated through specific mechanisms such as increased communication between the two sides. The inclusion of workers' voices and input about their working environments will allow both sides to have a better workplace. These varied topics in the area of labour and employment law in Canada will showcase the problems for workers but also the progress that has been achieved in the fight for workers' rights. The rise of the gig economy in Canada and elsewhere has created a new era of workers' rights which is decentralized. Rather than workers in full-time stable jobs fighting to belong to a union or greater protection outside the union setting, workers are now facing very uncertain times. Precarious work in the gig economy leads to workers not having set working hours, working in unsafe workplaces (and potentially on the boundaries of the law in the case of Uber and whether it is operating in compliance with the law).

I also discuss the plight of workers in other nations beyond Canada, who are tasked with producing goods for the North American market, but do not enjoy the same level of protection as the North American worker. Actually, sometimes the law on the books in these nations is relatively strong, but the enforcement mechanisms are not in place. The level of abuse suffered by these workers generally is far worse than workers in North America. However, just because workers in North America have better protections and rights does not mean that the situation is ideal. There is always more protection available for workers and greater control of their own work environments to possess.

1800s

Workers in the 1800s faced harsher conditions than current day, but that does not mean that current day workers live a utopian existence. There has been immense improvement since those days, but there still remains room for continued improvement.

Early cotton mill workers were pushed into the mills not by preference but by desperation and a lack of alternatives. Little skill was required for most jobs in the textile factories, so many workers were children from the 'poorhouses' who were sent by the parishes to earn their keep. Work in the cotton mills meant that children could be economically self-sufficient from the age of five.[51]

These sad stories were commonplace back in those times when children would be sent to work at factories to make sure that their families did not starve. Children were expected to earn their keep. In garment factories children were used to do dangerous tasks that only their small fingers could handle. Having a union to protect workers and restrict working hours was not likely due to union activities being criminalized or stigmatized as being too left leaning. Also, governments did not step in to enact legislation to protect workers in those days. With the advent of legislation to limit working hours and provide safety standards, workers have gained some protection from management. The 1800s was also before the advent of the welfare state, so if families were not able to provide for themselves, they would literally starve to death. With the introduction of a welfare system, families were able to provide enough to eat and a place to live and did not have to send their children to work in dangerous workplaces. Furthermore, workers may no longer face the same odds of losing hands, arms, and maiming as they did in the late 1800s, but factory work can still be quite dangerous. Workers still face higher risk of cancer if they are exposed to asbestos at work and other work hazards that are cancer causing.

Workers have made gains, but there is still much to be gained. The progress made by workers to avoid certain health and safety challenges continues to exist today. Stage collapses at music concerts still leave workers dead and injured;[52] workers stranded on the outside of buildings working as window cleaners still die and get injured.[53] While accidents can be reduced and never completely be gone, these incidents show management cutting corners to save money, and the end result is death for workers. There is a difference between an accident and a preventable accident. Workers pay the price. Sometimes with their very lives.

While progress is being made, the struggle goes on and on. Workers who fought for a 40-hour work week and better health and safety protections see those gains eroded by the replacement of full-time jobs with part-time jobs and contract work. Those gains are being diminished by the changing nature of work and the very loss of the title of 'worker.' If one is not a worker, then the protections in place for workers are unavailable to that person. They get caught in semantics and suffer the real-life consequences.

1900s

Workers in the beginning of the 1900s were not that much better off than workers in the 1800s. The slow increase in the acceptance of unions couples with the introduction of health and safety legislation allowed workers to access greater protection and helped to ensure safer workplaces. In developing nations there was a lag behind the developed world.

In the 1990s, Nike became the target for activists who claimed that they hired underage workers, violated safety requirements, etc. "Nike initially had responded to the barrage of criticism by saying, in essence: 'We don't own this problem. These are not our factories. . . . We simply buy their products.' "[54] Nike's insistence that it owes no duty to workers who produce their goods but are not employees of Nike rings hollow. With the rise of CSR and supply chain accountability, corporations are no longer able to distance themselves from abuses in factories that produce their goods—employees or not. Progress may be slow but seems to be coming. "The 1990s introduced a new phase in the history of global markets and market actors, exemplified by the expanding reach and role of multinational corporations."[55] The 1990s, also saw the rise of Students Against Sweatshops. This movement is larger in the United States where the market for college team merchandise is much larger than in Canada (think simply about the NCAA Championships). The group 'Students Against Sweatshops,' which sprang up across university and college campuses across North America, can be credited with bringing more attention to the anti-sweatshop movement alternatively called the 'sweatshop-free movement.' Once a school implements a code of conduct, it is ensuring that items bearing the university's logo are made under fair working conditions. The university usually adopts a Code of Conduct, which governs the relationship between the university and its suppliers and sub-suppliers. While it is generally thought that sweatshops are a developing world problem, this is not true as the working conditions even in certain parts of North America are horrendous. "The purpose of transnational protest is to connect corporate image with labor practices in order to improve the latter."[56] While sometimes activists in developed nations can lend their voice to those in developing nations, it must be noted that those trying to help must not force their values and ideals on to the others and have to avoid being paternalistic. The rise of CSR in the 1990s leads to questions about how best to regulate corporations in light of the power they hold on an international level. Even when schools implement a code of conduct, there must be a monitoring system that works well to ensure compliance of the code. The student movement fighting against sweatshops was quite successful as evidenced by the number of schools that are now 'No Sweat' campuses.

> Students across the US [the United States of America] have won public disclosure agreements from their administrations which require licensees to disclose factory locations. This relatively recent demand for public disclosure has been surprisingly successful (and would not have been predicted even two years ago).[57]

And attached to this new wave of codes is the monitoring system. How best to monitor the code can be described as: "They [Posner and Nolan] note that there are four critical characteristics in the monitoring process: 1) applying measurable, meaningful standards; 2) independence of monitors; 3) transparency in reporting; and 4) incorporation of local nongovernmental organization (NGO) and union dimensions."[58] The introduction of a code is important and is best served when there is also a monitoring system in place. There must be a form of compliance and a remedy for breaching the code.

2000s

The early 2000s saw the continued rise in CSR and more consumers caring about the products they purchase being made under fair working conditions as well as being ethically sourced. These two steps in the supply chain are equally important—both involve the use of labour from mining and picking cotton to sewing garments in factories.

The weight of monitoring the supply chain is of the utmost importance as each step in the process must be guaranteed sweat-free or made under fair working conditions. The image shows how the supply chain has dipped back into how the cotton farms are operated. As noted by Professor John Ruggie in his seminal text *Just Business: Multinational Corporations and Human Rights*, it is important that supply chains be rigorously managed to maintain that not only the worker who pieces together the end garment is working under fair working conditions, but also the worker who made the buttons and zippers in the first place and "most recently they have begun to address working conditions on cotton farms."[59] This backward looking process from the standpoint of retail companies like Gap and Nike means that they have to look backwards to how the products are sourced. The Civil Society Coalition on Garment Industry Transparency is made up of the Clean Clothes Campaign, the Workers' Rights Consortium, Human Rights Watch, Maquila Soldarity Network, etc. They devised a "Transparency Pledge" that corporations could use to make sure that they adhere to a certain standard. Without going into too much detail, the pledge forces companies to give all needed contact information for all factories used, the parent company, workers numbers at each site, and so on.[60]

The rise of the gig economy has allowed for workers who are seeking full-time employment to at least be making money on a smaller scale through picking up gigs. As noted by TD Economics in January 2017, there is a part-time conundrum in Canada as the report notes that although there have been solid employment gains, they are "solely part-time positions".[61] The report goes on to note that there have been job losses in energy-producing provinces due to the decline of the industry.[62] Alberta and Saskatchewan suffered from the lower costs of oil and the decline of the potash industry. In Canada, the manufacturing industry had slowly eroded to be replaced with jobs in the service industry. It used to be

Table 1.1 Codes and Enforcement

	Strong Code	Weak Code
Strong enforcement	Most effective	
Weak enforcement		Least effective

odd to see anyone besides teenagers and college students to be working at Starbucks or McDonald's, but is now commonplace. This change in the economy has a rippling effect on other sectors. The auto industry was intertwined with the steel industry, etc. The pace of job growth seems stalled as well. The job rate will slow and most of the new jobs are merely part-time ones not full-time.

So even with the decline of better paid manufacturing jobs with lower-paid service industry jobs the job rate is still bad. If every factory worker became a fast food worker that is still not ideal but even that is not the case—factory workers can remain unemployed. This forces workers into the gig economy to at least make a little money. "'The gig economy . . . is now estimated to be about 34% of the workforce and expected to be 43% by the year 2020,' Intuit [owner of TurboTax] CEO Brad Smith said."[63] It is difficult to determine how many giggers work full-time as giggers or just part-time as giggers. Also, some people may have 9–5 jobs and do gig work on the side. So it is a difficult number to determine in the absolute because of all of these differences. Also, it is difficult to determine how much of a worker's income is derived from one gig source. And the lack of full-time jobs may lead to lower salary per year compared to someone with full-time employment.

> As of 2015, 53 million Americans work as freelancers. Freelance workers and independent contractors earn 17% more per hour than conventional full-time employees. They will earn 28% less over the course of their career, however, because they work fewer hours.[64]

As mentioned earlier, the research shows that most of these workers do not enter the gig economy out of pure volition, but out of necessity. "Nearly 20 million gig workers do the work because they can't find better pay or jobs elsewhere, McKinsey found."[65] This is an important motivating factor to consider why workers enter the gig economy through choice or simply out of need.

So, what options are left for workers who lose full-time factory jobs to be replaced by part-time service industry jobs? Perhaps they also join the gig economy to pick up a "side hustle" of driving Uber. Uber's growth rate has been astronomical. Uber was started in 2009 in San Francisco and now operates in 600 cities in 81 countries. New Year's Eve 2016 Uber provided 15 million rides.[66] The growth of Uber costs taxi drivers fares as direct competition but is also linked with the decrease in stable jobs as more giggers turn to this new source of income. This continued rise of giggers is alarming. As noted by Professor Jeremias Prassl "As of August 2016 McKinsey's Global Institute estimate that numbers of workers for platforms ranged from 5000 Deliveroo drivers and 25,000 TaskRabbit service providers to 1 million Uber drivers and 12.5 million Upwork users."[67] And the money made by being a gigger is offset by the costs of being an independent worker who has to provide their own tools to work—a car, gas, and insurance in the case of Uber. The money made by Uber drivers is a pittance.

> Once all cost are subtracted, hourly wages quickly fall, often too far below minimum wage levels: spot checks of New York Uber drivers reveal takehome

pay of as little as $3.99 per hour or even a net financial loss (against a minimum wage of $ 10.50 in NYC).[68]

It is shocking that workers may be making less than minimum wage in North American cities like New York and Toronto once they account for the costs of operating their gig work. The overhead attached to work is not small. It is the case that "there are about 4 million quintessential gig workers, research from Intuit and Emergent show. They expect that to grow to 7.7 million workers by 2020."[69] So not only are part-time gig jobs the current wave, but economists expect that trend to continue on to 2020. This is alarming for people who care about workers' rights and people having stable, well-paying jobs.

In the transnational realm, workers face the problem of retaliation from management if they try to enforce their rights.

> When garment workers who are at the center of the transnational protest campaigns have been blocked from resolving their grievances, advocacy groups have stepped in and used their privileged networks, citizenship status, and access to language to carry out campaigns in support of labor rights.[70]

In some countries workers face severe consequences if they try to organize. This harkens back to the 1800s in Canada when workers were seemed deemed to be 'servants' of their 'masters'.

Canada is often compared to the United States and the unemployment rates between the two countries is not that far apart.

> Adjusted to the concepts used in the United States, the unemployment rate in Canada was 5.6% in May, compared with 4.3% in the United State. In the 12 months to May 2017, the unemployment rate fell by 0.3 percentage points in Canada and by 0.4 percentage points in the United States.[71]

The United States and Canada both suffer from the decline of the auto industry and the loss of manufacturing jobs overall. When someone used to be able to work for $20 an hour in a factory, and make even more if they could drive a forklift, the appeal of a job in fast food for minimum wage seems grave.

Nike

Nike has been covered endlessly perhaps not because they exploit workers more than the typical amount, but because they are such a large corporation. It may be the case that they are overobserved, and researchers have spent so much time on Nike and its working conditions.

> As early as the 1980s, Nike was criticized for sourcing its products in factories and countries where low wages, poor working conditions, and human rights problems were rampant. Then, over the course of the 1990s, a series of

public relations nightmares-involving underpaid workers in Indonesia, child labor in Cambodia and Pakistan, and poor working conditions in China and Vietnam—tarnished Nike's image. As Phil Knight lamented in a May 1998 speech to the National Press Club, 'The Nike product has become synonymous with slave wages, forced overtime, and arbitrary abuse.'[72]

So, Nike must change its image of being a sweatshop-using corporation to continue the best talent at the executive ranks and to make sure that consumers still buy their products. This is leaving aside 'what is right' and what is responsible as a separate ethical issue to be dealt with.

> In the mid-1990s, a variety of labor abuses came to light in factories that produced shoes and apparel for the Nike Corporation. Charges of underage workers, coerced or forced overtime, safety violations, and generally poor conditions began to surface, especially in factories in China and Indonesia. The factories, while supplying goods to Nike, were independently owned and operated. As a result, Nike argued, it bore no responsibility for conditions in its suppliers' factories.[73]

This goes back to Nike's argument that it cannot be responsible for its supply chain. But gone are the days when corporations can be willfully blind to the exploitation that occurs in factories where goods are produced for their corporation. " 'To some, the Nike swoosh is now as scary as the hammer and sickle'—Thomas Friedman, NY Times, 1999 'Foreign Affairs: The New Human Rights.' "[74] The new era of CSR and business ethics demands that corporations pay attention to its supply chain and ensure that workers are not being exploited at any stage in the process from sourcing materials to producing the garments in factories to shipping the goods to the North American market.

Arm's Length Exploitation

I thought I coined the term 'arm's length exploitation,'[75] but it has already been used in different circumstances. I use it to describe the phenomenon of companies that while not directly exploiting workers, they hire/contract with/ outsource, etc. with others who do exploit workers (the direct exploiters). This allows company A to escape liability because they are the not the actual wrongdoers, but they hire/contract with/outsource, etc. with company B who are the direct exploiters. A common example of this is Nike.

> Nike does not own any of the factories which manufacture its sports shoes or apparel. Direct control and regulation are thus not feasible. Instead, Nike must manage a network of over 350 factories around the world (employing approximately 500,000 workers) through incentives, suasion, and occasional sanctions.[76]

This allows for corporations to escape liability due to the distance between the corporation and the exploitation.

On the Factory Floor

Looking at governance mechanisms such as codes more generally, it can be argued that they do not fit with collective agreements as there is much overlap which leads to redundancy. Codes perform best when they act alone, not in combination with a CA. Codes can provide basic rights to workers who do not have the protection of a union. They can allow for those same workers to have a complaint-based process by which management is bound to listen to workers' concerns and try to remedy problems. Workers can be a useful means by which health and safety issues on the factory floor can be brought forward including problems which management might not be aware of due to not spending as much time on the floor. Professor Locke notes that the researchers affiliated with Oxfam and the Clean Clothes Campaign state that supply chains need more than compliance but also need to focus on the brands themselves and how upstream practices shape what happens on the floor.[77] He also notes that having workers included in the governing of the workplace and increasing worker voice will allow for better governance and regulation of the workplace. As noted by John Witte: "Workers will desire more participation in decisions directly related to their jobs and immediate working environments, and less participation in higher-level management decisions."[78] Workers gaining more freedom over their workplace will result in happier workers, which is linked to better output from the workers. Management may be able to get more from their workers simply by keeping them happy.

The ability of the law to shape corporate behaviour is an area that needs to be studied further. However, the power of the corporation itself may make it less of a regulatory target. The corporation as selective in its choice of which law to follow may be the result of efficient breaches where it is easier to pay a fine for not complying rather than paying the cost of compliance.

> Despite the oft-cited David vs. Goliath metaphor, anti-corporate activities pose a considerable threat to TNCs. Even if one assumes that corporations actually 'rule the world' (Korten 1995), their rule may well become self-defeating, as they then become a natural target for transnational social movement activities.[79]

While corporations may become greater targets for activists, that does not necessarily entail that activists are successful in reducing the power that corporations hold. Altering corporate behaviour is not the same as reducing power. While it may be said that the activists hold some power to get the corporation to change, it does not mean that the corporation's power has been reduced.

With the degradation of state-centred governance models, the move towards private regulation in the form of corporate regulation may be growing.

> In the absence of a global system of law, global norms cannot be as formal or binding as legal norms. Rather, they are part of a rather loose system of 'soft law' that is produced and elaborated by means of public discourse. The fact that world society remains a stateless (and thus, in some sense: a 'lawless') polity does not imply that there are no norms at all.[80]

If those in power enact laws that maintain that power the same can be said of corporate power. If corporations hold power akin to governments, then they may be able to push off formal regulation mechanisms in favour of soft law approaches. This in turn allows for corporate engagement in that activists can choose to have corporations become allies in their cause.

I will examine three different groups of workers: (1) Canadian workers working in Canada, (2) workers in other nations who are working for Canadian companies, and (3) migrant workers, those who are not Canadian working in Canada. The three different groups have some overlapping issues such as wages and working hours, and some differing concerns about immigration status, etc. The first group will be discussed with a focus on the Harris government in the 1990s and early 2000s. I then go on to discuss current problems facing workers such as the loss of full-time stable jobs that have been replaced by the gig economy, which is comprised of part-time unstable positions (ex. driving Uber). The second group will be discussed with an emphasis on the working conditions in Asia and other developing regions. These workers are still fighting for basic rights such as limits on overtime, etc. The third group will be discussed in light of the *Dunmore* decision from 2001.

The corporate code of conduct allows for a layer of governance to be included internally within the corporation. Having a code of conduct in place will allow these workers in the least protected segment that I look at to enjoy an increased level of governance and protection that would be otherwise absent. Legislation can accomplish the increase in wages, but it would be difficult to enact legislation that allows for isolation and inequality to be lessened, as the problem of isolation and inequality exists beyond the legal realm.

The distinction between 'basic rights' such as working conditions and more 'advanced labour rights' such as the right to strike and bargain collectively is important because workers in other nations are often still fighting for basic rights

Table 1.2 Categories of workers

	Canadian Citizen	*Non-Canadian*
Working in Canada	Group 1	Group 3
Working for a Canadian company	Can also be Group 1	Group 2

without the luxury to be concerned about advanced rights. The right to strike and withdraw one's labour is important.[81] Even in Canada in the early 1900s, it was not illegal to strike, but strikers faced harsh penalties that sometimes got inflated by claims about sedition.[82]

I use 'isolation and inequality' to describe a phenomenon akin to Marx's theory of alienation wherein both workers and management are left to view the other as somewhat of an enemy and forces the two sides to be distant and stop relating to each other as human. Marx's theory of alienation goes deeper than workers achieving mere wage increases and working fewer hours. Alienation, Marx argues, separates workers from other workers, from their manager, from their product and from themselves. Marx argues that in order for the worker to be truly free they must escape alienation. "The alienation of the worker in his product means not only that his labour becomes an object, an external existence, but that it exists outside him, independently, as something alien to him, and that becomes a power of its own confronting him."[83] For Marx, because of alienation, capitalism will never allow workers to have true freedom, and true freedom would only entail freedom from alienation, nothing less. This distance between workers and management can be bridged if workers are able to feel appreciated and acknowledged in the workplace. There have been studies that show that when workers are able to contribute to the workplace governance, they are more productive and morale increases.[84] This is a win-win situation for both workers and management. This allows for workers to have their voices acknowledged and included, while allowing management to adopt some of the ideas that encourage better productivity. These changes can be as simple as workers suggesting, which are the best safety shoes to wear to how to cut down on absenteeism in the workplace. Increasing morale has been shown to decrease absenteeism, and this is good for both workers and management alike.

Neoliberalism and Ontario Laws in the 1990s

Canada is not safe from the international rise of neoliberalism. Mike Harris was the Premier of Ontario from June 26, 1995, to April 14, 2002. The Harris government's rise to power led to the OPSEU strike in February–March 1996, where correctional officers were on strike for weeks. Labour legislation in Ontario under the Harris government will be discussed more in depth later on. From labour injunctions to halting picketing to back-to-work legislation aimed at striking workers, the law has often been on the side of management against labour. Management is able to turn to the courts and law more generally to take up their cause against labour.

> This brings us back to the Harris government's application for an injunction. It was losing or, at best, not winning, the political struggle. Given the way in which law favours the rich and disadvantages workers who try to use collective power, it is hardly surprising the government reached out to the court for help.[85]

As noted by Professor Glasbeek, the workplace is not immune from politics; actually; it is one of the most political environments at least how the workplace is governed is linked to the political ideology in power. Harris tried to justify the suppression of workers' rights by claiming that Canada had to remain competitive on the world market. But if all nations subscribed to this theory then a race to the bottom would become reality. If all nations support workers' rights, then no nation would feel the need to suppress its own citizens to increase profits; if all nations raised the standards to an appropriate level, then no nation would be made to start the erosion of rights in the name of profit.

Canadian Legislation—The Ontario Government Under Harris

The enactment of Bill 7, Bill 31, and Bill 139 by the Ontario Progressive Conservative government under Mike Harris changed labour laws to the detriment of workers across Ontario. Labour laws in Ontario were not ideal prior to the Harris government; however, they were vastly eroded after Harris left government. The enactment of Bills 7, 31, and 139 by the Harris government was to increase 'democracy' in the workplace. However, the effects have been to diminish workers' rights so that true democracy is stifled.

Prior to the enactment of Bill 7, Ontario had in place Bill 40 (under the New Democratic Party) which allowed workers' easier access to unionization. Bill 40 allowed for card-based certification given that at least 55 percent of the bargaining unit has signed union cards. Remedial certification was also in place, which gave the Labour Relations Board of Ontario the power to certify a union in the face of severe tampering of the organizing drive by the employer. These provisions allowed for workers to sign cards without their employer knowing, which allowed them to make a choice without threat of coercion from their employer. The enactment of Bill 31 removed the opportunity to sign cards without the employer knowing and further opened up the organizing drive to be influenced by employers.

Bill 7 (1995)

When the *Labour Relations Act, 1995* ("Bill 7") was enacted, the November 3, 2000, headline for the *Globe and Mail* was 'Ontario aims new law at unions' and *The Toronto Star*'s headline was 'Ontario renews war with unions.'[86] These seem to say that the government was biased when it chose to enact Bull 7, not that it was 'demoractizing' the workplace as claimed. The major changes enacted under Bill 7 include that

> When a trade union applies for certification, a representation vote will be required in every case in which more than 40 per cent of the employees in the prospective bargaining unit appear to be members of the union. If the union loses the vote, it will not be eligible to reapply for certification for one year.[87]

A strike vote was also imposed; this was to take power away from the union to call a strike and instead have workers decide by voting to strike. This may on the surface seem reasonable, but sometimes union officials know from past experience what is best to do in certain situations, not the workers. To make the union's ability to strike almost void is to deny an essential component of organized labour. As Pierre Elliott Trudeau said, "it is the possibility of the strike which enables workers to negotiate with their employers on terms of approximate equality."[88] To further disregard workers' rights to associate, the *Agricultural Labour Relations Act, 1994* was also repealed. This seemed to solidify the stronghold that owners have over their workers by denying the most vulnerable, migrant workers, the basic rights granted to other workers. If democracy was a true concern for the Harris government, then this Act would not have been repealed.

> The Harris government asserted that its reforms made the certification process more 'democratic'. . . . In order to be democratic, a vote must take place in a setting that is free from coercion and intimidation. The workplace is not such a place.[89]

To neglect the power imbalance that exists in workplaces is to condone the power imbalance. To be 'neutral' under an oppressive framework is to condone it. The imbalance that exists must be acknowledged, and legislation should be built to limit that imbalance.

The purpose of the enactment of Bill 7 was to curtail workers' rights to organize and decrease unionization. The card-based certification system, which had been in place since the 1950s, was eliminated and replaced by mandatory certification votes under Bill 7. This allows employers time to spread anti-union sentiment throughout the workplace when they become aware of workers trying to organize. Neo-liberalists argue that the 'invisible hand' will guide the market and that any injustices that arise are inevitable. But if the market is not truly free but masked as though it was, then what is to become of that theory? To deny the politicization of the economic sphere is to do an injustice to society at large. The beliefs that guide the market overlap with politics and every aspect of society.

The denial of workers' rights leads to lower rates of certification which is what the Harris government wanted but merely packaged as 'democracy.' For neo-liberalists equality entails "that all citizens have the same opportunity to engage in economic activity."[90] If the market were free and everyone were equal, then a just market would exist, but as long as there are connections and corporate profits is placed ahead of workers then any equality is merely an illusion. For true equality to exist, the workers would have real choices instead of artificial 'votes.' A vote does not truly matter if it is meant to cover true inequalities. Workers are often afraid to vote for the union because they are afraid of losing their jobs because owners sometimes make claims to allude to such. The only real choice a worker has is to choose among which owners he or she will sell their labour to.[91] This does not amount to true choice.

When Mike Harris became Premier of Ontario in 1995 he told Ontarians that he would enact changes that were outlined in his 'Common Sense Revolution 1994.' Harris told Ontarians that "there are more than half a million people unemployed in this province. The bottom line is that Ontario needs jobs."[92] One may disagree with this statement by countering that Ontario does not need jobs, but jobs that offer a decent living wage and allow workers the freedom to choose whether they want to unionize or not. Jobs alone are not the solution, instead *adequate* employment is. The Harris government also promised to

> repeal the NDP's labour legislation—Bill 40—in its entirety. Period. It's a proven job killer. We will replace it with a better, balanced labour law package that will restore the balance between labour and management. We will also shift the power from labour bosses to union members, restore individual choice and democratize internal union decision-making by introducing secret balloting for certification and strike votes.[93]

The promise to repeal Bill 40 in its entirety was upheld. The use of the word 'democratize' seems to be masking the true purpose of the provisions as they are taking away rights that workers once had. If a true democracy was to be achieved then Harris should have given workers a choice in the repealing of these laws. The neo-liberalist bias is evident in Harris' government, the laws he enacts and the actions that he makes. The decision to fire three vice-chairs at the Ontario Labour Relations Board midterm in October 1996 was held to be in violation of the requirement of 'just cause' under the *Labour Relations Act*.[94] When the government tried to appeal the decision, the Court of Appeal dismissed it. These vice-chairs were not terminated with cause, which leads one to believe that they were terminated due to political reasons, in that the Harris government did not like the decisions that they made. The enactment of Bill 7 is said to have set the labour movement back many years, as is told through numerous stories of past labour conflicts, as is the case of Kapuskasing.[95] Ontario labour laws had been progressing and allowing more freedom to unionize, but Bill 7 ended that progression. Canada ratified the International Labor Organization (ILO)'s Convention number 87 (Freedom of Association and Protection of the Right to Organize), however the Bills enacted under the Harris government go against that convention.[96] In a report by the ILO in 1997 it was noted that governments around the world chose to implement laws that curtailed unions:

> The report also says that in some case union membership is repressed for political or investment considerations. Some governments have 'adopted a restrictive policy with regard to recognizing unions in the hope of attracting foreign investment.'[97]

The last statement describes Ontario under the Harris government, which has hopes of attracting foreign investment by stifling workers' rights. By curbing freedom of association and making it harder to join a union, the Harris government was trying to adopt a global view of the workplace, which is not in the best interests of workers but of capital. Capital is more mobile than labour.

Bill 31 (1998)

In June 1998, the *Economic Development and Workplace Democracy Act, 1998* ('"Bill 31') brought further changes to the *Labour Relations Act, 1995*. The Harris government's repeal of the Board's power to order remedial certification came after the United Steelworkers of America–Canada (USWA–Canada) had succeeded in organizing a Wal-Mart store in Windsor. While it was quite a strong remedy, it was not often used. It served a dual role of rectifying unfair labour situations and trying to dissuade unfair labour practices (ULPs).

> The rationale for such a provision is obvious: first, once an employer has threatened the livelihood of employees if they choose to join a union, employees will never be able to join the union without the lingering fear that they shall be harmed. Second, the prospect of certification acted as a deterrent that prevented employers from threatening workers in the first place.[98]

Employers could also challenge the appropriateness of a bargaining unit or a union's estimates of the number of individuals in a proposed bargaining unit.

The essence of section 11, which gave the Board the power to order remedial certification, was voided with the implementation of Bill 31. Section 11 had been put in place to protect workers from fear of joining a union. If no remedy is available to properly correct this injustice, then what becomes of the union? If employers are allowed to commit ULPs and know that by doing so they are promoting fear and lack of support for the union unabated then what will stop them from doing so? Section 11 had acted as a preventative measure to help reduce ULPs. Instead under Bill 31, ULPs can be seen to be an efficient breach, as the penalty is not outweighed by the gain.

Bill 139 (2000)

The *Labour Relations Amendment Act, 2000* ('Bill 139') was enacted to allow for more information to be disclosed, this included listing union officers' salaries above $100,000 and information being posted in unionized workplaces on how to decertify. This requires employers in unionized workplaces to put up in the workplace a poster on how to decertify the union. It also requires that employers hand out that document to unionized employees once a year detailing the same information. "Bill 139 contains no parallel provision requiring the Minister to publish a document for non-unionized employees explaining how to join a union and to apply for certification."[99] The way in which labour is theorized in mainstream media tends to be anti-workers and workers themselves internalize neoliberal values, which act in direct opposition to their best interests. The worker is made to believe that working is a privilege and that they have to appreciate their job. This fosters an environment in which the worker is never made to feel quite worthy of his or her job and that they can be replaced at any time. This forces workers to behave in such a manner as to ensure employment and not to engage in activity that would cause the owner vexation.

The mandatory bar was changed to block not just the union that failed to get certification at a workplace, but also any union for one year after the failed attempt. The bar also tightened restrictions to say that no union could include an employee that was included in the past round of trying to organize. This forces unions to an almost standstill to wait out the one-year restriction, in which time workers may become less enthused about joining the union, as time is lost. The union also has to fund the organizing campaign to keep going through to wait out time to expire so that it can rally again.

Notes

1 Margaret McCallum, "Labour and the Liberal State: Regulating the Employment Relationship, 1867–1920" *Manitoba Law Journal*, 23(1996), 574–593, at 1.
2 For a comprehensive history of Corporate Law see Henry Hansman and Reinier Kraakman, "The End of History for Corporate Law" (2000), available on SSRN: <http://papers.ssrn.com/paper.taf?abstract_id=204528>.
3 *Salomon v Salomon & Co Ltd.* [1897] AC 22.
4 Section 119 of the *CBCA* allows for Directors to be personally liable for up to six-months unpaid wages.
5 Ewan McGaughey, "The Codetermination Bargains: The History of German Corporate and Labour Law" SSRN Online: <http://ssrn.com/abstract=2541877>, at 4: see footnote number 15.
6 See Fenner Stewart, "A History of Canadian Corporate Law: A Divergent Path from the American Model?" in Harswell Wells, ed. *The Research Handbook of the History of Corporate and Company Law* (Northampton: Edward Elgar, 2017), 8: "The Hudson's Bay Company was incorporated by Royal Charter on 2 May 1670. King Charles II granted the company an exclusive monopoly over an area that comprised approximately a third of modern-day Canada, as well as sections of present-day north-central United States. The company was given the authority to enact any laws and regulations in this area that did not run contrary to the laws of England, and served the purpose of maximizing profits for shareholders by "harvesting the natural resources of the empire" and maintaining "the interests of the crown by carrying out exploration, territorial expansion and law making." (Smandych and Linden, 1996)
7 Fenner Stewart, "A History of Canadian Corporate Law: A Divergent Path from the American Model?" in Harswell Wells, ed. *The Research Handbook of the History of Corporate and Company Law* (Northampton: Edward Elgar, 2017), 4.
8 Fenner Stewart, "A History of Canadian Corporate Law: A Divergent Path from the American Model?" in Harswell Wells, ed. *The Research Handbook of the History of Corporate and Company Law* (Northampton: Edward Elgar, 2017), 5.
9 Robert Flannigan, "Shareholder Fiduciary Accountability" *Journal of Business Law*, Issue 1(2014), 1–30, at 3.
10 Robert Flannigan, "Shareholder Fiduciary Accountability" *Journal of Business Law*, Issue 1(2014), 1–30, at 3.
11 Robert Flannigan, "Shareholder Fiduciary Accountability" *Journal of Business Law*, Issue 1(2014), 1–30, at 11.

12 Patrick Lupa, "The BCE Blunder: An Argument in Favour of Shareholder Wealth Maximization in the Change of Control Context" *Dalhousie Journal of Legal Studies,* 20 (2011), 1–34, at 4.

13 See Vanisha H. Sukdeo, *"Best Interests of the Corporation": Whose Interests Matter?* (Vancouver: University of British Columbia Press, 2018) (forthcoming).

14 *Manitoba Free Press,* 27 May 1918 as quoted in Craig Heron, ed., *The Workers' Revolt in Canada, 1917–1925* (Toronto: University of Toronto Press, 1998).

15 Manitoba, *Royal Commission to Enquire Into and Report upon the Causes and Effects of the General Strike Which Recently Existed in the City of Winnipeg for a Period of Six Weeks, including the Methods of Calling and Carrying on Such Strike* (Commissioner: Hugh Robson, 1919), 4.

16 *Health Services and Support—Facilities Subsector Bargaining Association v. British Columbia* [2007] S.C.J. No. 27; 2007 SCC 27; [2007] 2 S.C.R. 391.at para. 54.

17 Aloysius Balawyder, *The Winnipeg General Strike* (Toronto: The Copp Clark Publishing Company, 1967), Introduction.

18 The author uses the term 'alleged strike leaders' to refer to those men who later get charged however whether they were the *true* leaders is debated.

19 Jack Walker, *The Great Canadian Sedition Trials: The Courts and the Winnipeg General Strike 1919–1920* (Winnipeg: Legal Research Institute of the University of Manitoba, 2004), 11.

20 David Jay Bercuson, *Confrontation at Winnipeg: Labour, Industrial Relations, and the General Strike* (Montreal: McGill-Queen's University Press, 1990), 116.

21 James Edgar Rea, *The Winnipeg General Strike* (Minneapolis: Holt, Rinehart and Winston, 1973), 6.

22 *Merriam-Webster Dictionary,* Online, s.v. "revolution", Online: <www.merriam-webster.com/dictionary/revolution>: "a: a sudden, radical, or complete change b: a fundamental change in political organization; especially: the overthrow or renunciation of one government or ruler and the substitution of another by the governed."

23 *Merriam-Webster Dictionary,* Online, s.v. "rebellion", Online: <www.merriam-webster.com/dictionary/rebellion>.

24 D.C. Masters, *The Winnipeg General Strike* (Toronto: University of Toronto Press, 1950), 123.

25 Tom Mitchell and James Naylor, "The Prairies: In the Eye of the Storm" in Craig Heron, ed. *The Workers' Revolt in Canada, 1917–1925* (Toronto: University of Toronto Press, 1998), 307.

26 Norman Penner, ed., *Winnipeg 1919: The Strikers' Own History of the Winnipeg General Strike,* Second edition (Toronto: James Lorimer & Company, 1975), 225.

27 Irving Martin Abella, *Nationalism, Communism, and Canadian Labour: The CIO, the Communist party, and the Canadian Congress of Labour 1935–1956* (Toronto: University of Toronto Press, 1973), 31.

28 Peter Campbell, "'Making Socialists': Bill Pritchard, the Socialist Party of Canada, and the Third International" *Labour,* 30(Fall, 1992), 45–63, at 51.

29 Leslie Katz, "Some Legal Consequences of the Winnipeg General Strike of 1919" *Manitoba Law Journal,* 4.39(1970–1971), 39–52, at 40.

30 Mark Leier, *Where the Fraser River Flows: The Industrial Workers of the World in British Columbia* (Vancouver: New Star Books, 1990), 3.

31 Kenneth McNaught and David Bercuson, *The Winnipeg General Strike: 1919* (Don Mills: Longman Canada Limited, 1974), 32.

32 Gerald Friesen, " 'Yours in Revolt': The Socialist Party of Canada and the Western Canadian Labour Movement" *Labour,* 1(1976), 139–157, at 146.

33 Irving Martin Abella, *The Canadian Labour Movement, 1902–1960* (Ottawa: The Canadian Historical Society, 1975). Online: <www.collectionscanada.gc.ca/obj/008004/f2/H-28_en.pdf> at 11.

34 Harry Gutkin and Mildred Gutkin, *Profiles in Dissent: The Shaping of Radical Thought in the Canadian West* (Edmonton: NeWest Publishers Limited, 1997), 2.

35 Judy Fudge and Eric Tucker, "The Freedom to Strike in Canada: A Brief Legal History". Online: <www.law.utoronto.ca/documents/conferences2/StrikeSymposium09_Fudge-Tucker.pdf>, at 15.

36 Hugh Schwartz, *Rationality Gone Awry? Decision Making Inconsistent with Economic and Financial Theory* (Westport: Praeger Publishers, 1998), para. 6.

37 Peter R. Lederman, "Sedition in Winnipeg: An Examination of the Trials for Seditious Conspiracy Arising from the General Strike of 1919" *Queen's Law Journal*, 3.3(1976–1977), 3–24, at 6.

38 *Criminal Code*, Online: <http://laws.justice.gc.ca/en/C-46/>.

39 Ken Kehler and Alvin Esau, *Famous Manitoba Trials: The Winnipeg General Strike Trials—Research Source* (Winnipeg: Legal Research Institute, 1990), 2.

40 Royal Canadian Mounted Police History, Online: <www.rcmp-learning.org/history/history_mod2.htm>.

41 Koskie Minsky website <www.koskieminsky.com/upload/june_2001.pdf>.

42 Ellen Rosen's work "Making Sweatshops: The Globalization of the U.S. Apparel Industry" 2002. See also the report in *The Guardian* in 2012 about Apple factories also having mandatory pregnancy testing of women workers.

43 For more information about Rana Plaza see Chikako Oka, "Improving Working Conditions in Garment Supply Chains: The Role of Unions in Cambodia" *British Journal of Industrial Relations*, 2015, 1–26.

44 Russell Smyth et al., "Working Hours in Supply Chain Chinese and Thai Factories: Evidence from the Fair Labor Association's 'Soccer Project'" *British Journal of Industrial Relations*, 51.2(June 2013), 382–408.

45 See work of Maquila Solidarity Network, Maquila Solidarity Network: http://en.maquilasolidarity.org/resources/video/StopSweatshops.

46 A play on Derrida's title.

47 Sarah A. Donovan, David H. Bradley and Jon O. Shimabukuro, "What Does the Gig Economy Mean for Workers?" *Congressional Research Service*, R44365, February 5, 2016, Online: <www.fas.org/sgp/crs/misc/R44365.pdf> at 1.

48 Jagdish Bhagwati, *In Defense of Globalization* (New York: Oxford University Press, 2007), 148.

49 Unifor, *Community Chapters Handbook*, Online: <www.Unifor.org/Community Chapters> at 11.

50 Jagdish Bhagwati, *In Defense of Globalization* (New York: Oxford University Press, 2007), 208.

51 Pietra Rivoli, *The Travels of a T-shirt in the Global Economy Second Edition: An Economist Examines the Markets, Power, and Politics of World Trade* (Hoboken: John Wiley & Sons, Inc., 2009), 95.

52 See Radiohead concert in Toronto.

53 See the incident in Toronto.

54 John Ruggie, *Just Business: Multinational Corporations and Human Rights* (New York: W.W. Norton & Co, 2013), 5.

55 John Ruggie, *Just Business: Multinational Corporations and Human Rights* (New York: W.W. Norton & Co, 2013), 33.

56 Ethel Brooks, *Unraveling the Garment Industry: Transnational Organizing and Women's Work* (Minneapolis: University of Minnesota Press, 2007), in Introduction XV.

57 Charles Sabel, Dara O'Rourke and Archon Fung, "Ratcheting Labor Standards: Regulation for Continuous Improvement in the Global Workplace" 25, Online: <http://papers.ssrn.com/sol13/papers.cfm?abstract_id=253833>.

58 Robert J. Flanagan and William B. Gould, eds. *International Labor Standards: Globalization, Trade, and Public Policy* (Stanford: Stanford University Press, 2003), 11.

59 John Ruggie, *Just Business: Multinational Corporations and Human Rights* (New York: W.W. Norton & Co, 2013), 75.

60 Civil Society Coalition on Garment Industry Transparency, *Follow the Thread: The Need for Supply Chain Transparency in the Garment and Foot-wear Industry* (Civil Society Coalition on Garment Industry Transparency, 2017), Online: https://www.hrw.org/report/2017/04/20/follow-thread/need-supply-chain-transparency-garment-and-footwear-industry.

61 *TD Economics*, "Canada's Part-time Conundrum" January 4, 2017, Online: <www.td.com/document/PDF/economics/special/Part_Time_Conundrum. pdf>.

62 *TD Economics*, "Canada's Part-time Conundrum" January 4, 2017, Online: <www.td.com/document/PDF/economics/special/Part_Time_Conundrum. pdf>.

63 Patrick Gillespie, "Intuit: Gig Economy is 34% of US Workforce" *CNN* Online: <http://money.cnn.com/2017/05/24/news/economy/gig-economy-intuit/index.html>.

64 Time, "The Gig Economy, by the Numbers" June 4, 2016, Online: <http://time.com/money/4358945/gig-economy-numbers>.

65 Patrick Gillespie, "Intuit: Gig Economy is 34% of US Workforce" *CNN* Online: <http://money.cnn.com/2017/05/24/news/economy/gig-economy-intuit/index.html>.

66 Uber, Online: <https://newsroom.uber.com/nye2016/; https://uberestimator.com/cities>.

67 Jeremias Prassl, *Humans as a Service: The Promise and Perils of Work in the Gig Economy* (Oxford: Oxford University Press, 2017), 25.

68 Jeremias Prassl, *Humans as a Service: The Promise and Perils of Work in the Gig Economy* (Oxford: Oxford University Press, 2017), 84.

69 Patrick Gillespie, "Intuit: Gig Economy is 34% of US Workforce" *CNN* Online: <http://money.cnn.com/2017/05/24/news/economy/gig-economy-intuit/index.html>.

70 Ethel Brooks, *Unraveling the Garment Industry: Transnational Organizing and Women's Work* (Minneapolis: University of Minnesota Press, 2007), in Introduction XVII.

71 Statistics Canada, Labour Force Report, May 2017, Online: <www.statcan.gc.ca/daily-quotidien/170609/dq170609a-eng.htm?HPA=1>.

72 Richard M Locke, *The Promise and Limits of Private Power: Promoting Labor Standards in a Global Economy* (New York: Cambridge University Press, 2013), 49.

73 Pietra Rivoli, *The Travels of a T-shirt in the Global Economy Second Edition: An Economist Examines the Markets, Power, and Politics of World Trade* (Hoboken: John Wiley & Sons, Inc., 2009), 125.

74 Laura Hapke, *Sweatshop: The History of an American Idea*, at 144.

75 Spontaneous utterance? (IP?). At dinner, a friend of mine was describing her friend who works in the mining industry. I commented about him being an exploiter, and she said that he was not directly involved or something. I said, 'ah, arm's length exploitation. I should use that in my research.' After a quick Google search in December 2011 later, I realized that it has been used in other contexts.

76 Charles Sabel, Dara O'Rourke and Archon Fung, "Ratcheting Labor Standards: Regulation for Continuous Improvement in the Global Workplace" on SSRN: <http://papers.ssrn.com/sol3/papers.cfm?abstract_id=253833>, at 21.

77 See Richard M. Locke, *The Promise and Limits of Private Power: Promoting Labor Standards in a Global Economy* (New York: Cambridge University Press, 2013), 129: "These various studies—conducted both internally by global brands and externally by researchers affiliated with Oxfam and the Clean Clothes Campaign—suggest that promoting labor rights and improved working conditions in global

supply chains requires more than compliance and capacity building: we need to reexamine the upstream business practices of the brands and the nature and terms of relations among the key actors in global supply chains."

78 John Witte, *Democracy, Authority, and Alienation in Work: Workers' Participation in an American Corporation* (Chicago: The University of Chicago Press, 1980), 26.

79 Brian Holzer, *Moralizing the Corporation: Transnational Activism and Corporate Accountability* (Northampton: Edward Elgar Publishing Limited, 2010), 27.

80 Brian Holzer, *Moralizing the Corporation: Transnational Activism and Corporate Accountability* (Northampton: Edward Elgar Publishing Limited, 2010), 31.

81 See my work on The Winnipeg General Strike: The power of the strike, especially in the manufacturing industry, was critical. The ability to withdraw one's labour was detrimental to management who relied on the workers to produce goods. The ability of the strike to stop production was a financial penalty to management. The power of the strike used in the context of recognition strikes is truly important.

82 An effective way to curtail workers fight for rights is to criminalize behaviour that once expressed in regard to the labour movement becomes criminal—sedition charges against union organizers.

83 Robert Tucker, ed., *The Marx-Engels Reader, 2nd ed.* (New York: W.W. Norton & Co., 1978), 72.

84 Richard M Locke, *The Promise and Limits of Private Power: Promoting Labor Standards in a Global Economy* (New York: Cambridge University Press, 2013).

85 Harry Glasbeek, "Class Wars: Ontario Teachers and the Courts" *Osgoode Hall Law Journal* 37.4(1999), 805–842, at 832.

86 Law Society of Upper Canada, Online: <http://library.lsuc.on.ca/GL/stay_informed_general_00_4.htm>.

87 United Steelworkers of America–Canada (USWA), Online: <www.uswa.ca/eng/olra.04.htm>.

88 Leo Panitch and Donald Swartz, *The Assault on Trade Union Freedoms: From Wage Controls to Social Contract* (Toronto: Garamond Press, 1993), 1.

89 United Steelworkers of America–Canada (USWA), Online: <www.uswa.ca/eng/olra.04.htm>.

90 Barry Clark, *Political Economy: A Comparative Approach, 2nd ed.* (Westport: Praeger Publishers, 1998), 48.

91 See Karl Marx and the notion of the 'wage contract'.

92 Ontario Progressive Conservatives, "Common Sense Revolution, 1994", Online: <www.ontariopc.com/feature/csr/csr_text.htm>.

93 Ontario Progressive Conservatives, "Common Sense Revolution, 1994", Online: <www.ontariopc.com/feature/csr/csr_text.htm>.

94 *Hewat v Ontario* (1998) 37 OR (3d) 161 (Ont CA).

95 "Mr Len Wood (Cochrane North): This story began and ended on February 11, 1963, when the Spruce Falls Power and Paper Co bush workers, having been involved in a lengthy strike, were protesting the mill's buying of lumber from farmers and labourers in the district. The strikers arrived on the scene with the intention of stopping any loading that might take place on that day. The suppliers were aware of the plan, and shots were fired in the direction of the union men, killing three and wounding eight others. The strike ended soon after and the statue was erected three years later. Minister, your Bill 7 will take us back to the bad old days of labour strife, which workers in this province hoped we'd never see again and workers in Kapuskasing hoped they would never see again."

Hansard, Online: <http://hansardindex.ontla.on.ca/hansardeissue/36-1/1008.htm>.

96 International Labor Organization (ILO), Online: <http://www.ilo.org/ilolex/English/convdisp2.htm>.
97 ILO-UnitedStatesofAmerica,Online:<www.us.ilo.org/archive/press/pressrelease/1997/unions.cfm>.
98 USWA–Canada, Online: <www.uswa.ca/eng/policies/olra_04.htm>.
99 Ontario Federation of Labour, Online: <www.ofl-flo.on.ca/ftp/bill139.pdf>.

Bibliography for Chapter 1

Legislation

Criminal Code, Online: <http://laws.justice.gc.ca/en/C-46/>.

Caselaw

Health Services and Support—Facilities Subsector Bargaining Association v. British Columbia [2007] S.C.J. No. 27; 2007 SCC 27; [2007] 2 S.C.R. 391.
Hewat v Ontario (1998) 37 OR (3d) 161 (Ont CA).
Salomon v Salomon & Co Ltd. [1897] AC 22.

Secondary Sources

Books

Abella, Irving Martin. *Nationalism, Communism, and Canadian Labour: The CIO, the Communist Party, and the Canadian Congress of Labour 1935–1956* (Toronto: University of Toronto Press, 1973).

Abella, Irving Martin. *The Canadian Labour Movement, 1902–1960* (Ottawa: The Canadian Historical Society, 1975). Online: <www.collectionscanada.gc.ca/obj/008004/f2/H-28_en.pdf> at 11.

Balawyder, Aloysius. *The Winnipeg General Strike* (Toronto: The Copp Clark Publishing Company, 1967).

Bercuson, David. *Confrontation at Winnipeg: Labour, Industrial Relations, and the General Strike* (Montreal: McGill-Queen's University Press, 1990).

Bhagwati, Jagdish. *In Defense of Globalization* (New York: Oxford University Press, 2007).

Brooks, Ethel. *Unraveling the Garment Industry: Transnational Organizing and Women's Work* (Minneapolis: University of Minnesota Press, 2007).

Clark, Barry. *Political Economy: A Comparative Approach, 2nd ed.* (Westport: Praeger Publishers, 1998).

Flanagan, Robert, and William B. Gould, eds. *International Labor Standards: Globalization, Trade, and Public Policy* (Stanford: Stanford University Press, 2003).

Gutkin, Harry, and Mildred Gutkin. *Profiles in Dissent: The Shaping of Radical Thought in the Canadian West* (Edmonton: NeWest Publishers Limited, 1997).

Hapke, Laura. *Sweatshop: The History of an American Idea* (New Brunswick: Rutgers University Press, 2004) at 144.

Heron, Craig ed. *The Workers' Revolt in Canada, 1917–1925* (Toronto: University of Toronto Press, 1998).

Holzer, Brian. *Moralizing the Corporation: Transnational Activism and Corporate Accountability* (Northampton: Edward Elgar Publishing Limited, 2010).

Kehler, Ken and Alvin Esau. *Famous Manitoba Trials: The Winnipeg General Strike Trials—Research Source* (Winnipeg: Legal Research Institute, 1990).

Leier, Mark. *Where the Fraser River Flows: The Industrial Workers of the World in British Columbia* (Vancouver: New Star Books, 1990).

Locke, Richard M. *The Promise and Limits of Private Power: Promoting Labor Standards in a Global Economy* (New York: Cambridge University Press, 2013).

Masters, D.C. *The Winnipeg General Strike* (Toronto: University of Toronto Press, 1950).

McNaught, Kenneth and David Bercuson. *The Winnipeg General Strike: 1919* (Don Mills: Longman Canada Limited, 1974).

Panitch, Leo and Donald Swartz. *The Assault on Trade Union Freedoms: From Wage Controls to Social Contract* (Toronto: Garamond Press, 1993).

Penner, Norman. ed. *Winnipeg 1919: The Strikers' Own History of the Winnipeg General Strike*, Second edition (Toronto: James Lorimer & Company, 1975).

Prassl, Jeremias. *Humans as a Service: The Promise and Perils of Work in the Gig Economy* (Oxford: Oxford University Press, 2017).

Rea, James Edgar. *The Winnipeg General Strike* (Minneapolis: Holt, Rinehart and Winston, 1973).

Rivoli, Pietra. *The Travels of a T-shirt in the Global Economy Second Edition: An Economist Examines the Markets, Power, and Politics of World Trade* (Hoboken: John Wiley & Sons, Inc., 2009).

Ruggie, John. *Just Business: Multinational Corporations and Human Rights* (New York: W.W. Norton & Co., 2013).

Schwartz, Hugh. *Rationality Gone Awry? Decision Making Inconsistent with Economic and Financial Theory* (Westport: Praeger Publishers, 1998).

Sukdeo, Vanisha H. " *"Best Interests of the Corporation": Whose Interests Matter?* (Vancouver: University of British Columbia Press, 2018) (forthcoming).

Tucker, Robert ed. *The Marx-Engels Reader, 2nd ed.* (New York: W.W. Norton & Co., 1978).

Walker, Jack. *The Great Canadian Sedition Trials: The Courts and the Winnipeg General Strike 1919–1920* (Winnipeg: Legal Research Institute of the University of Manitoba, 2004).

Witte, John. *Democracy, Authority, and Alienation in Work: Workers' Participation in an American Corporation* (Chicago: The University of Chicago Press, 1980).

Book Chapters

Stewart, Fenner. "A History of Canadian Corporate Law: A Divergent Path from the American Model?" in Harswell Wells, ed. *The Research Handbook of the History of Corporate and Company Law* (Northampton: Edward Elgar, 2017).

Articles

Campbell, Peter. " 'Making Socialists': Bill Pritchard, the Socialist Party of Canada, and the Third International" *Labour*, 30 (Fall, 1992), 45–63.

Civil Society Coalition on Garment Industry Transparency. "Follow the Thread: The Need for Supply Chain Transparency in the Garment and Footwear Industry" (2017).

Donovan, Sarah A., David H. Bradley and Jon O. Shimabukuro. "What Does the Gig Economy Mean for Workers?" *Congressional Research Service,* R44365, February 5, 2016, Online: <www.fas.org/sgp/crs/misc/R44365.pdf>.

Flannigan, Robert. "Shareholder Fiduciary Accountability" *Journal of Business Law,* Issue 1 (2014), 1–30.

Friesen, Gerald. "'Yours in Revolt': The Socialist Party of Canada and the Western Canadian Labour Movement" *Labour,* 1 (1976), 139–157.

Glasbeek, Harry. "Class Wars: Ontario Teachers and the Courts" *Osgoode Hall Law Journal,* 37.4 (1999), 805–842.

Hansman, Henry and Reinier Kraakman. "The End of History for Corporate Law" (2000), available on SSRN: <http://papers.ssrn.com/paper.taf?abstract_id=204528>.

Katz, Leslie. "Some Legal Consequences of the Winnipeg General Strike of 1919" *Manitoba Law Journal,* 4.39 (1970–1971), 39–52.

Lederman, Peter R. "Sedition in Winnipeg: An Examination of the Trials for Seditious Conspiracy Arising from the General Strike of 1919" *Queen's Law Journal,* 3.3 (1976–1977), 3–24.

Lupa, Patrick. "The BCE Blunder: An Argument in Favour of Shareholder Wealth Maximization in the Change of Control Context" *Dalhousie Journal of Legal Studies,* 20, 1–34.

McCallum, Margaret. "Labour and the Liberal State: Regulating the Employment Relationship, 1867–1920" *Manitoba Law Journal,* 23 (1996), 574–593.

McGaughey, Ewan. "The Codetermination Bargains: The History of German Corporate and Labour Law" SSRN Online: <http://ssrn.com/abstract=2541877>, at 4: see footnote number 15.

Oka, Chikako. "Improving Working Conditions in Garment Supply Chains: The Role of Unions in Cambodia" *British Journal of Industrial Relations,* (2015), 1–26.

Sabel, Charles, Dara O'Rourke and Archon Fung. "Ratcheting Labor Standards: Regulation for Continuous Improvement in the Global Workplace" 25, available at <http://papers.ssrn.com/sol13/papers.cfm?abstract_id=253833>.

Smyth, Russell et al. "Working Hours in Supply Chain Chinese and Thai Factories: Evidence from the Fair Labor Association's 'Soccer Project'" *British Journal of Industrial Relations,* 51.2 (June 2013), 382–408.

Government Documents

Manitoba. *Royal Commission to Enquire into and Report upon the Causes and Effects of the General Strike Which Recently Existed in the City of Winnipeg for a Period of Six Weeks, Including the Methods of Calling and Carrying on Such Strike* (Commissioner: Hugh Robson, 1919), at 4.

Websites

Fudge, Judy and Eric Tucker. "The Freedom to Strike in Canada: A Brief Legal History", Online: <www.law.utoronto.ca/documents/conferences2/StrikeSymposium09_Fudge-Tucker.pdf>, at 15.

Gillespie, Patrick. "Intuit: Gig Economy is 34% of US Workforce", *CNN* Online: <http://money.cnn.com/2017/05/24/news/economy/gig-economy-intuit/index.html>.

Hansard. Online: <http://hansardindex.ontla.on.ca/hansardeissue/36-1/1008.htm>.

International Labor Organization (ILO). Online: <http://www.ilo.org/ilolex/English/convdisp2.htm>.

Koskie Minsky website <www.koskieminsky.com/upload/june_2001.pdf>.

Law Society of Upper Canada. Online: <http://library.lsuc.on.ca/GL/stay_informed_general_00_4.htm>.

Maquila Solidarity Network, Maquila Solidarity Network. http://en.maquilasolidarity.org/resources/video/StopSweatshops.

Merriam-Webster Dictionary. Online, s.v. "rebellion", Online: <www.merriam-webster.com/dictionary/rebellion>.

Ontario Federation of Labour. Online: <www.ofl-flo.on.ca/ftp/bill139.pdf>.

Ontario Progressive Conservatives. "Common Sense Revolution, 1994". Online: <www.ontariopc.com/feature/csr/csr_text.htm>.

Royal Canadian Mounted Police History. Online: <www.rcmp-learning.org/history/history_mod2.htm>.

Statistics Canada, Labour Force Report. May 2017. Online: <www.statcan.gc.ca/daily-quotidien/170609/dq170609a-eng.htm?HPA=1>.

TD Economics. "Canada's Part-time Conundrum", January 4, 2017. Online: <www.td.com/document/PDF/economics/special/Part_Time_Conundrum.pdf>.

Time. "The Gig Economy, by the Numbers" June 4, 2016. Online: <http://time.com/money/4358945/gig-economy-numbers>.

Uber. Online: <https://newsroom.uber.com/nye2016/; https://uberestimator.com/cities>.

Unifor. *Community Chapters Handbook.* Online: www.Unifor.org/CommunityChapters.

United Steelworkers of America-Canada (USWA). Online: <www.uswa.ca/eng/olra.04.htm>.

2 Current Structure of Labour and Employment Law

Canada

The current scheme that protects the rights of workers in North America is Employment Law, which is individual employees having a contract with their employer. In the Canadian context, each province or territory has its own provincial legislation that covers basic employment rights in the workplace such as working hours, overtime payment, etc. This is similar to the American framework, although it may be more state-centric than Canada is province-centric. In Ontario, the *Employment Standards Act* (ESA)[1], and other statutes guarantee certain working conditions for workers. Another form of regulation in Ontario (and other jurisdictions) is Labour Law, which covers the unionized workplace where the employer and employees have a collective agreement (CA) that governs the conditions of the workplace. Every CA in Canada incorporates the *ESA* as basic conditions and cannot be contracted out of unless it is for 'a greater benefit.' The Ontario *Labour Relations Act, 1995*[2] sets out when employer–union disagreements can be sent to the Ontario Labour Relations Board, which gets its power from the statute. International Law including the United Nations International Labor Organization Conventions lays out basic minimums for workers, but unless those rules and regulations are enacted in domestic law, they are unenforceable in Canadian courts.

When a union is trying to get certified to become the bargaining agent for a unit of workers, then they launch a union-organizing campaign at that worksite. During this campaign, there are certain rights protected under the *Ontario Labour Relations Act* that pertain to both sides (union and employer). The process of organizing a union can be difficult and can be made even more difficult if there is resistance from management that amounts to an unfair labour practice (ULP).

Right to Strike

This section argues that the right to strike, while important, may not be essential to workers to enforce their rights. The chapter examines the cases that comprise the 'Labour Trilogy'[3] from 1987. The chapter will demonstrate that if workers are given alternatives to the right to strike that enforce their rights effectively, then the right to strike becomes less important. These alternatives include binding arbitration. The author will examine the Framework of Fairness ('FFA') as a case study in examining the importance of the right to strike. The fact that some unionized workers do not have the right to strike raises the question of its true importance.

The strike is a tool that workers have used in the past to solidify their rights. Without the right to strike workers would have to devise other methods of enforcing their rights. In the changing economy, and with the rise of neoliberalism, the rights of workers continue to be eroded. To stop this erosion, different courses of action may be devised. While these different methods may not be ideal, they are worth considering and exploring to uphold the system of labour rights, as they currently exist. According to the *Merriam-Webster*'s dictionary, the word 'important' means "marked by or indicative of significant worth or consequence: valuable in content or relationship."[4] And essential means "1: of, relating to, or constituting essence; 2 a: of the utmost importance . . ."[5] While the right to strike is important, it may not be *essential* to build a labour system that truly values and protects workers. Unions must change to act in the best interests of workers when facing tough economic times, which may mean devising alternatives to the right to strike.

Background

While it is agreed that the right to strike is very important to the labour community, whether it is essential is debated. Many public sector employees do not enjoy the right to strike and instead have to resolve labour issues through binding arbitration. Binding arbitration is a process in which the two sides, union and management, take their unresolved issues to an arbitrator to settle the issue rather than go on strike or engage in other forms of work stoppage. The power of a strike must be examined in terms of the reasons for which workers go on strike. The main purpose of withdrawing one's labour when in a legal strike position is to force management to face economic consequences of not agreeing to terms of a new collective agreement with the union. If what the union aims to accomplish by going out on strike can be accomplished in another way, then the power of the strike must be questioned. Even for union members who have been deemed to be providing essential services, and who have their rights to work stoppages limited drastically, their voices are not silenced as there is still no outright curtailment of illegal strikes. The agreement is only as strong as the willingness of parties to respect it. To do so would be impossible. It is then up to the workers to decide if it is worth the consequences to take such extreme action.

Where does the Right to Strike Get its Legality?

The underlying legal basis for the right to strike are numerous and debatable. The first source to consider is the *Canadian Charter of Rights and Freedoms*[6] ('*Charter*'), in particular section 2(d), the second is caselaw, and the third is natural justice. The legitimacy of the right to strike may come from various sources.

Section 2(d) of the Charter

Section 2(d)[7] of the *Charter* states that: "Everyone has the following fundamental freedoms: . . . d) freedom of association."[8] The debate around whether
section 2(d) includes the right to strike is ongoing. Section 2(d) has been held to
guarantee a limited right to collective bargaining, but not yet the right to strike.
The caselaw helps to guide the discussion.
   Caselaw

The Labour Trilogy

The three cases that comprise the Labour Trilogy dealt with the interpretation of
section 2(d) and whether it covered collective bargaining. In *Reference Re Public
Service Employee Relations Act (Alberta)*, Justice Dickson writing for the dissent,
implied that only through collective bargaining and the right to strike do workers
have true expression of section 2(d). "Through association individuals are able to
ensure that they have a voice in shaping the circumstances integral to their needs,
rights and freedoms."[9] He goes on to state that, "[f]reedom of association is the
cornerstone of modern labour relations. Historically, workers have combined to
overcome the inherent inequalities of bargaining power in the employment relationship and to protect themselves from unfair, unsafe, or exploitative working
conditions."[10] Justice Dickson states that because the individual is free to refuse
work, the act of refusing work in concert should be protected:

> Since an employee is free as an individual to refuse to work, refusal to work
> by employees in concert is protected by freedom of association. With regard
> to the second element of freedom of association, the mental element of a
> strike is to compel an employer to agree to terms and conditions of employ-
> ment, not to inflict injury. Therefore, a person is free to associate in this
> manner, and accordingly the prohibition of strike activity in the Act violated
> freedom of association.[11]

In *Public Service Alliance of Canada v. Canada* Justice Dickson wrote, "[a]s
I have observed in the Alberta Labour Reference, the collective bargaining process serves important educative and democratic functions. The participation of
employees in determining their rights and obligations in the workplace cannot be
undermined without good reason."[12]

B.C. Health Services

The Supreme Court of Canada decision in *Health Services and Support—Facilities
Subsector Bargaining Association v British Columbia*[13] ('*B.C. Health Services*')
holds that workers have a constitutional right to collective bargaining.

> We conclude that s. 2(*d*) of the *Charter* protects the capacity of members of
> labour unions to engage, in association, in collective bargaining on fundamental

workplace issues. This protection does not cover all aspects of 'collective bargaining', as that term is understood in the statutory labour relations regimes that are in place across the country.[14]

The SCC decided that section 2(d) includes a right to collective bargaining. But the court goes on to state "[w]e note that the present case does not concern the right to strike, which was considered in earlier litigation on the scope of the guarantee of freedom of association."[15] The *Charter* only applies to government action so the impact for workers is still unclear. Does this mean that only in cases where the government is the employer will the right to collectively bargain be upheld? The SCC has not yet answered these questions. One prominent law firm described the expected impact of *B.C. Health Services* as follows: "We do not anticipate that the Court's decision will significantly impact private sector employers, although collective bargaining rights that currently exist under labour relations legislation have now been elevated to quasi-constitutional status and may be subject to more exacting review by labour tribunals in the future."[16] While *B.C. Health Services* was a major gain for union members, it did not entrench the right to strike as a constitutional right. It is possible that the SCC's decision has opened the door for another case to argue that the legal landscape has changed and that the gains accomplished in *B.C. Health Services* has laid the foundation for the right to strike to be entrenched. While the right to strike is important, it is not essential for workers as many union members do not have the right to strike and continue to have their rights protected.

> The Court does not go so far as to state that the *Charter* enshrines a right to strike. However, because the Court rejects the reasons relied on in previous cases to exclude striking from *Charter* protection, the issue of whether section 2(d) protects the right to strike will likely come before the courts again as a result of *Health Services*.[17]

As Professor Elaine Bernard of Harvard University states, "Unfortunately, this case did not involve the right to strike and so it remains an open question whether the Supreme Court, in a future case, will recognize 'the right to strike' as a constitutional right."[18]

Natural Justice

Some may argue that the right to strike is simply a fundamental right that does not have a basis in legislation or caselaw. It is impossible to absolutely prevent workers from withdrawing their labour collectively as evidenced by illegal strikes (or wildcat strikes). The fact that one can contract out their labour allows for the opposing right to withdraw their labour. Professor Brian Langille argues that the right to strike flows from the individual to the group. He states that because each individual can withhold their labour that the same right could be exercised in a group. Professor Langille seems to be arguing that whatever the individual has a right to do, they should have that same right when exercised collectively.

The Right to Strike—How Important is It?

Even if the right to strike is entrenched, a lack of enforcement dampens its strength. A right that has no remedy is a hollow right. Genuine enforcement of the right to strike needs to be explored. In order for a true right to exist, there must be an accompanying remedy that is granted when that right is infringed. Those workers who do not have the right to strike make the right less effective overall, as it lacks adequate enforcement. If the right to strike can be contracted out of then how important is it? How does one quantify the importance of a right? Must it be fundamental? The mere fact that some workers are not allowed the right to strike and instead go to interest arbitration means that the right loses strength. Also, if binding arbitration is an alternative it may work as well if not better. If there can be an alternative that is just as effective if not more so then the right to strike may not be indispensable.

Recognition Strikes

The power of the strike used in the context of recognition strikes is truly important. The reason that workers were striking in the early 1900s was to get the employer to recognize the union, the right to have a union, not a specific template of workers' rights. As the Supreme Court noted, "[w]hile employers could refuse to recognize and bargain with unions, workers had recourse to an economic weapon: the powerful tool of calling a strike to force an employer to recognize a union and bargain collectively with it."[19] Workplaces are so varied that what works in one workplace may not work in others. Even different bargaining units within the same workplace have very different needs, for example, office staff and janitors working for the same company. The way that unions and workers decide to have their rights organized in their workplace is varied and should be respected.

Collective Bargaining and the Charter

Many scholars have brought forward arguments in different ways that collective bargaining is guaranteed in the *Charter*. And if collective bargaining is guaranteed then the right to strike should follow. As Professor Jamie Cameron notes, "[i]f, as has been suggested, collective bargaining is meaningless unless workers can go on strike when negotiations fail, then in principle the right to strike should have the same status as collective bargaining under the *Charter*."[20] *B.C. Health Services* has guaranteed a limited scope of collective bargaining. But the case has yet been brought that will clearly articulate the SCC's stance on whether the right to strike is a *Charter* right.

> In the case of collective bargaining, the entitlement is a positive obligation which takes the form of a governmental duty to negotiate in good faith. By contrast, the right to strike is more akin to a negative entitlement which seeks freedom from governmental interference.[21]

Professor Brian Etherington notes that "[t]he Supreme Court of Canada declared very early in its reasons in *B.C. Health* that it was not dealing with the question of a constitutional right to strike, which had been found not to exist in the Labour Trilogy."[22] Future caselaw might one day grant a constitutional right to strike, but until that day, we live with the landscape created by the Labour Trilogy and shaped by *B.C. Health Services.* The progress is slow, and it may not ever be actualized. That is the harsh reality that must be faced: There may never be a constitutional right to strike. And the question becomes whether such a right is essential or even important? As noted by Professor Judy Fudge, "[i]n 1987 the majority of the Supreme Court dismissed collective bargaining as, at best, a mere legislative, and not a fundamental constitutional right, and, at worse, an activity akin to playing golf, as Justice McIntyre so disparagingly portrayed it."[23] Codes of conduct are a separate layer of governance that does not lend itself to working in conjunction with a collective agreement. Codes only exist in the absence of collective agreements. Collective agreements exist between management and union members to protect the rights of both parties as management is allowed to grieve using the grievance process although it is rarely used in that manner. Collective agreements usually contain a section on management rights, which ensures that certain decisions are left to the sole discretion of management. Unions have responded to the new economy after the economic downturn in 2008 and have been making significant changes in both how unions organize and how unions negotiate new collective agreements.

Even among unions, there are differences. Some unions can be described as more 'bread and butter' as the model they follow is more akin to members pay union dues and the union grieves for its members. Other unions are more social justice oriented or activist or militant. These unions tend to be more involved in advancing the concerns of all workers and may have social justice committees, women's committees, etc.[24] Just like corporations can vary from more profit driven to the socially responsible corporation so too can unions vary.[25] Unions have to adapt to changes in the economy, and codes are able to exist in places where it is difficult to unionize and attaches duty to the corporation itself rather than govern the workplace in each different jurisdiction in a disorganized manner. Codes exist where there is no union and allow for the governance void to be filled by having a place for workers to exist and thrive. When one thinks about workers' voice as a collective and the voice of shareholders, these two do not have to be at odds. There is space for both.

Framework of Fairness Agreement

I will examine the Framework of Fairness Agreement (FFA) as a case study in examining how CAs have changed including the fact that the FFA contains a works council.

The Framework of Fairness Agreement

The Framework of Fairness is an agreement negotiated between the Canadian Auto Workers (CAW) and Magna International Inc. (Magna). The deal struck between Magna and the CAW has been discussed at length within the labour community, and within society more broadly. Leaders and high-ranking officials of other unions have criticized the FFA as being too lenient and weak. The main aspect of the FFA that has drawn criticism is that there is no right to strike under the agreement, which is outlined on page 15 of the FFA.[26] Other points that have drawn criticism include the fact that union stewards are called 'employee advocates' and that the usual grievance process has been fundamentally altered and termed a 'concern resolution process.' The CAW's defense of the FFA includes many arguments with the main one being that times have changed and the environment under which old collective agreements were negotiated no longer exists. The slowdown in the economy and the general decline of the auto sector in North America has put the CAW in a more drastic position than other unions. The agreement itself acknowledges such changes.

> Dramatic changes in the global auto industry have created new technological, economic, and financial challenges for Canadian-based automotive producers. These challenges can be met most effectively, thus strengthening the Canadian industry, through a cooperative and productive working relationship between the employer and the union.[27]

Different unions have different ways of managing their organizations, and their varied union members may have different needs. For example, in the current auto industry, workers are likely more worried about keeping their jobs than about the right to strike and what it means to them. Within the document itself, the FFA is meant to be a "new, innovative, flexible, and efficient model of labour relations."[28]

One of the collective agreements under the FFA is between Windsor Modules and Magna. The Windsor Modules collective agreement incorporates the 'no strike' clause from the FFA into Article 2 of their collective agreement:

ARTICLE 2 CONTINUITY OF OPERATION

Section 1: No Strikes, Work Stoppages or Lockouts

Neither of the parties shall utilize any economic sanction to force its position on the other party over any issue. Further, no Employee or group of Employees shall individually or through concerted action, take part in any activity that impedes the operation of the business, except as otherwise authorized by this Agreement.

Should any person or group of people participate in any such unauthorized activity, upon notification of such occurrence, the Union or the Company, as the case may be, will direct such person or group of people to resume normal operations and will take effective means to cease the unauthorized conduct. Any employee or group of employees who participate in such unauthorized activity shall be subject to immediate dismissal, unless mitigating circumstances exist that are acceptable to the ERRC.

Should either party suffer financial damage as a result of such unauthorized activity, they may pursue compensation for such loss at the arbitration step of the Concern Resolution Process, and the arbitrator shall have full authority to remedy any violation of this Article.[29]

The purpose of the 'no strike' clause is to force the parties to use interest arbitration to settle disputes rather than with work stoppages. Whether this will prove to be effective for CAW members at Windsor Modules in the long term is still to be seen. As when new legislation is enacted and has to be put through the courts to determine how effective it is so too must the FFA be given a chance to develop at different workplaces to determine how useful it really is. As Jim Stanford, CAW economist, states:

> I think the bigger issue, the bigger unanswered question from the great Magna debate that went on, is the last one on this list: what is the labour movement's overall strategy to deal with falling density because that is, with no exaggeration, a threat to the survival of our movement and a threat to the fundamental nature of Canadian society. Finding creative ways to address that challenge and beat that challenge will be crucial to our future success.[30]

The true issue for the CAW and other unions is how to effectively fight for their members while helping to ensure those jobs for the future. One method introduced in the FFA is the works council.

The auto industry in Canada is very much attached to the US auto industry, as Canadian plants are dependent on the American counterparts. While the knee jerk reaction to workers losing rights and jobs is to push unions to be more militant and aggressive, the reality is that workers know that in this tough job market having a job with less rights is better than not having a job. The race to the bottom is allowed to continue and thrive. The desire to stop the erosion of workers' rights and build upon the established foundation seems to be a distant goal.

If workers do not have the right to strike then they must have something that adequately replaces it, usually in the form of binding arbitration. While it is beyond the scope of this chapter to study whether binding arbitration is comparable to the right to strike, it is worth acknowledging that the power attributed to the right to strike may be overblown. If other tools can be used to achieve the same result, arguably the enforcement of the terms of a collective agreement, then the right to strike may be adequately replaced by other vehicles. This draws attention to the point that the economy is in a downturn and that workers have to come to terms with that, and work within a new realization of society and what can and cannot be gained through negotiations. While it may seem like the wrong path to follow by making concessions, the reality is that workers who are union members in the end care more about keeping their jobs than the ability to strike.

The harsh reality is that with General Motors Corp., Ford Motor Company, and Chrysler LLC losing customers and money the workers are expected to take wage cuts to keep the business afloat. The CAW (now Unifor) was trying to make the best of a terrible situation for its members in the auto industry as the sector continues to bleed jobs. No one wants to think that workers are so distraught that they have to be concerned about keeping their job and, if they lose their current employment, that the ability to find another job that utilizes the skills that they have spent many years acquiring is rather non-existent. How do you reconcile the theory that the right to strike is important and worth fighting for, while watching Canadians lose jobs? It is a difficult and undesirable position to be in, to have to convince union members to make concessions and rather than fight for wage increases have to sometimes take wage cuts. With both the American and Canadian economies in a downturn, the future of the auto industry, as well as the manufacturing industry more broadly, seems bleak. The auto industry has many other plants that rely on it for jobs such as parts manufacturing so the ripple effect of the decline of the auto industry is felt throughout both countries.

The CAW was once the most socially active and militant union in Canada. The effect of current economic times has shaken it to its foundations. The once hard-won gains, the bitterly fought for improvements are all weakening. While it is easy to blame the union and its members for accepting the concessions and cuts, the truth is that even a bad job is often better than no job. Things are going to change for workers. Especially for members who have skills in making products that are no longer needed or at least are in the decline. What is to be done with the member who has spent 20 years making parts for Chrysler if Chrysler makes good on its threat to stop production in Canada?[31] Where are they to go?

The current economic climate is not allowing for workers' rights to thrive as, although workers as usually less powerful than management, they are facing management with even less power than previous times since the Depression. The ability of union members to negotiate collective agreements that allow for job protection seems to be paramount. And while the right to strike is absent from the FFA, the workers still may go on illegal strikes (wildcat strikes).The recognition strikes in the 1900s were about workers being allowed to have a union, not a union with a specific set of rights. The fact that more workers are able to enjoy the protection of a collective agreement in some form is progress. Not major progress, but progress nonetheless. The workers at Magna may one day have the right to strike, which is something that may be negotiated in the future. For the current time, most of the workers are probably happy to keep their jobs.

Criticism of the FFA

Sam Gindin's Critique of the FFA

Sam Gindin is a professor at York University who worked as an assistant to the National President at CAW. He is a major critic of the FFA.

> The right to strike is fully erased; it is gone *forever*. As the CAW press kit puts it: 'There will be no strikes or lockouts under this *system*' (emphasis added).

When the agreement ends, if the members reject the new offer, it goes to arbitration. Period. (The kit goes on to suggest that the strike weapon is, in any case, not really that important.)[32]

The fact that workers at Magna now have a collective agreement is a positive change. Not all change can be dramatic, and the CAW seems to be planning improvements for the Magna workers in the future. The CAW's role as being the leader of the union movement may at times be onerous and seems to hold them to a higher standard. Many other unions have collective agreements that have to be resolved by binding arbitration, yet the CAW is criticized for the FFA when other unions are not. "The CAW's abandonment of the right to strike at Magna has enormous implications in terms of the labour movement's struggles (including in the CAW) to win this democratic right."[33] The fact that one of the most militant unions in Canada has to make such concessions may herald a drastic change in the way that all unions have to negotiate, but the catalyst seems to be the economy not the weakness of the union. While the criticism of the FFA may be too strong, it is worth challenging unions to stay vigilant and not make too many concessions as the movement as a whole struggles. The alternative argument would be that unions should resist criticizing each other and instead show solidarity against bigger enemies than each other.

Other Critics

Other critics of the FFA include leaders from other unions such as Sid Ryan from the Canadian Union of Public Employees (CUPE) and Professor Eric Tucker from Osgoode Hall Law School who state that the process by which union representatives are selected is unfair. "The recent deal with Magna in which the CAW concedes the right to strike and the right of workers to select their own representatives is the clearest evidence of this trend [making an effort to staunch the bleeding of jobs]."[34] While Professor Tucker is right that the FFA seems to be a reaction to the loss of jobs in the auto industry, he is wrong about the FFA not allowing workers to select their own representatives. The FFA clearly states that the employee advocate is selected by workers.[35] The misreading or misinformation about the FFA is what is leading to many of the criticisms. A letter to the *National Post* signed by various union leaders states "The Magna-CAW pact not only eliminates the right to strike, it takes away the right of workers to elect their own representatives without the boss's participation—a vastly more insidious weakening of workers' rights because of its daily implications."[36] In response to the letter, Mr. Mitic wrote a letter to the editor stating "[c]ontrary to the false claims of these leaders, the language in our recently ratified collective agreement with Magna confirms that company managers play no role whatsoever in the selection of worker representatives."[37] This sort of in-fighting is not beneficial to the union movement overall. The time has come for unions to be more creative and stop job losses. If this means that the right to strike becomes less important, it is a sad reality, but it must be curbed in order for jobs to be secure. The right to strike does not exist in a vacuum, and it needs to be re-evaluated depending on the times. The current economic times signal a change in the union movement, and the right to strike loses its importance.

Works Councils and the German Model

Works councils allow for worker representation and permit workers to have a voice in how the organization is run. Germany is often held up as an example for works council administration as their legislation is thorough which can actually be a negative factor, "[b]ecause of the essentially inflexible one-works-council-fits-all-firms framework as provided by the German works council legislation, probably hampering tailor-made, firm-specific solutions."[38] The Works Constitution Act (*Betriebsverfassungsgesetz*) sets outs the legal basis for German works councils and was enacted in 1972 and revised in 2001.[39]

> The law affords works councils a bunch of legal rights, including the rights on information, consultation and even co-determination, whereas the number of rights increases with the number of employees in the plant. Employer and works councils meet frequently in order to discuss a broad range of topics, for example working conditions.[40]

Mueller notes that works councils are forbidden to call strikes, which links back to the FFA and the different role of the FFA compared to CAs.

The German Model

Germany uses a very different corporate governance model than other nation-states. This model is often determined to be effective due in part because of the increased worker participation. Works Councils allow for worker representation on the company Board. This model evolved from the 'codetermination' model that Germany adopted in the early 1900s. "The 'codetermination bargains' is a name that signifies the collective agreements between business and trade unions from 1918, and then from 1945 to 1951 to establish work councils and give workers a vote for directors on company boards."[41] The German story has many impediments due to governments that were problematic not just for the country but the entire world. This lead to policies that were eventually repealed so the entire story becomes halted because the laws were so reviled that they had to be replaced.

Building on the notion that workers should have a voice in regard to corporate governance, there is also the idea that workers are intrinsically tied to the corporation simply by virtue of being a worker. As noted by Ewan McGaughey, "In contrast, if a corporate is conceived as 'a combination of capital and labour', especially if capital derives from labour, then worker participation rights acquire absolute legitimacy."[42] This is a resonant point as the connection between corporate governance and labour has been central to some emerging theories grounded in CSR.[43]

As well as the theory about workers being a higher level of stakeholder than the average stakeholder due to the connection between many workers with their work, there is another idea about corporations only existing because of society granting them the power to exist. "Because the concession of the state creates a corporation, said Rathenau, shareholders' interests are not all-important."[44] Because society grants corporations the ability to even exist in the first place, there should be some acknowledgement that the corporation does not exist in isolation from the society which allows for its existence.

Factory Occupations

A factory occupation is when during the course of a strike or lockout, the workers takeover the factory and run the plant without management. Factory occupations serve an important function of informing other workers, and society at large, that workers are the backbone of the business and in essence do not require management to produce goods. This is merely an aside but worth mentioning in that the city[45] still continued to function, even without bread and milk delivery. Factory occupations, as well as general strikes, show that workers are able to run their workplaces without assistance from management, while the opposite may not be true. It highlights the importance of workers. This demonstrates that workers may be able to 'run the city' without help from management.

The gig economy demonstrates workers being able to work without management 'controlling the means of production' as in the typical factory setting; however, this new approach may be even worse than the alternative. Instead of a worker reporting to work and being provided the tools and training on how to do their job, in the gig economy, the worker must provide their own tools (a car in the case of Uber) and train themselves on how to do their job. This is more erratic than the factory worker setting of the past. What has the worker gained in the new economy? The ability to refuse certain passengers? The ability to choose when to work? These seem like small gains for the many tradeoffs. Gone is the predictability of work and gone is the stability of a full-time job. These new developments will leave lasting effects even if the gig economy were to evaporate tomorrow.

The United States

The American system is similar to the Canadian one, except that union density in Canada has always been greater than that in America. There are numerous reasons for this, but the most important might be the structure of federalism itself. In America, the rights of workers seems splintered and in the realm of state's rights.

> U.S. labor and employment laws—like similar laws in other wealthy nations— were designed in an era of industrial production, in which leading firms

directly employed hundreds of thousands of workers, and in which workers tended to stay with their employer for much of their career.[46]

Precarious Work

The term 'gig economy' or the 'sharing economy' is used to describe those workers who drive Uber, or rent out their homes on AirBnB when the actual shakiness of their employment is masked as choice. Perhaps those who are precariously employed do not choose to be that way, and instead of it being a decided choice, it is left as the only option. With the raise of part-time employment and people working contract to contract, it creates the notion of the worker as disposable and easily replaced. Even within industries where it was thought to be steady employment, such as Law and Medicine, there has been a rise in contract work and people being unable to find full-time employment.

Precarious conjures up notions of workers doing dangerous work and unsteady work in that the work is inherently risky or dangerous. Both of these definitions are apt as workers face more unsteadiness in employment than their parents' generation, yet should be able to benefit from increased protections for workers in some regards. What has created this duality? Workers arguably have better health and safety protections as workers were once exposed to asbestos in the workplace and now there are protections against such hazards. On the other hand more workers are working part-time and in situations where they work contract to contract. What has changed to create this hazardous situation for workers?

Independent Workers?

The notion that some workers choose to join the gig economy rather than it being a last resort shows the underlying power dynamics of the employment relationship. Are those who work for Uber classified as employees, workers, independent contractors, or this new label of independent workers? Who are the individuals who enter into the platform economy? "One recent proposal in this area would provide for the establishment of a third employment category for workers—called independent workers—who are not traditional employees, but who should not be considered independent contractors."[47]

The notion that some workers are independent while others are dependent has roots in the early 1900s.

> A turning point in that fight in the United States came courtesy of Henry Ford. In 1926, the Ford Motor Company adopted a regular five-day, 40-hour-a-week schedule for its factory workers, reducing their six-day-a-week schedule and the length of their shifts.[48]

This standardization of the 40-hour work week, Monday to Friday work, and 9–5 p.m. work day can be traced back to the factory setting where to power up the machinery meant that it should be worked for a set amount of time and powered down. Why turn on the machine for one person to work for two hours? This is distinct from modern work where someone can simply open up their notebook computer and start work right away.

The large study undertaken by MGI in 2016 outlines and describes the gig economy and how it has impacted the workers who choose to make a living within it. The study starts by providing a definition for independent work:

> Independent work has three defining features: a high degree of autonomy; payment by task, assignment, or sales; and a short-term relationship between worker and client. Our definition encompasses people who provide labor services as well as those who sell goods or rent assets.[49]

While on its face these components seem useful for workers, there is also the lack of ability to retain ratings which may be harmful if a worker leaves one platform for another.[50] This binds the worker to one platform if they worry about 'starting over' at another platform.

While MGI points out that some workers who are unemployed can at least make some money by entering the gig economy, this does not seem like a long-term solution.

> Independent work could have benefits for the economy, cushioning unemployment, improving labor force participation, stimulating demand, and raising productivity. Consumers and organizations could benefit from the greater availability of services and improved matching that better fulfills their needs. Workers who choose to be independent value the autonomy and flexibility.[51]

If workers choose to join the gig economy, they may actually be stuck within it without options of leaving. Workers would probably be more inclined to stay in the gig economy and simply work more hours to make more money than trying to get a job outside the gig economy. Because this is such a new area of research, there have not been enough studies done about the gig economy to draw conclusive results about whether workers stay permanently or enter (or re-enter) the average/typical workforce. How to even demarcate the gig economy from what was the typical or average workforce? If the gig economy is bright and shiny and new, does that mean that the mode of work left behind will become the 'antiquated workforce'? Key aspects: high degree of autonomy, payment by task, assignment, or sales, short-term relationship between the worker and the client.[52]

The MGI study acknowledges that there are disadvantages for workers in the gig economy.

> Despite its benefits, independent work involves some trade-offs. There is more work to do on issues such as benefits, income security measures, access to credit, and training and credentials. Some of these may call for policy

changes; others could be solved by innovators and new intermediaries. Tackling these challenges could make independent work a more feasible option for individuals.[53]

There is room for governments to set up a basic level of benefits for all workers so that gig workers would not be disadvantaged compared to other groups. Or insurance companies can set up plans that cater to the needs of gig workers so that they can purchase health benefits without having a standard workplace through which benefits could flow. MGI sets outs policy makers as one target for their report:

> Policy makers: The first policy priority is obtaining better data on the independent workforce through new and more regular government surveys, with up-to-date categories and criteria. More broadly, labor market policies developed for the industrial era often do not apply to the world of independent work. It may be time to modernize the safety net and worker protections to better reflect the realities of today's labor market.[54]

As well as workers themselves to take autonomy:

> Workers: Lifetime employment at one company is largely a relic of the past, putting the onus on individuals to map out their own career trajectories, looking for their own business opportunities and taking charge of developing their own skills along the way. Independent and traditional workers alike would be well served by developing differentiated skills and services to avoid becoming part of the low-wage generalist pool.[55]

One element absent from the McKinsey report is fissured workers and those who work short-term contracts with the same employer (permatemps) as researched by David Weil. As David Weil describes in his work on 'fissured work':

> The employment relationship in a growing number of industries with large concentrations of low wage workers has become 'fissured', where the lead firms that collectively determine the product market conditions in which wages and conditions are set have become separated from the actual employment of the workers who provide goods or services. Instead, the direct employers of low wage workers operate in far more competitive markets that create conditions for non-compliance.[56]

This describes the conditions that workers have been dealing with in regard to the rise of the gig economy. Professor Weil also raises the concern about where 'employment' resides.[57] Is the worker employed by the direct management or the company that is used to outsource labour? Which entity is ultimately responsible for the worker's wellbeing? Attached to the notion of fissuring is the notion of independent workers who are simply replacing work that was once full-time and permanent. "But today temporary or contract work reaches into a broader age group and many more occupations. In academia, for example, it is now harder to climb the tenure track as universities increasingly rely on lower-paid adjunct faculty."[58] This replacement is the underlying problem. The rise of jobs like Uber driver are a new creation, while rivals the taxi driver, but the aspect of being built on an app is new. However, the dismantling of permanent well-paying jobs to be broken into contract, low-paying positions is the difficulty.

> Multiple motivations underlie fissuring. In some cases, it reflects a desire to shift labour costs and liabilities to smaller business entities or to third-party labour intermediaries, such as temporary employment agencies or labour brokers. Employers have incentive to do so for obvious reasons.[59]

This undermines the integrity of the workplace relationship between worker and management if management is constantly replacing workers with 'independent workers' who cycle in and out of the workplace. "By offering the flexibility to work when and wherever participants want, platforms might have difficulty creating organizational commitment, work-group cohesion, and promotion opportunities— some of the typical predictors of employee retention in traditional jobs."[60] How can morale and collegiality be built when there is a constant influx of new people who then leave shortly afterwards?

Tied to the notion of the fissured workplace with its problems and dilemmas is the notion of workers not being well trained to do dangerous jobs.

> Reluctance to monitor behaviour of contracted entities can lead to profound workplace problems. For example, in a study regarding the petrochemical industry, Rebitzer (1995) found a series of major petrochemical explosions and worker fatalities were linked to the use of independent contractors.[61]

If needed services get contracted out, then that devalues the actual service being performed. When businesses try to offload liability by contracting out, they could face a situation where the temporary labour is not well trained and is simply a gig worker.

Similar to fissured work, is the fragmentation of work as described by Prassl and Albin: "The term 'fragmentation' is used in the literature to discuss the break-down of the traditional organization of work and of employment relations"?[62] This notion of further separation for the worker is problematic. Whether it is termed 'fissured' or 'fragmentation,' there is even more distance between the worker and management and between the worker and the work process as the worker becomes viewed ever more as interchangeable and easily replaced.

> In an era of fragmented work, British labour regulation has also become fragmented. This division signals a return to nineteenth-century labour law which was essentially selective in recognizing various categories of workers and affording them different degrees of legal protection.[63]

This notion of the category under which a worker fits being of the utmost importance demonstrates a method of providing loopholes for management to escape liability and responsibility towards their own employees.

These independent workers are different from those who simply supplement their income with outside sources beyond their job. "It is common for university professors to supplement their income by writing textbooks or consulting, activities that qualify as independent work."[64] Being a worker who supplements income is different from being a worker who only earns in the gig economy or otherwise as an independent worker. "Measuring the independent workforce is not a straightforward task, but our estimates indicate that up to 162 million people in the United States and Europe engage in some type of independent work."[65] These numbers are constantly shifting as the way to even measure the gig economy is fluid. Who gets counted as a gig worker, merely a part-time gig worker? Who is taking this survey to be counted?

The notion that the gig worker is a free soul who gets to work when they choose is a misnomer. "The app developer can code all night and sleep all day. The Uber driver can fit his hours around a class schedule or family priorities. These people enjoy the perks of being independent and would choose to remain so even if they had the option to switch to a traditional job."[66] This seems like a bold statement. How many gig workers would actually choose to remain gig workers? The MGI report outlines that highly skilled lawyers are also independent workers,[67] but this seems to be a half-truth as many lawyers are salaried at firms or in-house counsel. The only lawyers who are perhaps independent are the partners who may be considered as mini-businesses by themselves working in conjunction with other lawyers at the same firm.

Independent workers may lack benefits such as health care and a pension.

> Independent workers may also face other hurdles, such as access to credit. A would-be borrower without a steady paycheck from a traditional employer is likely to have to jump through additional hurdles when obtaining a mortgage or a car loan—and sometimes is shut out of the market altogether. It is not always easy for microbusinesses to access the credit they need to scale up.[68]

There are also problems with not getting paid. When a worker completes work for Uber, there is a contract between them and Uber indicating that they will get paid. However, with workers who sell products on Etsy or eBay, there is no guarantee that the buyer will actually pay. If this happens in the same jurisdiction and offline, there are contractual remedies, but this may be difficult in the online realm, where people can hide behind screen names. As well as non-payment independent workers have to be concerned about providing their own tools,

> Independent workers must also account for costs that reduce net earnings. These can include office space, equipment and tools, marketing, licensing fees, telecom costs, and other types of business expenses. Drivers who

work for Uber, Lyft, and similar services often must cover their own gas, repairs, insurance, and maintenance while absorbing the depreciation of their vehicles.[69]

Gig workers are merely the new proletariat—those who are forced to sell their labour to make enough money to sustain the cost of living. The gig world where workers are earning a small sum is not the new ideal, but a return to the left behind. The left behind days of meagre wages and dangerous work as

> over 40% earn a gross annual income of less than £20,000; a figure which is particularly troubling when considering the fact that crowd workers will usually bear the vast majority of cost associated with their work—from providing tools such as their cars or computers to paying for upkeep and running cost.[70]

Also, people who use these services and pay money for services not performed also lose out. What about customers who lose money on the platform?[71] It must be difficult to recover from the independent worker in a way that is different from recovering from a business which employs workers.

The MGI report concludes that the gig economy rather than replacing full-time jobs with gigs offers those who are unemployed a way to enter the workforce. However, the argument on the other side seems more concrete:

> We argue that within a regime that believes that labourers are not commodities, social exclusion must be strongly justified. In other words, the exclusion of workers from the institution called 'the contract of employment', or a parallel institution that provides equal rights with a universal view of those engaged in the activity of work, should be based on solid grounds.[72]

Albin and Prassl also voice concerns about the development of a the 'zero hour contract,' which in a sense binds workers to an employer but does not guarantee any working hours. "These work arrangements, marked by a lack of guaranteed work to be made available by the employer and (at least notionally) no obligation on the employee to undertake any work when offered, have challenged the legal domain."[73] This is similar to the gig workers where you can be an 'Uber driver' but not an 'Uber employee,' and neither seems to guarantee working hours. This allows employers to have a readily available set of workers without any corresponding duty on the 'employer' to provide work.

> In circumstances when clarification of the concept is requested to aid classification of an individual's working arrangement, respondents are provided with the following definition: '[A Zero-Hours Contract]' is where a person is not contracted to work a set number of hours, and is only paid for the number of hours that they actually work.[74]

This seems to be simply keeping workers ready to work without providing work.

Employees, Workers, or Something Else Entirely?

Which term best applies to the working relationship? Worker? Employee? Or something else? Is this new model of 'independent worker' going to be the new standard, or is this a temporary blip in the system? This could be akin to the change of work like the Industrial Revolution where work at its very foundation is forever changed. The question may be whether this change is temporary or fleeting.

> The structure of English employment law today has long outgrown the traditional 'binary' divide between employees working under a contract of service and thus entitled to the full range of employee-protective norms, and independent contractors, self-employed under contracts for services beyond the scope of employment law.[75]

Again, the question becomes whether the law is not keeping up or whether this is simply temporary.

In the MGI study, they define worker as "Worker/earner: Throughout the report, we use the terms 'worker' and 'earner' synonymously. In analyzing our survey respondents, anyone who reported earning income in the past 12 months was considered to be a worker."[76] This is different from the definition in Canadian law which is different from the definition in other jurisdictions. The importance of the word is because each different definition has attached to it a differing set of obligations and benefits.

Let us deconstruct the term 'gig,' which conjures up images of a band trying to get its break. They are only 'gigging it' until they get their break and sign a record contract with a music label. The gig part of their story is only temporary. To call it the gig economy does a disservice to those working within it. They are not waiting for their big break and record contract:

> the language of 'gigs' and 'tasks' and 'rides' devised by different operators must not obscure the reality of the underlying arrangements, which might— as we go on to demonstrate in this section—often closely resemble the working conditions found in traditional low-wage sectors.[77]

Seems better to call them gig workers than what it truly is: replacement, free-floating workers: "In the case of virtual crowdwork global competition and dislocated physical workplaces further aggravate these problems, as a lack of regulation leads to 'digital slaves' working away in their 'virtual sweatshops.' "[78] While workers are able to secure jobs easier than in the past, there must be recognition about how fluid those jobs are. Here today and gone tomorrow.

> Trend 2: Liquid Workforce. Companies are investing in the tools and technologies they need to keep pace with constant change in the digital era. But there is typically a critical factor that is falling behind: the workforce. Companies need more than the right technology; they need to harness that

technology to enable the right people to do the right things in an adaptable, change-ready, and responsive liquid workforce.[79]

Are crowdsourced individuals workers in the traditional sense? Are they independent contractors or a new approach?

> Whether a worker in the gig economy may be considered an employee rather than an independent contractor is significant for purposes of various federal labor and employment laws. In general, employees enjoy the protections and benefits provided by such laws, whereas independent contractors are not covered.[80]

The labour issues that flow from worker categorization is important, but there are also tax implications from being an independent contractors or small business owner.

Everyone's a Critic—Yet No One Is in Charge

Let Me Talk to Your Manager—Wait, You Don't Have One?

The gig economy has allowed for workers' rights to be eroded. In the hurry to find any job, some workers are forced to accept jobs with bad working conditions. In the gig economy, all customers become the boss as in the case of Uber, customers are able to rate their Uber driver, so every customer has the ability to make or break the career of their driver. Thus, all customers are management, yet at the same time, the worker is set aimless without a manager or boss to get instructions from. "Secondly, instead of the command-and-control systems inherent in 'traditional' employment relationships, crowdsourcers and platforms rely on 'digital reputation' mechanisms to guide the selection of crowdworkers and to ensure efficient performance control."[81] A manager is in the position to give the employee an unbiased review in relation to other employees. In regards to Uber, a driver may get bad customers and face bad ratings without it necessarily being their fault.

It is important to note that Uber is not legal in all the jurisdictions in which it operates. This is yet another problem about the gig economy—the lack of regulation. In some cities, Uber and AirBnB are regulated and legal, and in other cities, there is no regulation. Workers who work in cities where Uber is not regulated are in an even more unsteady situation. Perhaps this is even worse than precarious and can be termed 'wavering work,' which goes beyond merely having a job that is unsteady and toward having a job that is both unsteady and unsafe. Unsafe because it is acting outside the law. On the border of the law. The unregulated are able to be abused in a way that regulated workers are not. This allows management to operate without having to account to a higher body or a regulator or the law.

No Manager? Who Trained You?

While most workers do not want to be micromanaged, there is a need for some sort of management function being served by another person or training on the job. Without a manager, how is training to be accomplished? Who trains the Uber driver or the AirBnB host on how to be a host? Who trains the gig worker on how to best accomplish the tasks that they have been assigned? The resounding answer is 'no one.' This is a simple fact that no one has trained these people.

> Turnover is high within the online platform workforce. One in six participants is new each month and more than half of participants drop out within 12 months. This high turnover rate makes it harder to sustain growth in the supply of goods and services in the Online Platform Economy.[82]

The person who sells you a shirt at the local mall or hands you your Big Mac has been trained on how to do their job, but the person who is a gig worker has very likely received no training on how to do their job.

Not having a manager might seem like freedom to some workers, but not receiving any training or adequate training is problematic for the worker, as well as for the consumer of the service. The worker is never told how to complete tasks in the 'right way,' and consumers do not benefit from a well-trained worker. How can one provide good customer service if that has never been defined for you, and you have never been trained to do so?

> Employees of large companies may benefit from on-the-job learning, training, and opportunities for career advancement, but independent workers may have to seek out training on their own. Companies are often reluctant to hire independent workers for tasks they have never done, making it hard for them to build new career muscles.[83]

An Uber driver may be licensed to drive a car by the province or state in which they operate, but the licensing in being able to complete the task and being able to complete the task well are two separate issues. Also, the Uber driver is not just driving a car, but providing a customer experience for those who use their services—music, snacks, etc.

Recruitment seems to be separate from training.

> Talent is a key resourcing issue for Platform companies who compete with each other and the broader tech sector for the same limited pool of skilled people. Aggressive and innovative recruitment strategies are essential for attracting and retaining staff in addition to making that scarce talent as productive as possible.[84]

So, there is aggressive recruitment, but no move to train once workers have been recruited.

Leaving aside the built-in exploitation, there is no training. This person is doing a job without basic training on how to do that job. This is both unfair to the worker and dangerous for the person using the services. This is not disruption: This is disorder.

Who Is Immune?

There is a notion that those who are educated may escape this trap of becoming part of the precariat. If only they had stayed in school and gotten an education they would not be in this mess. Well, what about the unbundling of legal services? What about the medical doctor who only works 10 hours per work because older doctors will not retire?

These are more difficult conversations to have. To blame the poor and under-employed for their plight allows those with full-time jobs to rest easy—the masses are unaware of the inherent flaws and injustice in the system itself. As the saying goes, 'The system is not broken. It was built this way.' The system was flawed from the start. The system was exploitative from the start. As one of my friends told me 'the system is violence.' Only when we start at the beginning and challenge the underlying notions of the capitalist system from the bottom up do we begin to realize that the system was made to mask inequality so that those who fail within the system deem the failure to be their own fault and not the fault of the system.

How to keep the masses content or at least not discontent? Quiet their unease and unrest with whispers of individual responsibility and individual blame, rather than acknowledging the problems are systemic and difficult (and perhaps impossible) to unwind from the capitalist system itself. How to solve isolation and inequality when it is simply part of capitalism? Through worker voicing and workers being able to have their input included in the mechanisms that govern their workplaces and ultimately themselves. The ability to have one's voice heard is not the same as being counted or meaning that others are listening when one speaks. Speaking does not inherently mean that the audience is listening and absorbing what is being said.

The unbundling of legal services allows for a huge change in how legal services are provided. The typical route is that a client hires a lawyer by signing a retainer agreement and agrees that the client pays the lawyer a set amount up front and then on an hourly basis as the legal proceeding continues.

> Rapidly growing online platforms, such as Uber and Airbnb, have created a new marketplace for work by unbundling a job into discrete tasks and directly connecting individual sellers with consumers. These flexible, highly accessible opportunities to work have the potential to help people buffer against income and expense shocks. The 'Online Platform Economy' offers fewer worker protections than traditional work arrangements, however, which has led some to claim that the Online Platform Economy represents a fundamental shift in the nature of work.[85]

The new unbundling option means that lawyers can provide service on a single document to help those who cannot afford a lawyer for the entire proceeding. While on its face it seems like a solution for the barrier to access to justice for clients to afford to pay a lawyer for a bit here and a bit there, this devalues the work of lawyers as it no longer seems that a client needs a lawyer for the entire process but rather in a piecemeal and haphazard way. Who are the lawyers who will likely end up doing this work? It seems obvious on its face.

> The leading platforms for this kind of 'cognitive piece work' or 'Neo-Taylorism' include Amazon's *Mechanical Turk* and *Clickworker*. Survey research has shown that 25% of the tasks offered on Amazon *Mechanical Turk* are valued at $0.01, 70% offer $0.05 or less and 90% pay less than $0.10 per completed task; thus equalling an average wage of about $2 per hour.[86]

The doctors who are stuck working in small towns and stuck pulling together clinic hours probably look similar to the lawyer offering unbundled legal services. This is not unexpected. This is how the system was built. The inequality and unfair job prospects for graduates are not a mystery and unanticipated. The law school or medical school is able to praise themselves for admitting such students in the first place. Job prospects are divided from education, right?

Workers voicing is crucial, but appreciation and inclusion for their voice is the ultimate goal. Without a goal to be realized, the voicing might as well be in an empty room. Allowing workers to speak or encouraging workers to speak is important but without a goal or process in place there is no purpose to be served. If that voice gets captured in a jar and never heard that, did the worker even speak to begin with? Without more than simply an attempt to include but an actual inclusion process, the purpose of voicing is inconsequential. And without function.

Wavering Work

In the model I term 'wavering work,' workers operate on the boundary of the law. They do work that it is the absence of regulation. They do work that leaves them vulnerable and without order. They do work that is piecemeal and unpredictable. They do work that is unsafe. Uber and other such apps work on the boundary of the law, that is to say that they do not operate simply inside or outside the law because it depends on where you are and which city you are in. Some cities have legalized and regulated Uber, while others have found Uber to be operating illegally as a taxi service. And still other places have allowed a situation akin to legal limbo, where the government fails to take a stance one way or the other so Uber exists, but no one is sure whether it is legal. The argument from taxi drivers who are against Uber is that they pay fees to be able to run a legal business, and they have to be regulated and conform to certain guidelines—working seatbelts and other safety precautions must be met. In legal limbo cities, Uber drivers are able to avoid having to comply with such rules because they are on the boundary. At the same time, no one should really blame that individual Uber driver as he or she probably would rather do some other form of work but is put in this situation due to lack of other options.

Wavering workers do work that is not the work they desire to do. Do we have sympathy for the worker who does a job he or she hates? Should we? This is complicated but important to remember that perhaps empathy is important, so when a customer service provider is not able to bend to your request, maybe the better option than yelling at them is to remember that they too are human and deserving of dignity and respect. What is the role of the customer when interacting with gig workers? Is it separate from the usual role?

Gigging the Economy: What's Old Is New Again

When we critically explore the 'gig economy,' which is used to describe the development of such jobs as driving Uber and holding contract positions, we can understand how it arose. This is thought of as a new development. The actual fact is that certain positions have always been 'gigs,' and the only new development is that the proliferation of such jobs has grown. The 'gig' itself is not new. Writers have often written for serialization and are only paid on an inconsistent basis.

> Just as working models changed in the wake of the Industrial Revolution, the nature of work may be evolving again as the digital revolution takes hold. Digital platforms for independent earners are still in their infancy, but their rapid growth could accelerate the shift to independent work and even generate new demand.[87]

It is possible to turn gigs into full-time positions and whether all workers even desire such? Some workers may choose to hold small jobs over a full-time one because of child care, family care, illnesses, etc. While this may be true for some workers, it is probably likely that most 'giggers' want full-time employment. "When it comes to regulation of the workplace, however, it is not a turn to governance but a *return* to governance, or a shift in the nature of governance, that we are seeing today."[88]

Modern society convinces workers that work should not be enjoyed and that perhaps only the rich are busy 'doing what they love,' while others have to find jobs that are simply jobs and not their life work.

In a Communist paradise, Che Guevara writes that in the morning, you could be building a bridge, while then performing the work of a doctor in the afternoon. Che was a medical doctor, so he had that training. While it does seem utopian for everyone to be able to perform the work of everyone else, it is impossible. The training that goes into making someone a doctor or lawyer is so time consuming that it would take too long to train too many people. So specialization of labour becomes important. And then it becomes *too* important. Marx writes about the worker who is a shoemaker. That person used to be able to make an entire shoe. Now the process changed so that one person sews on the sole, while another one puts in the laces, etc. Each job is of such little importance that each person can be replaced without stoppage. If you make each worker so easily replaced that the routine keeps chugging along, then no one worker feels important. No one worker knows the secret behind making an entire shoe. No one worker has any transferable knowledge and becomes stuck in that one role. Each worker becomes that one role. That worker is not a shoemaker that worker is a sole sewer. That job becomes a soul wrecker.

If each worker is viewed as replaceable and easily forgotten, then any other worker will do. Any worker can replace that worker sewing on soles to the shoe. Any worker can accept the low wages and feel useless against the machine. However, if that one worker decides to strike and hold up production, then the company suffers as a result. Without that worker there to sew on the soles, there cannot be complete shoes made.

What is a shoe without a soul?

Platform Capitalism and the New Economy

The platform economy is the term used to describe the rise of online applications being used as a way to source labour and/or shop for goods. Companies that fall under this umbrella include Uber and Airbnb as among the most notable and easily recognized.

> Since its launch in 2008, Airbnb hosts have accommodated more than 60,000,000 guests worldwide. In the United States, the overall Airbnb host community has grown 85% year-over-year, with the typical host earning $7,350 in supplemental income per year on just a single property.[89]

These platforms can be divided between labour platforms and capital platforms. As noted by a research study conducted for the JPMorgan Chose & Co Institute, the breakdown between these two differing models is important.

The labour side of Uber versus the capital side of Airbnb both allow for individuals to become 'their own boss' but also allow for the distinction between home and work to die away. If one's home is now viewed as a business operation where strangers can stay in one's home for money and if one's car is not just for getting to the mall or the movies but instead is a way to make money to allow strangers in, this distinction becomes muddy. Where is the line between home and work? This is also an issue for people who work from home separate from the gig economy but becomes more pronounced when considering Uber and Airbnb where the individual has to supply their own car/house to make money. The issue is not about choice in that we should not feel sorry for the exploited Uber driver because he or she chooses to work this way but because they may not have other options. How factually correct is it to say that gig workers choose that way of life? With the shifts in how work is done and the movement from full-time jobs to more part-time jobs, the issue becomes that the very nature of work has shifted. And has this been an advantage to workers? Or are workers now facing harsher working conditions and less wages?

> As a primary source of income, however, the platform economy offers fewer workers protections than traditional work arrangements. The absence of benefits—such as employer contributions to Social Security, insurance, and other retirement accounts—have led some to claim that the platform economy represents a fundamental shift in the nature of work, and to propose the creation of a new class of 'independent worker' (Harris and Krueger, 2015).[90]

The new model of platform capitalism allows for workers to find gigs online while maintaining the opportunity to find other gigs.

> Platform companies start with a single product or service that has a clear value proposition: typically lower cost than existing offerings or convenience. Often, they face few direct competitors, but emerge as a disruptive force challenging incumbent competitors and traditional ways of doing things.[91]

This notion of disruption will be explored later in the book. Is Uber a disruptor? Is this something new and different? Or a return to forgotten days of low wages and unstable work?

We see how businesses go from being mundane towards growth and then on to the worldwide stage. "More than 2.5 million U.S. taxpayers are participating in the on-demand platform economy as small business owners every year, and that number is set to more than double in the next few years."[92] This statistic is from 2016, so it can be implied that the number is going up as more workers lose the opportunity to get full-time employment and are forced into the gig economy.

Labour Platforms

The best known labour platform is Uber. The rise and possible decline of Uber has been heralded as mainly a success in that drivers are able to set their own hours in deciding when to work and how long to work.

> Once the request has been accepted by a driver, she is directed to the passenger and onwards to the required destination, through her version of the *Uber* app. Payment is taken automatically from the customer by the platform, and after the taking of a commission between 20 and 30%, passed on to the driver. Customers and drivers rate each other anonymously following each journey; the resulting scores are displayed to passengers and operators respectively before the next trip commences.[93]

Uber keeps growing so the numbers are difficult to measure because they keep shifting and changing. "As of February 2016, Uber reported that it has more than 500, 000 drivers, who earned more than $3.5 billion in takehome wages in the first three quarters of 2015."[94]

The Uber driver as statistics show works less than 10 hours per week and makes on average about $15, 000 per year.

> Uber Technologies partnered with Economist Alan Krueger to analyze data collected from a sample of 601 Uber drivers in December 2014 and aggregate administrative data collected by the company from 2012 to 2014. Together, these data revealed that 162, 037 drivers were actively partnered with Uber in December 2014; the majority of Uber drivers were male (86.2%), more than half were between ages of 30–49, and 47.7% has at least a college degree. Many drivers did not use Uber as their sole source of earned income: 31% held a separate full-time job and 30% held a separate part-time job. The authors interpret survey data to show that the flexibility in work hours provided by Uber is a primary draw for drivers.[95]

The research shows that Uber drivers tend to be male, have some post-secondary education, and earn a low wage. This is not a sustainable model as gig workers will realize that the casual lifestyle offered by gigging cannot be maintained.

> As companies flourish, their base market will inevitability become saturated and new customer acquisition alone will no longer drive the same level of growth. 'On-demand companies' collect commissions from providers for jobs solicited through the company platform. Commissions often take the form of a flat percentage rate applied to job-earnings, but some companies employ more sophisticated models. For example, in 2014, Lyft announced that it would return a portion of its 20% commission on rides as a bonus to certain high-activity drivers.[96]

One strategy to increase users is to

> move into adjacent markets by applying core competencies in new ways. . . . In 2016 Uber launched UberEATS, using the same back-end technology behind the original Uber app and its existing network of drivers to enter the food delivery sector. The company later announced Uber Rush API to help merchants add the platform into delivery systems and has revealed plans to launch a line of self-driving cars.[97]

There was recently an accident in Arizona including a self-driving Uber hitting and killing a pedestrian. Uber has halted self-driving testing for the next 12 months. Uber has expanded into delivering food and might expand to offering other services as well.

Uber and Seattle

Seattle has come up with a new way to help solve problems in the gig economy. The solution that they allow for workers who would not ordinarily be covered by the same collective agreement as they do not work at the same workplace organize into units. This is similar to the approach taken by Unifor in Canada.

> A key idea behind the ordinance—the Seattle Solution—is that the most expedient way to improve the working conditions for these workers, who are regarded as ineligible for key employment protections yet who are powerless to bargain a better deal on an individual basis, is through increased collective leverage.[98]

This is similar to the work done by Unifor in Canada—organizing against the typical bargaining unit. "In December 2015, the Seattle City Council unanimously passed an ordinance (the 'ordinance' or 'driver bargaining ordinance') creating a collective bargaining system for for-hire drivers who were classified as independent contractors, including both app-based and traditional taxi drivers."[99] The difference between the so-called Seattle Solution as opposed to the London approach is that rather than re-certifying or re-classifying the type of worker that an Uber driver is works to change the ability of that individual driver to collectively organize. The individual worker becomes less important as opposed to the rights that flow from that individual worker in regards to union organizing. This allows for collective bargaining akin to the Unifor model in Canada. Community Chapters will be discussed elsewhere in this book, but it must be noted that there are difference models at work simultaneously. Which model works best for each worker? And which model works best for the industry as a whole? The two might not be the same.

In Seattle, many of the drivers are Somali or Sikh and were aided by Teamsters Local 117[100] in their quest to gain better working conditions and more rights.

> Additionally, Uber created a series of commercial and podcasts to discourage drivers from supporting a union drive, suggesting that collective bargaining might destroy Uber drivers' flexibility or even drive the company out of business, and threatened to pull out of Seattle if the ordinance took effect.[101]

We see anti-union tactics similar to those discussed surrounding employer free speech. This runs throughout all areas of work.

As noted by Professor Garden, "But while the ordinance is new, the strategy is familiar: the response to the increased prevalence of precarious work and fissured workplaces has often been the adoption of sub-federal level collective bargaining rights for workers left uncovered by the NLRA."[102] Workers are returning collective action to gain rights and freedoms that were buried. It is now getting resurrected.

Uber Loses Its License in London

Uber lost its license to operate in London. It has been found by a court of law to be acting like a taxi company and must be regulated as such.[103] This will have a big impact on other jurisdictions that are influenced by British law such as Canada. Uber has 40,000 drivers in London and claims that it has 3.5 million customers in the city.[104] This movement to recognize Uber as any other taxi company is monumental. In a world where companies like Uber see themselves as 'disruptors,' this is a return to the mundane. The notion of being a disruptor is that the gig economy or platform economy has disrupted mainstream businesses and how they operate. It can even be said to disrupt capitalism as we know it. Allowing companies to communicate directly and engage with consumers as business operators in the case of Uber allows for the notion of a boss with a worker working 9–5 p.m. being replace with flexible schedules and being your own boss.

> For example, in the case of platform capitalism, a neoliberal economic account tends to praise firms like Uber, Airbnb, TaskRabbit, and Postmates for promoting labor competition and improving quality, by telling a simple narrative about the incentives created by reducing transactions costs and creating more opportunities for individuals and firms to compete to provide services.[105]

In November 2017, the news got worse for Uber as a tribunal ruling held that Uber divers were not independent contractors and instead entitled to be paid like employees.

> The decision, which affirmed a ruling made last year, means Uber will have to ensure its drivers are paid a minimum wage and entitled to time off, casting doubt on the hiring model used by Uber and by other businesses in the so-called gig economy that rely on workers who do not have a formal contract as permanent employees.[106]

This ruling has great repercussions throughout Europe and beyond. North Americans markets where Uber operates have to re-examine their policies in regards to Uber. In Canada, are Uber drivers employees or independent contractors? Or those drivers are a new breed of worker with a new title and new set of rules? In the United States, are Uber drivers employees or independent contractors? As well, it depends on the individual province or territory in Canada and the individual state in the United States. Uber drills down to municipal laws, and it actually ends up being a city right to license Uber or not like in London. Uber may see the beginning of the end with the ruling in London.

> The company faces a similar challenge in Europe- the region's highest court is expected to rule by the end of the year in a case over whether the company should be regulated as a taxi service, which would make it subject to rigorous safety and employment rules, or as a digital platform that simply connects independent drivers to passengers.[107]

Capital Platforms

A capital platform versus a labour platform like Uber is that one can purchase hours for someone to complete a task like thought TaskRabbit.

> A 'peer economy' of platform-arranged production will break down old hierarchies. Gig workers will be able to knit Etsy scarves in the morning, drive Uber cars in the afternoon, and write Facebook comments at night, flexibly shifting between jobs and leisure at will.[108]

This notion of the gig worker being a free soul is problematic and may in fact be false.

> Social networks, search engines, cloud software providers and ride-sharing companies form an influential and fast-growing group of Platform companies which are reaping huge rewards by disrupting existing industries. Despite varied offerings and widely differing sector focus, these companies have much in common.[109]

Those not reaping those same rewards include the workers who provide the services or complete the tasks.

One of the leading capital platforms is Amazon's Mechanical Turk (MTurk) which has

> permitted purchases of 'human intelligence tasks' to pay almost nothing for labor-resulting in effective compensation far lower than the U.S. minimum wage. Scholars like Trebor Scholz and Miriam Cherry have discussed the sociological and legal implications of platforms that try to disclaim responsibility for following labor laws or other regulations.[110]

Again, we return to the notion of disruption. What takes the place after an industry has been disrupted? Not all change is good change.

> Should policy focus on encouraging competition or regulation? The two approaches are not mutually exclusive—many forms of regulation could assure a fairer playing field for competition. However, the standard neoliberal narrative of competition presumes that deregulation is a linchpin of truly open and contestable markets.[111]

While gig work does open up working options for workers, there must be critiques about what type of work is available through both labour and capital platforms:

> Online platforms like Uber and TaskRabbit now efficiently connect service providers and other workers with willing consumers. This new mode of transacting has transformed the landscape for twenty-first century workers.

No longer must they choose between working solely as an employee (subject to the restrictions and control of their employer) and starting their own business (requiring an investment of time and money to do things like advertise and find a customer base).[112]

Also, while unemployment may be difficult for workers, there is now the easier option of being a gig worker. So, it does lessen the ability to find a job.

The Online Platform Economy also adds an important new element to existing labor markets, where finding new or additional work typically involves a lot of effort and high transaction costs. Simply put, landing a platform job is often easier and quicker.[113]

The platform economy has changed the very nature of work. What is yet to be seen is if this is a permanent change.

The Platform Economy is considered one of the biggest transformations for business since the Industrial Revolution. It's a bold claim, but the speed and scale with which today's platform businesses have developed really only hint at the profound economic shifts that lie ahead.[114]

Most platforms categorize workers as independent contractors.

With some exceptions, on-demand companies view providers as independent contractors—not employees—using their platforms to obtain referrals and transact with clients. This designation is frequently made explicit in the formal agreement that establishes the terms of the provider-company relationship.[115]

While some workers would be fine with the categorization scheme, for an Uber however driver who relies on that as their main source of income, it seems unfair to not be an employee and enjoy the benefits that flow from being an employee. The Uber driver who works long hours and works only for Uber should be elevated to a higher level than the casual Uber driver.

Workplaces and Work Spaces

What does the 'typical' work space look like? What *should* it look like? There are certain legal requirements in a factory that fall under the heading of workplace health and safety and how such spaces are regulated. However, one's workplace may be changing due to open offices where workers no longer have separate offices and instead work communally in cubicles or open space desks. Also, with the rise of Uber and other such gig jobs, the nature of workplace has moved to simply a work space. I used the term 'workplace' to describe the typical place where one works often in an office or factory setting. I use the term 'work space' to connote a space where one works, but this space is fluid as in one day you are working at a Starbucks and the next day you are working at a park. This fluidity is both good and bad as workers have freedom to work where they want. However, this lack of distinction means that work is both everywhere and nowhere.

Open Offices

The idea of an open office may be problematic for lawyers where there are issues surrounding confidentiality and the need for client's to have privacy. Places like the new Deloitte office in Toronto are open offices which are supposed to encourage workers to work collectively. As the Robert Frost saying goes "good fences make good neighbours," and perhaps there is a level of privacy needed in the workplace for co-workers to get along. One does not need to hear everything about one's personal family issues, while someone is on the phone.

No Workplace and Just Space

If one is driving Uber then the workplace is one's car. This lack of distinction between work and personal life is problematic. The same issue arises for people who work from home. Where is the delineation? Is one ever 'off the clock' when the clock is on the dashboard or on one's desktop in the home office?

The vast majority of workers would rather be included in the governing process of their workplaces or places of work. I use 'place of work' to indicate that the place where workers work is not constant and is instead ever-changing.

Like a snail that carries its home with it everywhere, the Uber driver is turtle-like because they carry their workplace with them every time they get in their car. This lack of distance from one's work must have psychological impacts. The rate of anxiety seems to be increasing all the time.

Technology and the Ever-Lengthening Chain

Technology and the use/overuse of emails means that no one is ever truly 'away from the office' as every worker can be reached while at home, while sitting on a beach, etc. This ability to connect with anyone at any time means that time becomes changed. A worker should be able to leave work at work and not worry about it when he or she is at home.

This extends from not just the lowest ranking worker who feels devalued, but the highest employees at a firm or organization who are not allowed to be 'off the clock.' Since the invention of the BlackBerry by RIM in the early 2000s, there has been increasing encroachment of the work realm into the personal realm. Everyone is expected to be answering emails after work, at the dinner table (does anyone still eat dinner at a dinner table?), and right before you drift off to sleep. Perhaps the joke about the lawyer who asks if he can bill his client for a dream he had about the client's case is not so far off from becoming reality. Where does work end and personal begin? Where does the conscious mind and the subconscious separate? Can work not be shut off during sleep?

This is perhaps most pervasive at the high-income levels where we do not have pity for the surgeon making $500,000 a year who works long hours or the lawyer who works well into the night, but these are not compartments in the grouping of wage slaves as they are simply part of that world as well. Unless you are independently wealthy and do not have to work, you are part of the same group. The push to demarcate within this large group is artificial and pointless. Do you control the governance of your workplace? If not, should you?

Notes

1 *Employment Standards Act, 2000,* SO 2000, c. 41.
2 *Labour Relations Act, 1995,* SO 1995, c. 1, Sched. A.
3 *Reference re Public Service Employee Relations Act (Alta),* [1987] 1 SCR 313; *PSAC v Canada,* [1987] 1 SCR 424; and *RWDSU v Saskatchewan,* [1987] 1 SCR 460.
4 *Merriam-Webster Dictionary, s.v.* "important" Online: <www.merriam-webster. com/dictionary/important>.
5 *Merriam-Webster Dictionary, s.v.* "essential" Online: <www.merriam-webster. com/dictionary/important>.
6 *Canadian Charter of Rights and Freedoms,* Part 1 of the *Constitution Act, 1982,* being Schedule B, to the *Canada Act 1982* (UK), 1982, c.11.
7 While other subsections have been used to try to support a constitutional right to strike, the author chose to use 2(d) in interest of staying within the paper limit.
8 *Canadian Charter of Rights and Freedoms,* Part 1 of the *Constitution Act, 1982,* being Schedule B, to the *Canada Act 1982* (UK), 1982, c.11 at s 2(d).
9 *Reference Re Public Service Employee Relations Act (Alberta)* [1987] 1 SCR 313 at para 22.
10 *Reference Re Public Service Employee Relations Act (Alberta)* [1987] 1 SCR 313 at para 22. *Ibid* at para 23.
11 *Reference Re Public Service Employee Relations Act (Alberta)* [1987] 1 SCR 313 at para 22. *Ibid* at para 43.
12 *Public Service Alliance of Canada v Canada* [1987] 1 SCR 424 at para 47.
13 *Health Services and Support—Facilities Subsector Bargaining Association v British Columbia* [2007] SCJ No 27; 2007 SCC 27; [2007] 2 SCR 391.
14 *Health Services and Support—Facilities Subsector Bargaining Association v British Columbia* [2007] SCJ No 27; 2007 SCC 27; [2007] 2 SCR 391. *Ibid* at para 19.
15 *Health Services and Support—Facilities Subsector Bargaining Association v British Columbia* [2007] SCJ No 27; 2007 SCC 27; [2007] 2 SCR 391. *Ibid* at para 19.
16 Ogilvy Renault, "Supreme Court of Canada Declares Collective Bargaining a Charter Right" (15 June 2007), Online: <www.ogilvyrenault.com/en/resource Centre_965.htm>.
17 Ogilvy Renault, "Supreme Court of Canada Declares Collective Bargaining a Charter Right" (15 June 2007), Online: <www.ogilvyrenault.com/en/resource Centre_965.htm>.
18 Elaine Bernard, "Collective Bargaining as a Constitutional Right" *Our Times* (6 September 2007), Online: <www.ourtimes.ca/Features/printer_22.php>.
19 *Health Services and Support—Facilities Subsector Bargaining Association v British Columbia* [2007] SCJ No 27; 2007 SCC 27; [2007] 2 SCR 391.at para 54.

20 Jamie Cameron, "The Labour Trilogy's Last Rites: *B.C. Health* and a Constitutional Right to Strike" *Canadian Labour and Employment Law Journal*, 15(2009–2010), 297 at 303.

21 Jamie Cameron, "The Labour Trilogy's Last Rites: *B.C. Health* and a Constitutional Right to Strike" (2009–2010) 15 Canadian Lab & Emp LJ 297 at 303. at 309.

22 Brian Etherington, "Does Freedom of Association under the *Charter* Include the Right to Strike after *B.C. Health*? Prognosis, Problems and Concerns" *Canadian Labour and Employment Law Journal*, 15(2009–2010), 315 at 318.

23 Judy Fudge, "Brave New Worlds: Labour, The Courts and the *Canadian Charter of Rights and Freedoms*" *Windsor Yearbook of Access to Justice*, 28(2010), 23 at 27.

24 Just my inside information having articled at OPSEU (a public sector union) and prior to that spending time in the legal department at then CAW (now Unifor) the largest private sector union in Canada.

25 As an aside, I recall a union organizer telling me that management "gets the union you deserve" in that management who is mean to their workers gets a more militant union compared to management that is nice to its workers may get a more diplomatic union.

26 Framework of Fairness Agreement, November 19, 2007, at 15 states:
"No strike-no lockout

- Neither party shall utilize any "economic sanctions" to force its position on the other party for any reason
- No employee or group of employees shall individually or through concerted action, take part in any activity that impedes the operation of the business
- Any employee or group of employees who participate in such unauthorized activity shall be subject to immediate dismissal, unless mitigating circumstance exist which are satisfactory to the ERRC
- The parties shall negotiate the resolution of all issues in good faithAny issue regarding the National Agreement unable to be resolved through negotiation shall be referred to the Neutral for binding arbitration on the basis of final offer selection."

27 Framework of Fairness Agreement, November 19, 2007 at 4.

28 Framework of Fairness Agreement, November 19, 2007 at 3.

29 Framework of Fairness Agreement, November 19, 2007 at 33.

30 Jim Stanford, "New Union Strategies for Tough Times: The CAW-Magna Deal and other Responses" (Lecture at Sefton Memorial Lectures, University of Toronto, March 2008), Online: <www.chass.utoronto.ca/cir/library/seftonlectures/ SeftonLecture26th_2008_Stanford_openingstatement.pdf>.

31 "Chrysler President Tom LaSorda has said that the company will consider a complete pull-out of Canada if it doesn't reach an acceptable agreement with the CAW and if it doesn't receive government funding."
Source: CTV, "No deal yet between CAW and Chrysler Canada" (27 March 2009) Online:<http://toronto.ctv.ca/servlet/an/local/CTVNews/20090327/caw_ chrysler_090327/20090327/?hub=TorontoNewHome>.

32 Sam Gindin, "The CAW and Magna: Disorganizing the Working Class" *The Socialist Bulletin* (19 October 2007), Online: <www.socialistproject.ca/bullet/ bullet065.html>.

33 Sam Gindin, "The CAW and Magna: Disorganizing the Working Class" *The Socialist Bulletin* (19 October 2007), Online: <www.socialistproject.ca/bullet/ bullet065.html>.

34 Eric Tucker, "The Constitutional Right to Bargain Collectively: The Ironies of Labour History in the Supreme Court of Canada" *Comparative Research in*

Law & Political Economy Research Paper 03/2008, 04.01(2008) Online: <www. comparativeresearch.net/servlet/Controller?Action=DownloadPDF&pape rid=100000049> at 37.

35 Framework of Fairness Agreement, November 19, 2007

36 Wayne Fraser, et al. "The Magna Sell-out: The CAW Deal is a Threat to Independent Unionism" *The National Post* (23 November 2007) Online: <www. financialpost.com/story.html?id=e9163705-0d0b-4664-bdcb-0d4c7ea5f5c8>.

37 Hemi Mitic, Letter to the Editor, *The National Post* (1 December 2007), Online: <www.labourwatch.com/forms/no_sell-out_at_magna.pdf>.

38 Steffen Mueller, "Works Councils and Labour Productivity: Looking beyond the Mean" *British Journal of Industrial Relations*, 53(2 June 2015), 308–325 at 308.

39 Steffen Mueller, "Works Councils and Labour Productivity: Looking beyond the Mean" *British Journal of Industrial Relations*, 53(2 June 2015), 308–325 at 309.

40 Steffen Mueller, "Works Councils and Labour Productivity: Looking beyond the Mean" *British Journal of Industrial Relations*, 53(2 June 2015), 308–325 at 309.

41 Ewan McGaughey, "The Codetermination Bargains: The History of German Corporate and Labour Law" SSRN Online: <http://ssrn.com/abstract=2541877>, at 2.

42 Ewan McGaughey, "The Codetermination Bargains: The History of German Corporate and Labour Law" SSRN Online: <http://ssrn.com/abstract=2541877>, at 4.

43 See my own research agenda for about a decade which focuses on the connections between labour and employment law and corporate law.

44 Ewan McGaughey, "The Codetermination Bargains: The History of German Corporate and Labour Law" SSRN Online: <http://ssrn.com/abstract=2541877>, at 5.

45 See Winnipeg General Strike.

46 Brishen Rogers, "Fissuring, Data-Driven Governance, and Platform Economy Labor Standards" October 2017, SSRN online: <http://ssrn.com/abstract=3057635>, at 2

47 Sarah A. Donovan, David H. Bradley and Jon O. Shimabukuro, "What Does the Gig Economy Mean for Workers?" *Congressional Research Service*, R44365, February 5, 2016, Online: <www.fas.org/sgp/crs/misc/R44365.pdf> at 14.

48 McKinsey Global Institute, *Independent Work: Choice, Necessity, and the Gig Economy* (McKinsey & Company, October, 2016), 24. Online: https://www.mckinsey.com/featured-insights/employment-and-growth/ independent-work-choice-necessity-and-the-gig-economy.

49 McKinsey Global Institute, *Independent Work: Choice, Necessity, and the Gig Economy* (McKinsey & Company, October, 2016), viii.

50 Jeremias Prassl offers a solution of having a system where ratings attach to the worker even if they leave a platform to work on another platform.

51 McKinsey Global Institute, *Independent Work: Choice, Necessity, and the Gig Economy* (McKinsey & Company, October, 2016), viii.

52 McKinsey Global Institute, *Independent Work: Choice, Necessity, and the Gig Economy* (McKinsey & Company, October, 2016), 20.

53 McKinsey Global Institute, *Independent Work: Choice, Necessity, and the Gig Economy* (McKinsey & Company, October, 2016), viii.

54 McKinsey Global Institute, *Independent Work: Choice, Necessity, and the Gig Economy* (McKinsey & Company, October, 2016), 15.

55 McKinsey Global Institute, *Independent Work: Choice, Necessity, and the Gig Economy* (McKinsey & Company, October, 2016), 16.

56 David Weil, "Enforcing Labour Standards in Fissured Workplaces: The US Experience" *The Economic and Labour Relations Review*, 22.2, 33–54 at 33.

57 David Weil, "Enforcing Labour Standards in Fissured Workplaces: The US Experience" *The Economic and Labour Relations Review*, 22.2, 33–54 at 34.

58 McKinsey Global Institute, *Independent Work: Choice, Necessity, and the Gig Economy* (McKinsey & Company, October, 2016), 51.
59 David Weil, "Enforcing Labour Standards in Fissured Workplaces: The US Experience" *The Economic and Labour Relations Review*, 22.2, 33–54 at 37.
60 Farrell, Diana and Fiona Greig, 2016, JPMorgan Chase & Co. Institute, "The Online Platform Economy: Has Growth Peaked?" Online: <www.jpmorganchase.com/corporate/institute/document/jpmc-institute-online-platform-econ-brief.pdf> at 11.
61 David Weil, "Enforcing Labour Standards in Fissured Workplaces: The US Experience" *The Economic and Labour Relations Review*, 22.2, 33–54 at 48.
62 Einat Albin and Jeremias Prassl, "Fragmenting Work, Fragmented Regulation: The Contract of Employment as a Driver of Social Exclusion", SSRN Online: <http://ssrn.com/abstract=2709569>, at 2.
63 Einat Albin and Jeremias Prassl, "Fragmenting Work, Fragmented Regulation: The Contract of Employment as a Driver of Social Exclusion", SSRN Online: <http://ssrn.com/abstract=2709569>, at 32.
64 McKinsey Global Institute, *Independent Work: Choice, Necessity, and the Gig Economy* (McKinsey & Company, October, 2016), 20.
65 McKinsey Global Institute, *Independent Work: Choice, Necessity, and the Gig Economy* (McKinsey & Company, October, 2016), 38.
66 McKinsey Global Institute, *Independent Work: Choice, Necessity, and the Gig Economy* (McKinsey & Company, October, 2016), 45.
67 McKinsey Global Institute, *Independent Work: Choice, Necessity, and the Gig Economy* (McKinsey & Company, October, 2016), 42.
68 McKinsey Global Institute, *Independent Work: Choice, Necessity, and the Gig Economy* (McKinsey & Company, October, 2016), 90.
69 McKinsey Global Institute, *Independent Work: Choice, Necessity, and the Gig Economy* (McKinsey & Company, October, 2016), 91.
70 Mark Freedland and Jeremias Prassl, "Employees, Workers, and the 'Sharing Economy': Changing Practices and Changing Concepts in the United Kingdom" SSRN Online: <http://ssrn.com/abstract=2932757>, at 6.
71 McKinsey Global Institute, *Independent Work: Choice, Necessity, and the Gig Economy* (McKinsey & Company, October, 2016), 94.
72 Einat Albin and Jeremias Prassl, "Fragmenting Work, Fragmented Regulation: The Contract of Employment as a Driver of Social Exclusion", SSRN Online: <http://ssrn.com/abstract=2709569>, at 15.
73 Einat Albin and Jeremias Prassl, "Fragmenting Work, Fragmented Regulation: The Contract of Employment as a Driver of Social Exclusion", SSRN Online: <http://ssrn.com/abstract=2709569>, at 18.
74 Abi Adams, Mark Freedland, and Jeremias Prassl, "The 'Zero-Hours Contract': Regulating Casual Work, or Legitimating Precarity?" SSRN Online: <http://ssrn.com/abstract=2507693>, at 8.
75 Jeremias Prassl, "Pimlico Plumbers, Uber Drivers, Cycle Couriers, and Court Translators: Who is a Worker" SSRN Online: <http://ssrn.com/abstract=2948712>, at 1.
76 McKinsey Global Institute, *Independent Work: Choice, Necessity, and the Gig Economy* (McKinsey & Company, October, 2016), 99.
77 Mark Freedland and Jeremias Prassl, "Employees, Workers, and the "Sharing Economy": Changing Practices and Changing Concepts in the United Kingdom" SSRN Online: <http://ssrn.com/abstract=2932757>, at 4.
78 Jeremias Prassl and Martin Risak, "Uber, TaskRabbit & Co: Platforms as Employers? Rethinking the Legal Analysis of Crowdwork" SSRN Online: <http://ssrn.com/abstract=2733003>, at 8.

79 Accenture, "Accenture Technology Vision for Oracle 2016: Trend 3: Platform Economy" Online: <www.accenture.com/t20160929T023540Z__w__/us-en/_acnmedia/PDF-26/Accenture-Tech-Vision-for-Oracle-Trend-3.pdf> at 4.

80 Sarah A. Donovan, David H. Bradley and Jon O. Shimabukuro, "What Does the Gig Economy Mean for Workers?" *Congressional Research Service*, R44365, February 5, 2016, Online: <www.fas.org/sgp/crs/misc/R44365.pdf> at 8.

81 Jeremias Prassl and Martin Risak, "Uber, TaskRabbit & Co: Platforms as Employers? Rethinking the Legal Analysis of Crowdwork" SSRN Online: <http://ssrn.com/abstract=2733003>, at 7.

82 JPMorgan Chase & Co. Institute, "The Online Platform Economy: Has Growth Peaked?" November 2016 Online: <www.jpmorganchase.com/corporate/institute/document/jpmc-institute-online-platform-econ-brief.pdf> at 17.

83 McKinsey Global Institute, *Independent Work: Choice, Necessity, and the Gig Economy* (McKinsey & Company, October, 2016), 91.

84 Accenture, "Platform Companies: Treading the Path from Early Disruptor to Platform Titan, Part 3: Overcoming the Obstacles to Growth" 2017 Online: <www.accenture.com/t20171003T093751Z__w__/us-en/_acnmedia/PDF-62/Accenture-Platform-Companies-PoV-Part3.pdf> at 8.

85 Farrell, Diana and Fiona Greig, 2016, JPMorgan Chase & Co. Institute, "Paychecks, Paydays, and the Online Platform Economy: Big Data on Income Volatility" February 2016 Online: <www.jpmorganchase.com/corporate/institute/document/jpmc-institute-volatility-2-report.pdf> at 2.

86 Jeremias Prassl and Martin Risak, "Uber, TaskRabbit & Co: Platforms as Employers? Rethinking the Legal Analysis of Crowdwork" SSRN Online: <http://ssrn.com/abstract=2733003>, at 6.

87 McKinsey Global Institute, *Independent Work: Choice, Necessity, and the Gig Economy* (McKinsey & Company, October, 2016), 19. Online: https://www.mckinsey.com/featured-insights/employment-and-growth/independent-work-choice-necessity-and-the-gig-economy.

88 Cynthia Estlund, "A Return to Governance in the Law of the Workplace (and the Question of Worker Participation)" July 2010, SSRN Online: <http://ssrn.com/abstract=1640566>, at 3.

89 Caroline Bruckner, "Shortchanged: The Tax Compliance Challenges of Small Business Operators Driving the On-Demand Platform Economy" May 2016, Online: <www.american.edu/kogod/research/upload/shortchanged.pdf> at 2.

90 Farrell, Diana and Greig, Fiona, 2016, JPMorgan Chase & Co. Institute, "Paychecks, Paydays, and the Online Platform Economy: Big Data on Income Volatility" February 2016 Online: <www.jpmorganchase.com/corporate/institute/document/jpmc-institute-volatility-2-report.pdf> at 8.

91 Accenture, "Platform Companies: Treading the Path from Early Disruptor to Platform Titan, Part 2: The Road to Maturity" 2017 Online: <www.accenture.com/t00010101T000000Z__w__/au-en/_acnmedia/PDF-62/Accenture-Platform-Companies-PoV-Part2.pdf> at 4.

92 Caroline Bruckner, "Shortchanged: The Tax Compliance Challenges of Small Business Operators Driving the On-Demand Platform Economy" May 2016, Online: <www.american.edu/kogod/research/upload/shortchanged.pdf> at 1.

93 Jeremias Prassl and Martin Risak, "Uber, TaskRabbit & Co: Platforms as Employers? Rethinking the Legal Analysis of Crowdwork" SSRN Online: <http://ssrn.com/abstract=2733003>, at 6.

94 Caroline Bruckner, "Shortchanged: The Tax Compliance Challenges of Small Business Operators Driving the On-Demand Platform Economy" May 2016, Online: <www.american.edu/kogod/research/upload/shortchanged.pdf> at 2.

95 Sarah A. Donovan, David H. Bradley and Jon O. Shimabukuro, "What Does the Gig Economy Mean for Workers?" *Congressional Research Service*, R44365, February 5, 2016, Online: <www.fas.org/sgp/crs/misc/R44365.pdf> at 7.

96 Sarah A. Donovan, David H. Bradley and Jon O. Shimabukuro, "What Does the Gig Economy Mean for Workers?" *Congressional Research Service*, R44365, February 5, 2016, Online: <www.fas.org/sgp/crs/misc/R44365.pdf> at 3.

97 Accenture, "Platform Companies: Treading the Path from Early Disruptor to Platform Titan, Part 3: Overcoming the Obstacles to Growth" 2017 Online: <www.accenture.com/t20171003T093751Z__w__/us-en/_acnmedia/PDF-62/Accenture-Platform-Companies-PoV-Part3.pdf> at 5.

98 Charlotte Garden, "The Seattle Solution: Collective Bargaining by For-Hire Drivers & Prospects for Pro-Labor Federalism" Online: <http://harvardlpr.com/wp-content/uploads/2018/01/Garden-SeattleSolution.pdf> at 1.

99 Charlotte Garden, "The Seattle Solution: Collective Bargaining by For-Hire Drivers & Prospects for Pro-Labor Federalism" Online: <http://harvardlpr.com/wp-content/uploads/2018/01/Garden-SeattleSolution.pdf> at 2.

100 Charlotte Garden, "The Seattle Solution: Collective Bargaining by For-Hire Drivers & Prospects for Pro-Labor Federalism" Online: <http://harvardlpr.com/wp-content/uploads/2018/01/Garden-SeattleSolution.pdf> at 2.

101 Charlotte Garden, "The Seattle Solution: Collective Bargaining by For-Hire Drivers & Prospects for Pro-Labor Federalism" Online: <http://harvardlpr.com/wp-content/uploads/2018/01/Garden-SeattleSolution.pdf> at 8.

102 Charlotte Garden, "The Seattle Solution: Collective Bargaining by For-Hire Drivers & Prospects for Pro-Labor Federalism" Online: <http://harvardlpr.com/wp-content/uploads/2018/01/Garden-SeattleSolution.pdf> at 16.

103 See Prashant Rao, "Uber Loses Its License to Operate in London" *New York Times*, September 22, 2017.

104 See Prashant Rao, "Uber Loses Its License to Operate in London" *New York Times*, September 22, 2017.

105 Frank Pasquale, "Two Narratives of Platform Capitalism" *Yale Law & Policy Review*, 35.1, Article 11, Online: <http://digitalcommons.law.yale.edu/ylpr/vol35/iss1/11>, at 309.

106 Prashant Rao, "Uber Drivers Aren't Independent Contractors, U.K. Tribunal Rules" *New York Times*, November 10, 2017.

107 Prashant Rao, "Uber Drivers Aren't Independent Contractors, U.K. Tribunal Rules" *New York Times*, November 10, 2017.

108 Frank Pasquale, "Two Narratives of Platform Capitalism" *Yale Law & Policy Review*, 35.1, Article 11, Online: <http://digitalcommons.law.yale.edu/ylpr/vol35/iss1/11>, at 312–313.

109 Accenture, "Platform Companies: Treading the Path from Early Disruptor to Platform Titan, Part 1: The Industry We Can't Live Without" 2017 Online: <www.accenture.com/t20171109T094151Z__w__/us-en/_acnmedia/PDF-62/Accenture-Platform-Companies-PoV-Part1.pdf > at 2.

110 Frank Pasquale, "Two Narratives of Platform Capitalism" *Yale Law & Policy Review*, 35.1, Article 11, Online: <http://digitalcommons.law.yale.edu/ylpr/vol35/iss1/11>, at 313.

111 Frank Pasquale, "Two Narratives of Platform Capitalism" *Yale Law & Policy Review*, 35.1, Article 11, Online: <http://digitalcommons.law.yale.edu/ylpr/vol35/iss1/11>, at 316.

112 Kathleen Delaney Thomas, "Taxing the Gig Economy" presented at NYU Tax Policy Colloquium April 3, 2017 Online: <www.law.nyu.edu/sites/ . . . /Taxing%20the%20Gig%20Economy_%20Thomas.pdf> at 1.

113 Farrell, Diana and Fiona Greig, 2016, JPMorgan Chase & Co. Institute, "Paychecks, Paydays, and the Online Platform Economy: Big Data on Income Volatility" February 2016 Online: <www.jpmorganchase.com/corporate/institute/document/jpmc-institute-volatility-2-report.pdf> at 29.
114 Accenture, "Accenture Technology Vision for Oracle 2016: Trend 3: Platform Economy" Online: <www.accenture.com/t20160929T023540Z__w__/us-en/_acnmedia/PDF-26/Accenture-Tech-Vision-for-Oracle-Trend-3.pdf> at 6.
115 Sarah A. Donovan, David H. Bradley and Jon O. Shimabukuro, "What Does the Gig Economy Mean for Workers?" *Congressional Research Service*, R44365, February 5, 2016, Online: <www.fas.org/sgp/crs/misc/R44365.pdf> at 2.

Bibliography for Chapter 2

Legislation

Canadian Charter of Rights and Freedoms, Part 1 of the *Constitution Act, 1982*, being Schedule B, to the *Canada Act 1982* (UK), 1982, c.11.
Employment Standards Act, 2000, SO 2000, c. 41.
Labour Relations Act, 1995, SO 1995, c. 1, Sched. A.

Caselaw

Health Services and Support—Facilities Subsector Bargaining Association v British Columbia [2007] SCJ No 27; 2007 SCC 27; [2007] 2 SCR 391.
PSAC v Canada [1987] 1 SCR 424.
Reference re Public Service Employee Relations Act (Alta) [1987] 1 SCR 313.
RWDSU v Saskatchewan [1987] 1 SCR 460.

Books

Articles

Adams, Abu, Mark Freedland, and Jeremias Prassl. "The 'Zero-Hours Contract': Regulating Casual Work, or Legitimating Precarity?" SSRN Online: <http://ssrn.com/abstract=2507693>.
Albin, Einatm and Jeremias Prassl. "Fragmenting Work, Fragmented Regulation: The Contract of Employment as a Driver of Social Exclusion", SSRN Online: <http://ssrn.com/abstract=2709569>.
Bruckner, Caroline. "Shortchanged: The Tax Compliance Challenges of Small Business Operators Driving the On-Demand Platform Economy" May 2016, Online: <www.american.edu/kogod/research/upload/shortchanged.pdf>.
Cameron, Jamie. "The Labour Trilogy's Last Rites: *B.C. Health* and a Constitutional Right to Strike" *Canadian Labour and Employment Law Journal*, 15 (2009–2010), 297.
Donovan, Sarah A. David H. Bradley and Jon O. Shimabukuro. "What Does the Gig Economy Mean for Workers?" *Congressional Research Service*, R44365, February 5, 2016, Online: <www.fas.org/sgp/crs/misc/R44365.pdf>.

Estlund, Cynthia. "A Return to Governance in the Law of the Workplace (and the Question of Worker Participation)" July 2010, SSRN Online: <http://ssrn.com/abstract=1640566>,.

Etherington, Brian. "Does Freedom of Association under the *Charter* Include the Right to Strike after *B.C. Health*? Prognosis, Problems and Concerns" *Canadian Labour and Employment Law Journal*, 15 (2009–2010), 315.

Freedland, Mark and Jeremias Prassl. "Employees, Workers, and the 'Sharing Economy': Changing Practices and Changing Concepts in the United Kingdom" SSRN Online: <http://ssrn.com/abstract=2932757>,.

Fudge, Judy. "Brave New Worlds: Labour, The Courts and the *Canadian Charter of Rights and Freedoms*" *Windsor Yearbook of Access to Justice* 28 (2010), 23.

Garden, Charlotte. "The Seattle Solution: Collective Bargaining by For-Hire Drivers & Prospects for Pro-Labor Federalism" Online: <http://harvardlpr.com/wp-content/uploads/2018/01/Garden-SeattleSolution.pdf>.

McGaughey, Ewan. "The Codetermination Bargains: The History of German Corporate and Labour Law" SSRN Online: <http://ssrn.com/abstract=2541877>.

Mueller, Steffan. "Works Councils and Labour Productivity: Looking beyond the Mean" *British Journal of Industrial Relations*, 53.2 (June 2015), 308–325.

Pasquale, Frank. "Two Narratives of Platform Capitalism" *Yale Law & Policy Review*, 35.1, Article 11, Online: <http://digitalcommons.law.yale.edu/ylpr/vol35/iss1/11>.

Prassl, Jeremias. "Pimlico Plumbers, Uber Drivers, Cycle Couriers, and Court Translators: Who is a Worker" SSRN Online: <http://ssrn.com/abstract=2948712>,.

Prassl, Jeremias and Martin Risak. "Uber, Task Rabbit & Co: Platforms as Employers? Rethinking the Legal Analysis of Crowdwork" SSRN Online: <http://ssrn.com/abstract=2733003>.

Rogers, Brishen. "Fissuring, Data-Driven Governance, and Platform Economy Labor Standards" October 2017, SSRN Online: <http://ssrn.com/abstract=3057635>.

Thomas, Kathleen Delaney. "Taxing the Gig Economy" presented at NYU Tax Policy Colloquium April 3, 2017. Online: <www.law.nyu.edu/sites/ . . . /Taxing%20the%20Gig%20Economy_%20Thomas.pdf>.

Weil, David. "Enforcing Labour Standards in Fissured Workplaces: The US Experience" *The Economic and Labour Relations Review*, 22.2, 33–54.

Reports

Accenture. "AccentureTechnologyVisionforOracle2016:Trend3:PlatformEconomy" Online: www.accenture.com/t20160929T023540Z__w__/us-en/_acnmedia/PDF-26/Accenture-Tech-Vision-for-Oracle-Trend-3.pdf.

Farrell, Diana and Fiona Greig. "The Online Platform Economy: Has Growth Peaked?" JPMorgan Chase & Co. Institute, 2016. Online: <www.jpmorganchase.com/corporate/institute/document/jpmc-institute-online-platform-econ-brief.pdf>.

Framework of Fairness Agreement. November 19, 2007.

McKinsey Global Institute. *Independent Work: Choice, Necessity, and the Gig Economy* (McKinsey & Company, October, 2016). Online: https://www.mckinsey.com/featured-insights/employment-and-growth/independent-work-choice-necessity-and-the-gig-economy.

Websites

Bernard, Elaine. "Collective Bargaining as a Constitutional Right" *Our Times,* 6 September 2007. Online: <www.ourtimes.ca/Features/printer_22.php>.

CTV, "No Deal Yet between CAW and Chrysler Canada", 27 March 2009. Online: <http://toronto.ctv.ca/servlet/an/local/CTVNews/20090327/caw_chrysler_0 90327/20090327/?hub=TorontoNewHome>.

Fraser, Wayne et al. "The Magna Sell-out: The CAW Deal is a Threat to Independent Unionism" *The National Post,* 23 November 2007. Online: <www.financialpost. com/story.html?id=e9163705-0d0b-4664-bdcb-0d4c7ea5f5c8>.

Gindin, Sam. "The CAW and Magna: Disorganizing the Working Class" *The Socialist Bulletin,* 19 October 2007. Online: <www.socialistproject.ca/bullet/bullet065. html>.

Merriam-Webster Dictionary, s.v. "important" Online: <www.merriam-webster.com/ dictionary/important>.

Mitic, Hemi. Letter to the Editor, *The National Post,* 1 December 2007. Online: <www.labourwatch.com/forms/no_sell-out_at_magna.pdf>.

Ogilvy Renault. "Supreme Court of Canada Declares Collective Bargaining a Charter Right", 15 June 2007. Online: <www.ogilvyrenault.com/en/resourceCentre_965. htm>.

Rao, Prashant. "Uber Loses Its License to Operate in London" *New York Times,* September 22, 2017.

Rao, Prashant. "Uber Drivers Aren't Independent Contractors, U.K. Tribunal Rules" *New York Times,* November 10, 2017.

Stanford, Jim. "New Union Strategies for Tough Times: The CAW-Magna Deal and other Responses" *Lecture at Sefton Memorial Lectures,* University of Toronto, March 2008. Online: <www.chass.utoronto.ca/cir/library/seftonlectures/ SeftonLecture26th_2008_Stanford_openingstatement.pdf>.

Tucker, Eric. "The Constitutional Right to Bargain Collectively: The Ironies of Labour History in the Supreme Court of Canada" *Comparative Research in Law & Political Economy Research Paper 03/2008,* 04.01 (2008), 37. Online: <www.comparativeresearch.net/servlet/Controller?Action=DownloadPDF&pape rid=100000049>.

3 How Can the Law Be Changed

Legislative Framework

While legislative changes and stronger labour laws in other countries may be the best approach and the most stringent with the power of the state behind such laws, there are ways that legislation can be hard to implement: (1) It is difficult to get new laws passed, (2) it is time consuming, (3) laws can be repealed, and (4) laws need an enforcement mechanism. The changes to a corporate structure are not dependent on political changes in the same manner that legislative changes are impacted by changes in the political climate.

Firstly, passing news laws involves tabling bills then having them pass through readings and then get implemented and out into force. Laws are of the utmost importance, but when the goal is to strengthen workers' rights in other nations because they produce goods for the Canadian market, then strengthen Canadian laws will not have the desired impact. Even if laws are strengthened in Thailand and Honduras, they may not be strongly enforced.

Secondly, the time it takes for a Bill to become law is time consuming. To effect change as quickly as possible, it may be easier to get the corporation to adopt a code, which can take less time. A corporation can make that decision quite quickly, and it does not have to go through the lengthy process like a Bill does.

Thirdly, even if a law gets passed, it can get repealed. This may seem like a simple argument to make in that anything that can be changed can be changed back, but it is important to recognize that laws do not necessarily last forever. Laws can be repealed, and it may be less likely that a code of conduct, an internal mechanism, gets removed than for a law to get repealed. The abolition of a law is also outside the power of the corporation, and it is impacted without any say. The decision to remove a code of conduct may be met with resistance by those internal to the corporation, be it customers, shareholders, etc. A current example is PETA buying shares of Canada Goose when it went public—the purpose was to try to get Canada Goose to stop using coyote fur on its coats. A group such as that shareholder group will protest and try to stop any internal changes to the corporation.

Fourthly, in order for a law to be effective, it needs a strong enforcement mechanism. A law on the books that is not well enforced is not useful. So, the task is not just to get a law implemented, but to make sure that there are governmental resources enough to pay for the enforcement of the law. In the code of conduct context, the corporation has to pay for the monitoring agency so that government resources are not used.

My research looks at how to increase the rights of workers in the era of union decline (see the decline of the auto industry in North America) and attaches responsibility to the corporation itself, which forces the corporation to abide by the code of conduct no matter what jurisdiction. The book will show how workers can have a greater voice by using methods outside of the standard labour and employment law schemes. Many sources put pressure on the corporation such as shareholders, activists, NGOs, etc. This compels the corporation to adopt a code of conduct which guarantees certain working conditions. In the unionized context, the employees also have the union on their side, but in the scheme I developed, the employees are without a union. There is no 'protection' beyond the code and its internal resolution procedure. The code may be enforced by an external monitoring agency such as the Fair Labor Association (FLA) or Workers Rights Consortium (WRC), but they are not legal 'protection' for the worker in the same way that the Union is in the unionized setting. The code of conduct is somewhat similar to the CA in Labour Law but does not have the power of the state to enforce such as the role of the Ontario Labour Relations Board, etc. This is what takes the rights of workers into the realm of soft law unlike Labour Law. This model is able to be adopted in workplaces where unionizing is difficult as it offers a basic level of protection that workers would otherwise be without. There is room for a discussion about hard law versus soft law and how codes occupy a space in the middle. The work of Professor Larry Cata Backer will be used to show how this governance gap may be filled.

Fiduciary Duty to Workers

To expand the fiduciary duty of the corporation to workers following from *Peoples* and *BCE* will allow for workers to gain an increased level of protection that did not exist before.

Fiduciary Duties

Holding multiple fiduciary duties seems to be a paradox; however, in Europe there are multi-stakeholder agreements that demonstrate that this can be accomplished. As noted by Bradley,

> [i]n this context, fiduciary duties are generally owed to the dependent person(s) whose reasonable expectations they are intended to protect, while the statutory fiduciary duty in corporate law is always owed to the corporation itself; the reasonable expectations of others are external to this relationship.[1]

Fiduciary duties arise in the law of trusts, within parent–child relationships and are held to be the utmost duty of one towards another. It should be noted that not all duties under the law are fiduciary duties. Also note that some legal duties are based in legislation termed 'statutory duties,' while other legal duties are based in common law. Even if it can be said that society expects directors and officers to have duties and obligations to the corporation, it must be determined whether these are duties or fiduciary duties: "The basic nominate function of directors is to manage or direct the business of the corporation. Fiduciary accountability attaches to every aspect of that function. Each power (more broadly, each aspect of limited access) is capable of being turned to personal ends."[2] While it may be said that directors and officers have fiduciary duties to the corporation, the duties to other stakeholders may be duties but not fiduciary duties.

The term 'fiduciary duty' only appears 16 times in eight different federal statutes[3] (appearing twice in each of the eight statutes). This not a vast landscape for fiduciary duties as defined at the federal level. This movement from state-made law to judge-made law through legislation to the common law system is tantamount in Canadian law. Only when the courts receive further guidance from the legislature about fiduciary duties will it be clearer to understand the extent of the duties owed to the corporation and to whom those duties are owed. It will be easier to understand whose interests the corporation does serve and whose interests matter to directors and officers.

Expanding on the decision in *Peoples* the Court held that where there is conflict among stakeholders that directors and officers must treat each stakeholder group fairly. The Court's distinction of whether the Directors owe a duty to shareholders or the corporation itself is rather hollow as the corporation itself encompasses shareholders plus other stakeholders. A duty to just the corporation is rather meaningless as the corporation is a separate legal entity which contains no people, etc., and having a duty to such an entity must mean that others are owed the duty instead. As noted by Bradley, statutory fiduciary duties are owed to the corporation itself,[4] which may isolate the corporation's directors and officers from considering interests beyond the corporation. While reasonable expectations may not occupy a paramount position in regards to corporate law, the nature of the mundane duties needs to be drawn out. Professor Richardson's work in socially responsible investment is significant for its research on fiduciary duties. According to Richardson, "the fiduciary's foremost duty is one of loyalty to the beneficiary—to act in their sole or best interests."[5]

Expanding the fiduciary duty in the corporate law context will ultimately dilute the duty. So perhaps there can be another method way by which there would be increased protection for workers within corporate law through a more stakeholder-focused version of corporate law theory. Shareholder primacy model is akin to shareholder dominance because the theory states that shareholders will be given the utmost importance when corporate decisions are made. Perhaps it is time to replace shareholder primacy model not with stakeholder theory, but with a shareholder-focused model that allows shareholders to be lowered from the level in shareholder primacy but not as low as to be considered directly alongside stakeholders. This model of shareholder-focused governance would allow for the theory to be described more broadly as placing shareholders at the forefront, but not the only interests that count.

This movement from shareholder wealth maximization and/or shareholder primacy model can move into the shareholder-focused model then onwards to stakeholder theory actualized. This would allow for a smoother transition from rather divergent models that of shareholder primacy and stakeholder theory to have a bridging model that allows for laws to be changed without being drastic.

Shareholder primacy model → shareholder-focused model → stakeholder theory actualized

And this also allows for corporate culture to change to keep pace with the law. Also, elements can be added in slowly and allow for everyone to adapt rather than a sudden shift from one model to another. *Peoples* and *BCE* has helped to usher in this new model, which is not exactly as I have described. This transition model that I am describing does not describe the current Canadian landscape. There would need to be elements changed.

How Traditional Corporate Governance Has Failed Workers

Because workers have been viewed as outsiders to corporate governance in that the position they occupy is not considered internal in the typical sense of being directors or officers then the place they have occupied is on the periphery. They are not given the status of shareholders and the protection that follows from "being the true owners of the corporation," neither are they bondholders to occupy that esteemed position as enunciated in *BCE*. Workers get grouped in with other stakeholder groups and are not given any further status. At the domestic level in Canada, workers are only able to claim a limited amount against directors of a corporation for unpaid wages. At the international level, workers are exploited outside the protection of Canadian law and instead are treated according to their domestic laws, and often abuses go unpunished. The rise of CSR holds promise for workers that consumers will continue to demand ethical products and that shareholder activists will continue to draft shareholder proposals that can impact corporate behaviour. The movement is in the right direction and if that momentum remains and gets better, then workers may gain from corporate governance changes. With more unions and other ethical groups looking for corporations to invest their pension plans in there may be progress for corporations to become more accountable and transparent about how they treat their workers. Also, when younger businesspeople get promoted and move up in the ranks, they may govern with a view to a profit, but with good values alongside. There are studies that show that young graduates leaving business schools with MBAs have a desire to work for ethical corporations and are willing to take a pay cut to work somewhere that is 'doing good by being good' rather than work somewhere that is less ethical. See also the MBA Oath where students graduating with an MBA take an oath to be good and ethical businesspeople.

Codes of conduct are a separate layer of governance that does not lend itself to working in conjunction with a collective agreement. Codes only exist in the absence of collective agreements. Collective agreements exist between management and union members to protect the rights of both parties as management is allowed to grieve using the grievance process although it is rarely used in that manner. Collective agreements usually contain a section on management rights, which ensures that certain decisions are left to the sole discretion of management. Unions have responded to the new economy after the economic downturn in 2008 and have been making significant changes in both how unions organize and how unions negotiate new collective agreements.

Unions have to adapt to changes in the economy, and codes are able to exist in places where it is difficult to unionize and attaches duty to the corporation itself rather than govern the workplace in each different jurisdiction in a disorganized manner. Codes exist where there is no union and allow for the governance void to be filled by having a place for workers to exist and thrive. When one thinks about workers' voice as a collective and the voice of shareholders, these two do not have to be at odds. There is space for both.

Corporations as Citizens

The Supreme Court of Canada introduces the notion of the 'good corporate citizen' and the notion that corporations are citizens and enjoy the rights of citizens accordingly. To delve deeper into this concept, one must ask questions about how the corporation functions as a citizen—do we expect corporations to be active and engaged citizens, or would we expect corporations to be a domicile and blasé citizenry. Corporations have, perhaps unwillingly, been drawn into the political sphere by its decisions to invest, to hire more staff, to move the location of factories and offices, etc. Crane, Matten, and Moon postulate that corporate concerns now include issues such as climate change, poverty, human rights, and social justice.[6] They go on to note that citizens do not merely enjoy rights and freedoms, but also have duties and responsibilities to the society in which they exist.[7] The relationship is symbiotic and ongoing. Corporations as citizens are also social actors.

> [French] argues that the corporation, and not just the people within it, are moral actors and thus the proper subject of ethical evaluations (French 1970). He illustrates this with reference to the evidence that corporations have intentions and thus undertake moral responsibility.[8]

The corporation must act ethically as well as the individuals who work within the corporation. If the corporate citizen exists within a democracy, then there is room for the corporation to consolidate power in the form of an oligarchy and can create something close to a monopoly by takeovers and mergers.[9]

Corporations taking over governmental responsibilities in the form of providing clean water for the mining community within which they operate, etc. can be seen as a positive in that people can access clean water or negative in that the government has failed to provide clean water to its own citizens. Certain roles of the government like the armed forces and police are still hard to be taken over by corporations. However, some corporations hire their own security personnel such as Shell in Nigeria.[10] Even such core functions of the government can be appropriated by corporations.

Corporations are only able to become involved with governance when government ceases to do so, when government has not yet assumed the task of governing and when it is beyond the reach of the state to govern.[11] The government may be failing when corporate philanthropy is used to improve schools and neighbourhoods in that this may be viewed as stepping into the welfare state.[12] Privatization of public services is another example of the corporation acting when the government decides not to—which is distinct from the government failing to act. When the government has not yet assumed the role, then corporations may be forced to start providing health care for their workers and making sure that they receive a living wage. Finally, globalization has made it so that some roles are beyond the role of government. Governments can choose to act to stop climate change, but corporations may also have an important role to play in regard to such issues. For example if Shell decided to cut carbon emissions in their worldwide operations, this may be more influential than Nigeria forcing Shell to cut carbon emissions—nation-state versus the world.

'Good Corporate Citizen' versus 'Good Samaritan Corporation'

I use the term 'Good Samaritan Corporation' to denote that we expect corporations to not just be good corporate citizens, which is acknowledged in the text of *Peoples* and *BCE*, but rather we expect them to be good Samaritans who help those in need and are beyond simply citizens, but also good citizens.

The *Good Samaritan Act*[13] in Ontario truly only acts to protect individuals who try to help those in peril from being held responsible for negligence as subsection 2 (2) reads "[n]ot liable for damages that result from the person's negligence in acting or failing to act while providing the services."[14] There is no law that requires people to act to assist someone in danger or in an accident. Doctors are often thought to be required to offer assistance due to their obligations flowing from the Hippocratic Oath and possibly the regulations of their regulatory body like the College of Physicians and Surgeons. The fact that there is no duty to act in Ontario seems consistent with other laws that shelter individuals from legal liability if you attempt to help someone who is injured, etc. Laws that have compelled action to help others have been challenged successfully in court.

Forcing someone to act in a positive manner is very different from requiring individuals to refrain from bad actions—do not steal and do not assault someone or face the consequences is different from requiring someone to take positive action to help someone in need. There may be an ethical argument to be made that you should help someone in need but the legal argument is different. What if there is a duty? How would it be enforced? Would it span across all ages? Could you require someone who is a child to act? Someone who is an elderly adult? Would you have to take heroic measures to save a drowning person or merely call 911? This goes back to our earlier discussion about establishing a duty and then fulfilling the standard of care associated with the duty.

Obviously, the extent of the duty and the actual language for a statute about this topic would have to be fleshed out, but it is worth considering thinking about the direction in which corporations might be willing to move to become more 'good.' Or maybe to move from being a good corporation to being a great corporation in regards to social responsibility.

Good Samaritan Corporation

What would a Good Samaritan Corporation look like? It would possibly resemble a Benefit Corporation's increased duty to disclose and have a third-party standard. The Benefit Corporation is intended to act in the benefit of society, not just corporate interests. So this seems very close to the purpose of a Good Samaritan Corporation—one that exists not solely to make a profit, but to make a profit while acting honestly, caring about the environment, and caring about workers. This type of corporation is even beyond the Benefit Corporation in terms of caring about others and acting somewhat as a guardian towards others. This may seem idealistic and naïve, but the trend towards increased social responsibility may support such a new corporate form—one that exists not just for shareholders, but truly for all stakeholders. The Board may include workers like in Germany but also an environmental steward, which would be new and unique. So, the focus would be not just on workers, but there would be a designated seat for environmental concerns to reside in.

There would still be the corporate veil that allows for liability to vest in the corporation and not with individuals like the standard corporation. These basic aspects of the corporation should be retained to help protect individuals from being personally liable for the actions of the corporation. Perhaps the Good Samaritan Corporation would have a special reserve of money simply for community outreach programs and other such corporate philanthropy projects. If there are ten Board members then one is already designated as the worker representative and another for the environmental steward which leaves eight members to be 'normal' members. This just carves out two members to be 'special representatives,' which is not onerous in the least. This helps to brand the corporation as beyond CSR and instead more in line with CSR principles: CSR principles being that corporations do not exist solely for their shareholders to become more wealthy and that its duties are greater than internal actors of the corporation.

People working with and for the Good Samaritan Corporation could be bound by a code of conduct to ensure that they are acting ethically at all times. They could also be required to swear an oath similar to the MBA Oath, even if they do not have MBAs.

Layering Governance

What might be ideal is in fact a process of layering governance. In the context of rights in relation to the corporation, this new mode of governance might be useful and

> the layering of private voluntary initiatives on existing legal structures (labor courts, labor regulations)—promote an effective alternative to weak or absent state regulation. At the same time, it can provide a more efficient vehicle through which workers can actually exercise their citizenship rights.[15]

This notion of layering governance so that one corporation has multiple duties to multiple stakeholders may allow for a broader range of control and for the corporation to be more flexible in its approach to being governed. For some aspects of being governed, the corporation has strict legal obligations that it must comply with, while other governance mechanisms may be more variable and open to input from the very stakeholders who are impacted. This level of variability may include more stakeholders than those merely able to wield political power or have a seat at the boardroom table. Those stakeholder groups may include workers, customers, etc.

This allows for there to be extra layers on top of the mandatory legal requirements to be adhered to. This means that management may have to abide by the domestic law, international norms, as well as a code of conduct, and maybe compliance is enforced through the use of a monitoring agency. Thus, it creates many layers of governance that when all are complied with create a more effective regulatory scheme.

Employer Free Speech

This section critically explores whether the 'captive audience speech' given by management in workplaces in an attempt to dissuade workers from unionizing is actually legislated intimidation. Some members of management will force workers to listen to a speech about the ills of unionization and the detriment to job security if the union is implemented. This speech is a form of intimidation. While employers may argue that they have a right to free speech, 'captive audience speeches' are a form of advertising in that the underlying message is about economic rights. The employer is not exercising free speech, but rather is selling a union-free workplace by scaring workers by using threats of job loss, etc. By granting any form of employer free speech, the government is effectively legislating the right to intimidate.[16] While labour and employment law can be thought of as union versus management in the unionized context or employer versus employee in the non-unionized context, the true dynamic is one of struggle on the part of the worker. While labour law is not usually constructed as an 'us against them' scheme, it is worth noting then when workers fight for greater rights management is not quick to acquiesce thus situating the two parties on opposite sides. While the employment relationship is often an ongoing one and one in which both parties are frequently working towards similar, if not the same, goals, it is a site of intimidation as well.

This section investigates whether employers right to speech is truly serving the purpose of allowing employers the ability to speak against the union's claims and promises, almost a rebuttal, or if it is a form of economic intimidation. One reason that employers may want to block the union is that some employers think that unions are focused on trying to usurp the powers of management. Other employers may think that unions drive up wages and lower profits or revenue.

Section 70 of the *Labour Relations Act, 1995*[17] outlines that employers are not to interfere with unions under the umbrella term of 'unfair practices.'

> 70. No employer or employers' organization and no person acting on behalf of an employer or an employers' organization shall participate in or interfere with the formation, selection or administration of a trade union or the representation of employees by a trade union or contribute financial or other support to a trade union, but nothing in this section shall be deemed to deprive an employer of the employer's freedom to express views so long as the employer does not use coercion, intimidation, threats, promises or undue influence. 1995, c. 1, Sched. A, s. 70.[18]

The true essence of employer freedom is grounded in section 70. Particularly, "nothing in this section shall be deemed to deprive an employer of the employer's freedom to express views so long as the employer does not use coercion, intimidation, threats, promises or undue influence." Well, what constitutes coercion? Intimidation? Threats? Promises? These issues need to be addressed by the legislature to ensure that management is not manipulating their workers to not join a union.

> The Windsor case also raised issues of employer free speech when the union was awarded automatic certification due in part to charges that Wal-Mart had acted unfairly when it refused to answer the employees' questions about whether the store would close if the union campaign succeeded.[19]

In that case, the OLRB found that not answering questions, what could be termed an omission, runs against the nature of the Act as well. If the employer will sit idly by while another makes claims seems to lead the listener to the conclusion that what is being said by another is true. The failure of management to correct untrue statements. The true purpose of a captive audience meeting in the organizing context is to try to dissuade workers from supporting the union and trying to not have the union become certified as the bargaining agent.

The two parties, union and management, are not equals. The employer holds economic power over the workers in the form of job security, termination, decrease in wages, etc. To try to hold employers to be at a disadvantage if they did not have a right to free speech is not true. Not all unions are alike. Some are more activist than others. Depending on which union tries to organize or has been approached to organize depends on how your workers view the employer. You had a chance to run this union-free and you could not. Interpret that as you may.

> Most prominently, Senator Wagner denounced the free speech amendment arguing that it would suppress, rather than enhance, the exercise of free speech in American society: 'The talk of restoring free speech to the employer is a polite way of reintroducing employer interference, economic retaliation, and other insidious means of discouraging union membership and union activity.'[20]

In the United States their *National Labor Relations Act* is referred to as the Wagner Act after its sponsor Senator Robert Wagner and was enacted in 1935. This was a quote from Senator Wagner denouncing the Taft–Hartley Act enacted in 1947, which eroded some of the rights outlined in the 1935 Act. "Unwilling listeners have received some protection through the captive audience doctrine. Under this doctrine, a listener's right to privacy may trump a speaker's right to communicate."[21] The right to privacy has actually really grown as an area in light of the digital revolution, the increased usage of social media, and the right to be forgotten. What constituted privacy in the 1970s or even in the 1990s has evolved to now include the right to be forgotten when someone dies. They can choose to be erased from the internet. The right to privacy in the realm of discrimination has also increased protection for workers—whether management can use surveillance to spy on their workers is a contested ground. It depends on whether the worker is absent for medical reasons, or perhaps has lied to their employer about being sick and then running a business on the side, etc. It is a balancing act between management's right to know if an employee is being truthful versus the employee's right to privacy.

When does trying to persuade someone to do something cross into the more ethical ambiguous area of manipulation? In the employment context this is a difficult line to draw.

> Moreover, the Board's oft-used mantra in other areas of labor law—that persuasion is not coercion—should apply with equal force in union representation campaigns. An employer's ability to deliver on its promises made during a union campaign does not constitute coercion solely because such promises may more effectively convince employees to vote against a union.[22]

The courts and tribunals have not been able to decide unanimously about what constitutes coercion or not.

> The fine distinction between coercion and persuasion is not unique to the Board's prohibition on employer promises. In various other contexts, the NLRB has often held that persuasion is not coercion. That is, speech designed to influence a party is not equivalent to coercion.[23]

It becomes an issue of semantics whether manipulation and persuasion are the same as coercion. In the workplace context, it is not difficult to picture that a worker who fears losing their job will give in to the request of management to not join a union. This masks the inherent inequality of the employment relationship. These are not two equal parties with equal power and monetary budgets. This is the difference between one party that controls the process and another that merely participates. One party dictates the terms and the another acquiesces.

Unions also have to contend with being left out of the process entirely as the rules around whether unions can access employee information is not settled. Can a union access that information for members? What about during the course of an organizing campaign? Well, it depends on the jurisdiction. And it depends on how much time and money the union has to invest in such negotiations. If the task is too difficult it might be yet another obstacle in the way of organizing potential members. "Because unions are generally not guaranteed access to employer property to share their pro-union message with employees, organized labor rightly believes such meetings give employers the ability to effectively intimidate and harass employees during union organizational campaigns."[24] Without better protections in place to gain access to employee information, union-organizing drives will continue to more difficult than need be. With management sometimes trying to sell employees on a 'union-free workplace' coupled with the ability to say what they want without reproach then management is able to dominate the message to their employees: Do not join a union. And workers are not able to hear the other side to make an informed decision for themselves.

This infantilizes workers and disallows them true choice. Even if workers are told that they can leave when management holds a captive audience speech, this is not true choice.

> Although in a formal sense employees are free to walk away from such speech or not attend such meetings, in reality, employees risk being fired if they are considered to be insubordinate to their supervisors by failing to listen [sic] them or by not attending anti-union assemblies.[25]

The best way forward is to protect not just the right of management to free speech to inform their employees about the benefits and disadvantages of joining a union, but would be to protect those employees who choose to walk away.

> Following the lead of the AFL-CIO, a number of states have considered Worker Freedom Act (WFA) legislation. This legislation would 'give employees the freedom to walk away from political or religious indoctrination meetings—and would bar employers from firing or disciplining workers who choose not to attend or who report unlawful forced meetings.'[26]

Having such legislation enacted would help secure the rights of employees to walk away from management 'free speech' without fear of repercussion. Workers are the less powerful party in the relationship and this should not go unrecognized during the course of union-organizing drive. Why allow management to sway workers who want to join a union? The other side of being pro-union gets silenced or at least the volume gets turned way down. Why not allow workers to hear both sides and make an informed choice knowing the gains and losses from joining a union?

As noted by Kate E. Andrias, "[E]mployer free speech not only limits the statutory rights of workers to unionize, but also silences worker speech and pro-union messages."[27] If free speech is to truly be upheld, then it follows that both sides have an equal ability to assert that right. Those who want to hear more about the union should be able to do so without fear of losing their job or other consequences. "Attendance at captive audience meetings is compelled: Employees must listen to anti-union speeches or face termination."[28] Imagine being forced to listen to a message that you do not want to hear. This is borderline harassment or at least an annoyance. What about the employee's right to be free from harassment? This balancing of rights is complex, but the greater weight should be given to the worker who is in the position of less powerful. There should be recognition given for the fact that workers have to be at work and should not be compelled to forcibly listen to anti-union messages while at work. This creates a rather toxic workplace.

> While employers may be free to cast aspersions against trade unions (and vice versa), they must be careful not also to suggest or speculate without a factual foundation, however subtly, that unionization will necessarily undermine the viability of the enterprise, and thus compromise employees' job security.[29]

Management will often scare workers with untruths about the plant shutting down or cutting jobs if they get unionized. "For these reasons, we are satisfied that the union ought to be certified pursuant to section 11."[30] What is termed a remedial certification when the ULP or contravention of the Act is so egregious that no other remedy will suffice. This forces management to be careful about their language usage during an organizing campaign.

Increasing Labour Standards on a Worldwide Level

International Labor Organization

The International Labor Organization (ILO) Conventions outline core labour standards. However, even Canada is not signatory to all of the conventions. Even if a country signs on to the ILO Conventions, the task of enforcing such standards operates on the domestic front. How are breaches of a country's ILO obligations treated? What is the remedy for a breach?[31]

Also, the inclusion of ILO Conventions in corporate codes may be misreading the intent of the ILO. As stated by Professor Jill Murray:

> ILO conventions are designed to place obligations on states. That is so in a purely technical sense, because conventions are instruments which are

'addressed' to states. Each member state of the ILO must decide whether or not it ratifies an individual convention, and the form which implementation of a ratified convention will take.[32]

Trying to get corporations to adopt conventions that are geared at states is ineffective as the state may possess the proper mechanisms for enforcement that a corporation may lack.[33]

Jenkins argues that codes are very much connected to globalization. "The emergence of voluntary corporate codes is both a manifestation of, and a response to, the process of globalization."[34] With corporations expanding to other parts of the world the cry of trying to regulate beyond borders arose. "The second wave of corporate codes, which emerged in the early 1990s, focused on labour conditions. As with the first wave in the 1970s, the new trend for companies to adopt codes was prompted by scandals about corporate practices."[35] It seems as though corporations wait to react to demands about increased regulation rather than be proactive and take the steps necessary to satisfy the activists. Jenkins also describes how ethical consumers may be a small group.[36] Again, the notion of the ethical consumer becomes typified as an affluent person rather than merely an informed person. "One important indicator of the nature of different voluntary codes is the extent to which they incorporate the ILO's core labour standards, or even go beyond those standards."[37] As noted by Murray, the ILO Conventions were not intended to be adopted by companies but rather nation-states. "They [codes of conduct] should be seen as a contested terrain which can be used to advance the cause of workers in the South and to carve out space for them to organize and to struggle to improve their own wages and working conditions."[38] This is important as the codes act as a voice for workers. One in which they can alter the message to suit their own purposes and needs. Voice is not static.

As noted by Barrientos, "[t]racing the supply, or value chain allows us to situate employment within the context of global sourcing, and helps to understand the different factors affecting conditions of work (Barrientos, forthcoming)."[39] Work, like capital, is able to transcend borders—although in a different way. Workers are less likely to move to another jurisdiction, but the nature of work has changed. A single product can be sourced and then assembled in numerous jurisdictions and then shipped to another country to be purchased.

> Yet there are others who are more optimistic, seeing codes as offering a potential tool in efforts to promote worker organization and education. However, this will only be possible if workers have a sense of ownership, if they feel that codes are actually there to support them.[40]

If workers are able to be involved with the drafting of the code and implementation of the code, then they may feel more connected to it.

Transportable Law/Portable Law

The law has become so transportable or portable across jurisdictions. This may be advantageous with regard to stopping abuses on the international level. If a Canadian company can be bound by Canadian laws and/or duties and responsibilities, then perhaps this can alleviate some of the abuses faced by workers and other stakeholders. Imagine a suitcase full of laws and that suitcase can be transported to any other country to bind a corporation to those laws whilst operating in another jurisdiction. This would force corporations to be bound by Canadian law. This is opposite of the fundamental distinction in law of the recognition of sovereignty of nations and the ability to make their own laws to bind their own citizens. Well, if a corporation is a citizen, then it too should be bound by laws in the same way that a citizen can be bound while abroad. This may be similar to laws about Canadian and Australian citizens not being able to engage in unlawful activity abroad otherwise face criminal prosecution when they return to the nation of their citizenship. This privilege of citizenship is restricted by reasonable terms and one of them may be that the citizen cannot commit crimes in another jurisdiction and return home without punishment. The corporation seems immune from extradition proceedings, while an individual citizen may face such punishment. Returning to one's homeland does not grant one sanctuary from facing punishment from behaviour committed abroad.

Allowing the law of one nation to be transplanted into another nation may be reminiscent of colonialism and other forms of domination; however, in this context, the aim is to be able to regulate the behaviour of a corporation while operating abroad, so it is the ability of one government to control a corporation domiciled within its territory and abroad. Perhaps the transportable briefcase containing the law is not the right image, but instead, imagine a tentacle from an octopus being able to grab something far away due to its long grip or ability to extend. The item that the octopus is grabbing rightly belongs to the octopus.

The idea of being able to transplant law is different as this has existed for eons, and it easily demonstrated by looking at colonialism and the ability of the ruling power to enact laws in foreign jurisdictions that either mimicked the law in their home nation or at least enabled them to hold power/increase power. Transplanted law is about abusing power of one nation over another—perhaps with resistance to this intrusion. My idea of transportable law is beneficial to both nations in that the nation moving into another nation for whatever period of time is able to be governed by the home nation while abroad. This home nation's laws are likely more rigourous than the host nation, so they bound the home nation no matter what country. This will cut down on the use of sweatshops, forced labour, and other abuses that are able to be exploited by those who do not live in these nations being exploited. The corporation does not act alone as the case in sweatshops where governments are complacent and do not do anything to stop the corporations from operating on their soil.

> Although corporations often take advantage of low labour standards and weak human rights regimes, for instance by imposing long working hours and neglecting work place security, they are usually not the ones who created the underlying socio-political conditions in the first place.[41]

The impact of the corporation versus the government in developing countries needs to be explored further. What are the conditions that give rise to the sweatshop? Why are individuals so desperate for work that they accept jobs in sweatshops?

To allow Canadian law to follow Canadian corporations into other jurisdictions is to hold those corporations to account in a very basic manner. This would decrease the use of sweatshops and forced labour as Canada has strict laws against such methods of labour. This may result in those same corporations choosing to manufacture their products in Canada rather than choose what was the cheaper alternative by manufacturing in other nations. This will still allow corporations to manufacture because of special natural environments, etc. to source the best coffee or chocolate but will require the labour laws and environmental laws of Canada to be adhered to. This may cut down on outsourcing and other drains on the Canadian economy.

To allow for laws to be transported throughout other jurisdictions binding citizens to the laws of their homeland might seem bizarre and untenable. Corporations are also citizens and should be bound in the same way. Consider countries like Canada and Australia where citizens of their respective nations potentially face criminal charges if they leave the country to engage in illegal activity with children in other countries. This instance shows that the law is already used in a transportable manner in that the behaviour engaged in within other nations may be legal in those countries or not properly enforced, but the citizen faces consequences when returning to the country of their citizenship. This is a small segment of the grand laws of Canada and Australia, but it demonstrates that the law is much like a bungee cord or elastic and can travel with citizens not to be left behind to be forgotten and ignored.

Collective Agreement as Certification Scheme

I have developed a theory that the collective agreement can act as a certification scheme so that the changes in standard union contracts does interact/intersect with certification schemes. If one thinks of the collective agreement for a certain workplace it can be described as a certification scheme that guarantees that all products produced are (1) union made and (2) sweatshop free. If a customer buys a coat made by workers with a collective agreement, then that customer can be confident that the coat is made under fair working conditions, and this acts as a certification of the product much like a certification scheme with a branding logo such as the FSC or Rainforest Alliance. The only difference is that the coat or its labels will not identify it as union made. There was a movement started by the garment workers that customers should 'look for the union label,' but such branding has died off and is no longer used in the same marketing way. However, with the rise of certification schemes, there may be market space for unions to bring back the customers need to 'look for the union label' if the union chooses to brand its products to display the fact that it is union made.

This allows for unions to capitalize on the growing market for certification systems to appease ethical consumers. This gets unions to move into the space occupied by corporations that sell to ethical consumers so unions are able to compete in a similar way as the corporation. Ultimately the union is not producing the product in the same way that the company which the union members work for is producing, but it allows for union to rebrand to follow the CSR trends. This means that unions can keep pace with changing times by tapping into a new market.

Consumer Autonomy

Perhaps the notion that consumers hold much sway in regard to corporate power is a fallacy.

> If the consumer wields any power at all it must derive from the ability to choose from a range of options. Yet if those options are dependent on the range of choice offered by the producers, what remains of the power and influence of the consumer? Is it a mere illusion? Or does it exist, if only in a limited and secondary form?[42]

How much power do consumers truly yield? Perhaps, the power is less than originally conceived. Perhaps if one consumer chooses not to purchase one product does not mean that the next consumer will also refuse. Basically, this is the same problem with shareholders who sell their shares when faced with a 'bad' corporation—the share still exists on the market for someone else to purchase. The reduction in overall 'bad' products is not reduced in and of itself. That product stays on the shelf for someone else to purchase. "From the perspective of social movements, individual consumers 'lend' their purchasing power to them and thus enable them to establish effective threats on the marketplace."[43]

Unifor and Community Chapters

Unifor has been able to devise a new way of organizing workers that allows for workers to be in the same bargaining unit without sharing the same workplace. Under normal labour and employment law, there are requirements that bargaining units be made of up workers who are employed by the same employer at the same workplace, etc. With this new mode of organizing workers are able to come together without those necessities. This allows for an Uber driver to team up with someone who works in another gig job to become one group. This novel way of organizing acts in the opposite way from organizing like with like and deciding who gets to be included. I came up with the term 'unclude' to describe those who do not get included in these typical working scheme and instead get 'uncluded' through new mechanisms.

Worker Voice

Codes also flow through different disciplines from law and business to political science. Who drafts the code (the rulemaker), and who is regulated by it (the ruletaker)? Whose voice is heard and whose voice is silenced? How much influence, if any, does the voice of the worker have on codes? As Locke notes, "[w]e found that the opportunity to participate in decisions related to work process had a strong and positive effect on work climate."[44] And as author Arundhati Roy notes, "we know of course there's really no such thing as the 'voiceless'. There are only the deliberately silenced, or the preferably unheard."[45]

Whose voice is silenced in the labour and employment law context? The voice of the worker is not silenced but instead lowered, or the volume knob is turned down. Way down. To the point of not being heard at all. Worker voice is not silenced by accident. This is intentional. If workers were able to voice their concerns to management, then management may feel compelled or guilted into acting on those words. If workers keep complaining about workplace accidents, then management may feel the need to install safety procedures. Worker voice costs money. It is both easier and cheaper to keep workers silenced.

> These findings echo a large body of academic work pointing to the importance of choice, autonomy, and self-agency as key drivers of worker satisfaction. While most of these studies have looked at the importance of allowing employees more autonomy and flexibility in the traditional workplace, their findings resonate when we consider the appeal of independent work for millions of people.[46]

When talking about worker voice, it is important to note that workers are not a homogeneous group who speaks with one voice. "At the very minimum, the opportunity to have voice is dependent upon receiving information and/or having entitlement to consultation."[47] Those who work in the public sector often have different concerns than those who work in the private sector. One can look at the different unions that cover the two sectors to see a difference in how the union treats the two groups as they have divergent concerns.

Governance Models

The aim is to strengthen existing labour laws and create new laws, and the best way forward may be to construct methods for implementing CSR changes that involve changes to corporations themselves by either external or internal sources.

This can be achieved in two ways, the first being through changes to legislation (hard law), which can be accomplished by expanding duties of directors and officers beyond shareholders to include employees. This can be attained by implementing a mandatory code of conduct for companies, possibly embedded in the *Canada Business Corporations Act* (CBCA).[48] This still leaves the question as to what form this would take and what an ideal code would look like. The second option would be to strengthen existing voluntary codes of conduct (which is a move from soft law to hard law), which is often termed a 'hardening of soft law.'

Answers to these questions can be used to direct policy and should be useful for government when deciding how best to implement new rules or laws and how to strengthen existing rules and laws. Option 2 of implementing more voluntary codes of conduct and strengthening existing ones is the best way forward. Trying to change legislation is more time consuming and less rewarding. Even if legislation is passed by one government, it can be easily removed by the next government as is often the case in regard to labour legislation. Because labour issues are politically isolating the government in power may choose to curtail workers' rights in their administration that the next party in power may change. In the case of codes of conduct there is less chance of codes being changed as key officials may remain in those positions of power. Also, the potential consumer backlash against changing the codes may be anticipated and fought against. Codes do not have the same force that hard law offers but are a good alternative for those who are often left out of the political decision-making process.

Once codes are implemented, their force and effect comes from having external monitoring agencies that are paid to monitor compliance. Depending on the code itself, the remedy for breach usually amounts to an effort to have the company fix the problem by meeting the standards of the code in question, rather than terminating the contract with the supplier automatically. The nature of the code varies from corporation to corporation, but most codes identify that suppliers and sub-suppliers must be governed by the code: Otherwise, the efficacy is reduced. If the attempt to try to rectify the wrong does not happen, then the relationship may be terminated. "The ultimate sanction against non-compliance is the threat of being de-listed as a supplier. Codes are thus only 'voluntary' to the suppliers in that the alternative is to find new outlets."[49] This is often stipulated in the language of the code itself.

Codes are essential in current society as the reach of transnational corporations is vast, and domestic laws are not able to fully provide a regulatory system that is needed for policing such an organization. Critics may argue that codes allow corporations to get away with behaviour that hard law mechanisms would punish (possibly severely so). However, as Teubner explains, "voluntary codes take the process one step further: they allow corporations to make something resembling 'law' without state approval ex ante or ex post."[50] The question becomes more akin to what corporations should do when the state fails to act, rather than corporations vying to usurp the power of the state. "What, then, is the relationship of corporate codes to law? As I have tried to show, corporate codes may be used to deflect state law, to create the illusion of law while fending off the reality of regulation."[51] However, while it may be true that corporations turn to self-regulation as opposed to calling for state regulation, it is not necessarily true that self-regulation is futile. Self-regulation may also be a first step towards increased regulation.

Codes do not offer the protection that hard law does but may allow coverage for areas that legislation does not. While legislation may govern hours of work, there is room within a code to allow for formation of advantages akin to those gained in a collective agreement. In jurisdictions where union organizing is difficult there may be ground covered in a code that may not be able to be achieved through hard law. While the future outcome of numerous codes is yet to be realized, the potential of codes is compelling. Only through the establishment of voluntary codes and onwards towards getting those same rights entrenched in legislation will the fight for workers' rights move forward. "They [codes of conduct] should be seen as a contested terrain which can be used to advance the cause of workers in the South and to carve out space for them to organize and to struggle to improve their own wages and working conditions."[52] Again, a first step in the fight for workers' rights is better than waiting for a perfect model to emerge.

Codes of Conduct as Tools to Increase Workers' Rights

I critically explore how to implement changes to corporate behaviour in regard to labor-related issues through codes of conduct ('code' or 'codes') that would strengthen the rights of workers. The corporation essentially allows for its own reformation from within. There are many ways the link between corporate governance or CSR, and workers' rights can be explored. The term CSR is used to differentiate from the alternate shareholder primacy model of a corporation existing solely for its shareholders and to increase profit. It stands for the idea that corporations have duties to other stakeholders beyond shareholders. Those stakeholders include, but are not limited to, employees and those who produce goods and provide services,[53] environmental agencies, and government. Codes are a soft law mechanism that may be used to create a voluntary standard or set of rules to which corporations are bound. While this may be viewed as rather insubstantial compared to legislation, codes have value in terms of allowing the two (or more) parties that are bound by the code to have direct input in drafting the code. While the inherent imbalance of power involved in the dynamics of the employment relationship between management and workers must be acknowledged and must have an impact on the creation of the code, it does allow for involvement at a level which legislation does not.

Corporations may rally around CSR to appease the masses, and in recognition of the shift towards ethical consumption. This may force corporations to put substance behind their claims to be socially responsible. Because consumers are becoming more knowledgeable about products, the demand for ethical products may put pressure on corporations to adopt the same. Professor Lance Compa credits Levi's and Reebok for adopting internal codes of conduct in the 1990s.[54]

But he also notes that "[c]ompanies monitoring and enforcing their own codes of conduct led inevitably to charges that the fox was monitoring the henhouse."[55] This is also shown by such organizations as the FLA, which was essentially created by the US government under President Bill Clinton, so the FLA is questioned as to whether it is as effective as it could be. The FLA is viewed as a governmental soft mechanism to counter critics rather than an effective monitoring agency. Professor Compa goes on to state that "[t]oday a new generation of codes called 'multi-stakeholder' initiatives has appeared. Companies, unions, human rights groups, community and development organizations, and other NGOs participate in formulating a code of conduct."[56] And these groups can be described as "seeking improvement and compliance, rather than cutting off business and hurting the workers they are trying to help."[57] This illustrates the potential for negative repercussions resulting from efforts to help workers: If a corporation is not able to meet certain standards, then it might shut down, resulting in workers losing jobs. The emphasis is often on trying to reform corporate practices, not putting corporations out of business.

Corporate codes of conduct (also referred to as 'codes of conduct') outline duties and responsibilities that flow from the corporation to stakeholders (employees, customers, etc.). These codes can be narrow in scope (ex. dealing only with environmental issues) or broad in scope (ex. environmental, labour, and social issues). The codes can be superficial or multifaceted. A more fulsome code would be broad in scope and quite detailed in regard to the language of the code itself and compliance mechanisms. A rather shallow code would be narrow in scope and use language that is vague and non-specific, perhaps such a code would be void of an enforcement mechanism. Codes can be internal, external, or third-party codes. The compliance and enforcement mechanisms used to monitor the code can also be weak or strong or somewhere along the continuum. Bondy, Matten, and Moon note that code characteristics can be sorted as follows: (1) Specific versus general and that model codes contain more sweeping language; (2) comprehensive versus selective as multi-stakeholder codes tend to be more comprehensive and include a broader set of issues; (3) positive versus negative in that some codes may be more principles based, while others are more rules based and include language that is negative about what companies should abstain from doing; (4) voluntary versus mandatory which is self-explanatory; and (5) equilegal versus supralegal as to what codes reflect existing laws and which move beyond minimal requirements.[58]

While I argue that codes of conduct are the best way forward for workers, critics of CSR may argue that codes may not be the best way to secure or increase the rights of workers. With the rise of capitalism and what may be termed 'corporatism,' workers must be willing to acknowledge that power and the ability to gain strength in their collective ability allows for speaking truth to power. Only through engaging with corporations will workers be able to forge ahead. The labour movement in many forms has accepted this new mode and has adapted as a result. For workers to have a seat at the table like in the German model may be just one option, and other options may prove useful to other workplaces; no one solution will work in every single workplace. If workers are given increased autonomy and voice about their workplaces then they would be able to choose which model works for their individual workplace. Corporations are only able to become involved with governance when government ceases to do so, when government has not yet assumed the task of governing, and when it is beyond the reach of the state to govern.[59] The governance gap has allowed for corporations to avoid state regulation and instead devise methods of self-regulation. This may be viewed as beneficial in that corporations will bear the cost of regulation and perhaps lend their expertise. Or this can be viewed as corporations being able to fend off actual governmental regulation.

Codes of Conduct

Another tool that is available to corporations that want to put substance behind claims of being socially responsible is to adopt a code of conduct. This allows corporations to be more in line with the BCE requirements and signals to consumers and investors that the corporation is serious about CSR. The corporation can adopt an internal code that governs employee/corporate behaviour within. The corporation can also adopt a code of conduct that governs how the corporation operates internationally such as a supplier code of conduct. This allows for the corporation to be bound to a certain set of guidelines no matter where they are operating. This is a form of transportable law. Or even portable law that can be carried wherever the corporation goes.

The depth of research and studies on codes of conduct cannot be covered enough in this book, but it does build on the reasoning and logic of recent court cases that corporations do have obligations beyond shareholders and should be 'good corporate citizens' meaning that they should be contributing to society in a beneficial way. Being a corporate citizen is different from being a good corporate citizen as the second one provides that the corporation should be acting in a good way by benefiting society at large. Codes of codes are on a spectrum from very weak codes to very strong ones—arguably stronger than hard law alternatives in some cases. Along with the degree of strength for the code itself is the relative strength and effectiveness of an enforcement mechanism that ensures that the code is being adhered to. A code of conduct allows for another layer of governance on top of the existing hard law requirements. This may lead to a stronger version in the future but having a soft law mechanism in place to start with allows for some increased regulation which can be fortified in the future. It can be said that codes are effective and having a strong code in place is somewhat akin to having hard law protections, and in the case of a weak code, it can be replaced in the future with a better code. This spectrum on which both codes and enforcement mechanisms exist is important because it allows us to question how useful the existing structure is and what that same structure can become in the future.

A weak code can be amended to be a stronger code or can be completely replaced with a stronger code. It does not have to be the case that a code will be constantly amended as it could simply be replaced. Of course, it can be that a strong code can be replaced with an inferior code as well. The pressure from both consumers and investors of the corporation may hold the corporation account-able and not allow that to happen. This type of ethical consumption holds that through using transparency and accountability corporations will remain com-mitted to being more ethical or becoming more ethical because, otherwise, they might lose consumers or investors if they fail to be ethical.

This layering of regulation and governance creates a more complete model of regulation for the corporation. New court cases were focused on balancing the interests of shareholders versus investors (bondholders), which is difficult because of the stale model of the corporation with its focus on shareholder wealth maxi-mization. As corporations change so too must corporate law as well as securities law. The ability of the law to change to reflect the changing values of society and citizens is practical because the law cannot remain stagnant and inflexible. As society expects corporations to be more socially responsible and to act in the interests of the many rather than the few, the law must adapt to reflect these changes. The reflection of the law in society also flows the other way in that change in values and beliefs in society must be accommodated into law.

This raises questions about the underlying purpose of the corporation as a profit-making enterprise—how much does that 'view to a profit' extend to cover being good in society and being good to society? How far should that extend? Shareholders and other stakeholders probably would not want the duty to be so diluted that the duty is ineffective and inconsistent. It can be argued that it is easier to attribute directors and officers duties to be towards shareholders for the simplicity of having one single group to be concerned about. Having to take into consideration multiple groups with multiple concerns that may not overlap may lead to confusion. Directors and officers are very concerned with fulfilling their duties and need clarity in order to do so well. By including other stakeholder groups into the duty-driven focus on shareholders leads to a balancing of interests.

Bondy, Matten, and Moon note that

> [s]elf-regulatory initiatives offer a means to control corporate behaviour across borders as they are not tied to any particular political system or ter-ritory, and therefore can be applied in a variety of locations within corpora-tions, industries or sectors, depending on the scope of the initiative and the will of the corporation in implementation.[60]

The Clean Clothes Campaign outlines four major faults in codes of conduct: (1) They are vaguely defined; (2) they are incomplete—may exclude right to organize; (3) not implemented—may lack information about how the codes are employed or monitored; and (4) not independently monitored—an internal monitoring system may not be sufficient.[61] The authors offer a definition of codes of conduct:

> CoCs can be defined as a voluntary set of commitments that either influence corporate attitudes and behaviours or are undertaken by the corporation to

define their intentions and/or actions with regard to ethical and other issues, or towards a range of stakeholders from a market-based perspective.[62]

Codes of conduct offer a breadth and scope that hard law may lack, and codes can be tailored to fit individual corporations, workplaces, and so on.

Ivanka Mamic's book notes that there are numerous types of codes of conduct.[63] She makes the distinction between (a) company codes, (b) multi-stakeholder initiatives (MSIs), (c) intergovernmental codes, and (d) framework agreements. What she calls 'company codes,' I refer to as codes of conduct which are codes that are voluntarily adopted by individual corporations. She notes that sometimes, there is external pressure to develop such codes and uses the example of Nike.[64] She defines MSIs as

> Developed through the co-ordination of diverse stakeholders including NGOs, trade unions, companies or industry associations and on occasion governmental bodies, these codes represent a more progressive approach to addressing concerns such as independent monitoring and the overall effectiveness of codes.[65]

MSIs such as Social Accountability International (SAI) and Ethical Trading Initiative (ETI) may not certify performance or conduct audits. Intergovernmental codes such as Organisation for Economic Co-operation and Development (OECD) and ILO have no binding effect on governments unless they are adopted into domestic law. Framework agreements are usually between a union and a corporation.

Mamic notes that there is a feedback loop by which monitoring allows for the companies to gain insight into what violations, if any, can be remedied and how. This allows for the company to receive feedback on how it is complying with its own code. This mechanism is described as:

> This feedback loop exists in many instances as the code of conduct is not static once in place as it can be amended and improved upon. Also, the feedback loop as outlined above includes ongoing dialogue with different stakeholder groups. This allows for the code and process to be adaptable. As Professor Locke notes, the supply chain is best managed when there is collaboration between all groups, and each group feels valued within the discussion.[66]

Once codes are implemented, the real force and effect comes from having external monitoring agencies that are paid to monitor compliance with the code. Depending on the code itself the remedy for a breach of the code is usually to try to get the company to fix the problem rather than terminating the contract with the supplier automatically. The nature of the code varies from corporation to corporation, but most identify that suppliers and sub-suppliers must be governed by the code, otherwise the efficacy is reduced. If the attempt to try to rectify the wrong does not happen then the relationship may be terminated. "The ultimate sanction against non-compliance is the threat of being de-listed as a supplier. Codes are thus only 'voluntary' to the suppliers in that the alternative is to find new outlets."[67] This is often stipulated in the language of the code itself.

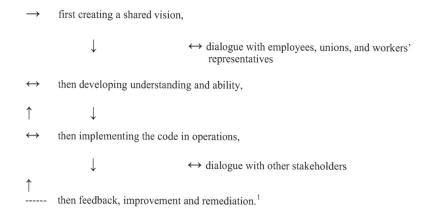

→   first creating a shared vision,

↓   ↔ dialogue with employees, unions, and workers'
                                  representatives

↔   then developing understanding and ability,

↑   ↓

↔   then implementing the code in operations,

↓   ↔ dialogue with other stakeholders

↑

------   then feedback, improvement and remediation.[1]

---

[1] Adapted from Ivanka Mamic, Implementing Codes of Conduct: How Business Manage Social Performance in Global Supply Chains, (Geneva: Greenleaf Publishing, 2004) at 121.

Figure 3.1 Code of conduct feedback loop

As noted by Professor Larry Cata Backer, codes of conduct do not share the special characteristics of hard law (perhaps a more comprehensive enforcement structure) but they also do not suffer the weakness of law: "They reflect a potentially enforceable private law among the parties consenting thereto, provide a more robust basis in consent legitimacy than that offered by the more remote process of law making."[68] He goes on to state that

> Corporate Codes and soft law generally are criticized as undemocratic, as dangerous because of asymmetries in bargaining power and in the difficulty of using the mechanics of state power to enforce. More importantly, soft law is viewed, like contract, as party specific and thus of little help when attempting to harmonize conduct norms over large groups of enterprises and individuals.[69]

Many different codes acting in isolation can one day become industry-wide standards, and then true change can be actualized on a large scale. The idea of creating uniformity across industries in a global sense may be more productive than changing domestic laws in separation from others. Attaching the governance at the site of the corporation will force that corporation to comply with the code in any jurisdiction as opposed to getting various laws to become standardized simultaneously.

While codes of conduct may be effective tools in strengthening the rights of stakeholders, they are but a few tools among many available, and that many tools being used at the same time for the same purpose will prove more effective than a single tool. Codes of conduct are an effective tool in increasing the rights of workers. When paired with a monitoring agency that is rigourous and conducts spot audits in factories, then it creates a scheme that very much models hard law with the code being akin to legislation and the monitoring agency being like the government to enforce the code. This is particularly helpful in jurisdictions where it is difficult to unionize. Within jurisdictions where unionizing is not difficult, the code of conduct model offers greater malleability than legislation and other hard law mechanisms. The ability for a code of conduct to reflect the voice of workers may be greater than that within a unionized context where it may be said to be more rigid than the flexible code which can be altered from one corporation to another. There may be greater buy-in from workers about the governance of the workplace environment if they are involved with the creation of said governance rules. Also, the ongoing feedback from workers about how the code of conduct can be improved allows for ongoing discussions between management and workers. This sense of worth in the workplace environment and having workers' voice be acknowledged can lead to greater worker productivity (see Locke and the two Mexican factories).

Codes Versus Certifications

Because of the ability of capital to cross borders in a distinct way from laws it may be easier to regulate the corporation through codes, which traverse borders, than to bind it to national laws.

> The effect of these developments has been to give multinational corporations remarkable freedom to choose the legal systems that will govern their operations. Corporations are now free to seek out those environments in which the laws in place provide the most favourable conditions for maximizing profits.[70]

There should be a rule/law that moves with the corporation such as a code. The code is in place no matter what jurisdiction the company is in. This bridges the divide between host nations and home nation as the corporation is bound by the code no matter what border it crosses. This allows for consistency and predictability as the code is the same in every jurisdiction rather than trying to navigate and manage the differing employment laws that exists in different nations.

Corporations do not have the same availability of enforcement that is available to the state.

> It is argued here that it is both valid and useful to study the ILO Conventions in their own right, independently of their ratification and implementation at the national level. The Conventions can be studied as a body of rules which reflects the views of the tripartite delegates of the ILO Member States at the International Labour Conference in any given year.[71]

Because of the malleability of the Conventions, she argues that they are not quite as useful as planned.

The character of transnational labour rules of the ILO and the Community is thus at times rather difficult to capture. For the most part, they are not instruments of direct 'governance', and they do not 'regulate' as national legislation does. The details in international rules are often templates for multiple outcomes within and between national jurisdictions.[72]

Codes as Corporate Reformation

Codes do not offer the protection that hard law does, but may allow coverage for areas that legislation does not—while legislation may govern hours of work there is room within a code to allow for formation of advantages akin to those gained in a collective agreement. In jurisdictions where union organizing is difficult there may be ground covered in a code that may not be able to be achieved through hard law. While the future outcome of numerous codes is yet to be realized, the potential of codes is compelling. Only through the establishment of voluntary codes and onwards towards getting those same rights entrenched in legislation will the fight for workers' rights move forward. "They [codes of conduct] should be seen as a contested terrain which can be used to advance the cause of workers in the South and to carve out space for them to organize and to struggle to improve their own wages and working conditions."[73] Again, a first step in the fight for workers' rights is better than waiting for a perfect model to emerge.

Governance

The intersection between corporate law and labour law is not frequently discussed as labour law is often left out of corporate law textbooks and classrooms. Labour law may be left out of boardroom discussions too. Simon Deakin noted that "[w] hile labour law and corporate governance could once have been thought as discrete area for analysis, it is clear that this is no longer the case."[74] This should not be the case as the worlds are not so separate and distinct. The intersections and interconnections are becoming more apparent and noteworthy. Professor Peer Zumbansen notes that codes of conduct challenge "traditional understandings of law making, an analysis of voluntary codes of conduct further illuminates the complex nature of the regulated and self-regulating firm."[75] This makes explicit the need for the discussion to be regularly maintained and makes note that the corporation is multifaceted.

This movement from nation-state as the fundamental source of authority has given way to the corporation as a new form of governance. The rise of the corporation and the power and wealth contained therein allowed the corporate form to dominate on the world stage. This corporatization of the world has allowed for corporate power and greed to thrive and takeover the power of the state. As noted elsewhere, the question becomes whether the state has voluntarily given away its power to the corporation or whether the corporation has stolen this power. The two forces can be acting at the same time as well. It is not an either or situation.

The rise of international law and transnational governance regimes has also lead to the decrease in state power. The ability of goods and services to transcend borders has also allowed for exploitation to carry across borders more easily.

Ethics Codes

Ethics codes are intended to govern employees of the company through the usage of terms such as 'responsibility, duty, etc.' As Wes Cragg notes,

> [w]hat all ethics codes have in common is the belief that those whose behaviour is designed to guide have ethical responsibilities, obligations, rights and duties. Where codes typically differ is in their understanding of the nature of those responsibilities, obligations, rights and duties.[76]

Codes of conduct play a very important role in shaping behaviour, outling the rules of conduct, and possibly setting out punishment for violating the rules.

> Corporate ethics codes are a relatively recent addition to the pantheon of ethical codes of conduct. This is not surprising since the modern corporation is itself of relatively recent vintage. Corporate codes themselves predate globalization. However it is globalization that has thrust them into the limelight and made them objects of scrutiny in a new and urgent way.[77]

Globalization has allowed companies to expand their markets and consumers. However this also increases the attention given to huge companies as the limelight is brighter on a bigger stage.

> The effect of these developments has been to give multinational corporations remarkable freedom to choose the legal systems that will govern their operations. Corporations are now free to seek out those environments in which the laws in place provide the most favourable conditions for maximizing profits.[78]

While it may be true that corporations were once able to 'get away' with behaviour on foreign soil that would not be tolerated on domestic soil that may soon be changed. With increased usage of codes of conduct, increased pressure to build on workers' rights, increased discussion about companies and human rights, those companies that choose to be stagnant may face the consequences as a result.

> The real issue here is whether corporations are likely to honour commitments where risk reduction or enhanced profitability is unlikely to follow.

The record in this respect is not encouraging. This, of course, is why many critics have argued that self-regulation is no substitute for legal regulation.[79]

While self-regulation is not a perfect substitution for legal regulation, it is a good approach. It is also trite to say but true that *some* regulation is better than *no* regulation. As Harry Arthurs notes, "[h]owever voluntary codes take the process one step further: they allow corporations to make something resembling 'law' without state approval *ex ante* or *ex post* (Teubner 1997)."[80] However this idea raises the issue of whether corporations need the approval of the state. If the state is failing to regulate corporations effectively then what alternative is there for a corporation besides self-regulation? "What, then, is the relationship of corporate codes to law? As I have tried to show, corporate codes may be used to deflect state law, to create the illusion of law while fending off the reality of regulation."[81] Regulation by the state is held up as the ideal, but the state often lacks the resources and jurisdiction to govern on the soil of other nations.

> If corporate codes were to become more closely entangled with state law, they would inevitably lose their distinctive 'corporate' or voluntary character. This is likely to make them less attractive to key actors. After all, corporations initially adopted these voluntary codes precisely because they preferred self-regulation to state regulation.[82]

While the issue of preference is debatable, the corporation had to devise some sort of regulation in response to critics, consumers, etc. The real issue is whether the state should stand idly by while corporations self-regulate.

> As some commentators have argued, a second and third generation of codes may overcome the defects of the first (Compa and Hinchcliffe-Darricarrere 1995), and each partial victory in the struggle against exploitation ultimately contributes to a more effective regime of transnational labour standards (Trubek et al. 1999).[83]

This argument is the most correct in that the first wave of codes may be inferior to the next generation of codes and so on until a near perfect model is achieved. Each new code allows others to see how their own codes can be improved and amended accordingly. I recall bargaining a new collective agreement while articling and how my union steward told me that if he was able to get International Women's Day as a paid holiday in my C.A. then he could use that when bargaining for others. This notion of leading by example and minimum setting often encourages others to follow. One does not need to be the first, but you better not be the last to adopt minimal standards.

> In such a context, one might argue, half a voluntary code is better than no regulation. But while this argument may have merit, it does not address a

further concern of labour, human rights advocates and social movements: that to acknowledge the potential of corporate good intentions and to accept employer self-regulation, even as a transitional measure, is to legitimate the existing global economic system and its ultimately unpalatable manifestations in workplaces and communities around the world.[84]

Codes are an element of governance that extends beyond simply those who the code targets, but extends beyond. Whether this extension (arguably over-extension) of the code's scope is needed or desired is another issue. Whether those beyond the code are impacted by the code depends on the individual circumstances and how connected the specific individual or organization is to the proponents of the code. Does a particular supplier provide a lot of business to a certain company? Or is this particular company just one of many?

The Gig Economy or the Rig Economy?

While the 'gig economy' is heralded as a way for millennials to be able to be creative and allow them free time to explore the world through travel or to work on their music denies the fact that workers would like full-time employment. While some workers may choose to work part-time and have flexible work schedules due to family obligations, illness, or simply personal choice it is a disservice to act like those who are precariously employed desire to be so.

Isolation and Inequality

Alienation is about the distance between management and workers. This is similar to Marx's theory of alienation as he outlined that higher wages and shorter working hours will not rid the system of alienation. It is something more intrinsic and difficult to simply remove. Workers are separated from their work product in that if one builds for a living then one must sell those products. Workers are also separated from their fellow co-workers as they compete for promotions. Workers are separated from management because the ability of management to keep workers at a distance allows management to not feel too much sympathy for workers. If one developed a liking for their workers, then it becomes more difficult to terminate those workers or decline to increase wages, etc.

Incessant noise and movement cannot be good for human existence. Otherwise there would not be a premium placed on silence and relaxation. A day at the spa for relaxation is only priced so high because humans crave peace and quiet. The noisiest and dankest workplaces still exist. They have not gone the way of Dickens' workhouses. Those jobs have simply been sent overseas—away from North American eyes. If one does not see that person toiling away to make your $10 t-shirt, then that person may not even exist. Why should you care about them? Who are they to you?

The noise of the factory floor is against the human desire for quiet. It does not allow for deep thoughts or reflection. Instead, it has a numbing effect. As described by L.M. Montgomery,

> For the transfer and change department, in the middle of the big hardware basement, was the noisiest place in the great hive. There were all kinds of noises-ceaseless, meaningless noises that hammered on her tired brain and numbed her soul.[85]

This numbing of the soul is important as the incessant noise is tiresome and tedious. Offices tend to be less noisy than the factory setting. What is the noise level of driving Uber all day?

Notes

1 Sarah P Bradley, "BCE Inc. v. 1976 Debenture-holders: The New Fiduciary Duties of Fair Treatment, Statutory Compliance and Good Corporate Citizenship?" *Ottawa Law Review,* 41(2009–2010), 325–349 at para 23.
2 Robert Flannigan, "Fiduciary Duties of Shareholders and Directors" *JBL* (May 2004), 277–302 at 283.
3 *Bank Act* SC 1991, c 46, s 106 and s 125, *Bankruptcy and Insolvency Act* RSC 1985, c B-3, s 13 and s 14, *CBCA*, s 61 and s 75, *Canada Cooperatives Act* SC 1998, c 1, s 214 and s 236, *Canada Not-for-profit Corporations Act* SC 2009, c 23, s 71, *Cooperative Credit Associations Act* SC 1991, c 48, s 113 and s 132, *Insurance Companies Act* SC 199, c 47, s 110 and s 129, *Trust and Loan Companies Act* SC 1991, c 45, s 109 and s 128.
4 Sarah P. Bradley, "BCE Inc. v. 1976 Debenture-holders: The New Fiduciary Duties of Fair Treatment, Statutory Compliance and Good Corporate Citizenship?" *Ottawa Law Review* 41(2009–2010), 325–349 at para 23.
5 Benjamin J. Richardson, "Do the Fiduciary Duties of Pension Funds Hinder Socially Responsible Investment?" *BLFR* 22.2(2007), 145–201 at 150.
6 Andrew Crane, Dirk Matten and Jeremy Moon, *Corporations and Citizenship* (Cambridge: Cambridge University Press, 2008), 1.
7 Andrew Crane, Dirk Matten and Jeremy Moon, *Corporations and Citizenship.* (Cambridge: Cambridge University Press, 2008), 7: "By bringing in the Aristotelian assumption about duties of citizenship, to each other and to the polity as a whole, we understand the citizen's participation in politics not simply as a right to vote or hold office, but also as a contribution to personal development and to societal flourishing."
8 Andrew Crane, Dirk Matten and Jeremy Moon, *Corporations and Citizenship* (Cambridge: Cambridge University Press, 2008), 31.
9 I use 'close to a monopoly' because the competition bureau and other such organizations are tasked with ensuring that monopolies do not form/exist.
10 Andrew Crane, Dirk Matten and Jeremy Moon, *Corporations and Citizenship* (Cambridge: Cambridge University Press, 2008), 5.
11 Andrew Crane, Dirk Matten and Jeremy Moon, *Corporations and Citizenship* (Cambridge: Cambridge University Press, 2008), 64.
12 Andrew Crane, Dirk Matten and Jeremy Moon, *Corporations and Citizenship* (Cambridge: Cambridge University Press, 2008), 65.
13 *Good Samaritan Act, 2001*, S.O. 2001, c. 2.

14 *Good Samaritan Act, 2001,* S.O. 2001, c. 2, s 2.
15 Richard M. Locke, *The Promise and Limits of Private Power: Promoting Labor Standards in a Global Economy* (New York: Cambridge University Press, 2013), 166.
16 George W. Adams, *Canadian Labour Law*, Second Edition (Aurora: Canada Law Book, 1993), Chapter 10.
17 *Labour Relations Act, 1995* S.O. 1995, c. 1, Sched. A.
18 *Labour Relations Act, 1995* S.O. 1995, c. 1, Sched. A.
19 Ogilvy Renault, "Wal-Mart, Unions and Free Speech in Canada" Online: <www.ogilvyrenault.com/files/unionfreespeech01oct04.pdf>, at 1.
20 Kate E. Andrias, "A Robust Public Debate: Realizing Free Speech in Workplace Representation Elections" *The Yale Law Journal*, 112(2003), 2415 at 2429.
21 Caroline Corbin "The First Amendment Right Against Compelled Listening" *Boston University Law Review*, 29, 939 at 941.
22 Daniel V. Johns, "Promises, Promises: Rethinking the NLRB's Decision Between Employer and Union Promises During Representation Campaigns" *University of Pennsylvania Journal of Business and Employment Law*, 10(Winter 2008), 433 at 434–435.
23 Daniel V. Johns, "Promises, Promises: Rethinking the NLRB's Decision Between Employer and Union Promises During Representation Campaigns" *University of Pennsylvania Journal of Business and Employment Law*, 10(Winter 2008), 433 at 447.
24 Paul M. Secunda, "United States: Towards the Viability of State-based Legislation to Address Workplace Captive Audience Meetings in the United States" *Comparative Labor Law Journal & Policy Journal,* 29(Winter 2008), 209 at 209–210.
25 Paul M. Secunda, "United States: Towards the Viability of State-based Legislation to Address Workplace Captive Audience Meetings in the United States" *Comparative Labor Law Journal & Policy Journal,* 29(Winter 2008), 209 at 215.
26 Paul M. Secunda, "United States: Towards the Viability of State-based Legislation to Address Workplace Captive Audience Meetings in the United States" *Comparative Labor Law Journal & Policy Journal,* 29(Winter 2008), 209 at 226–227.
27 Kate E. Andrias, "A Robust Public Debate: Realizing Free Speech in Workplace Representation Elections" *The Yale Law Journal*, 112(2003), 2415 at 2432.
28 Kate E. Andrias, "A Robust Public Debate: Realizing Free Speech in Workplace Representation Elections" *The Yale Law Journal*, 112(2003), 2415 at 2439.
29 *Communications, Energy and Paperworkers Union of Canada v. Boehmer Box LP* (2010) 0474–08-R (OLRB) Vice-Chair Patrick Kelly at para. 53.
30 *Communications, Energy and Paperworkers Union of Canada v. Boehmer Box LP* (2010) 0474–08-R (OLRB) Vice-Chair Patrick Kelly at para. 77.
31 See Charles Sabel, Dara O'Rourke and Archon Fung, "Ratcheting Labor Standards: Regulation for Continuous Improvement in the Global Workplace" Online: <http://papers.ssrn.com/sol3/papers.cfm?abstract_id=253833> at 4: "The open and crucial questions, then, is how to construct a regulatory framework that protects vulnerable groups against the abuses identified in core labor standards?"
32 Jill Murray, "Labour Rights/corporate Responsibilities: The Role of ILO Labour Standards" in Rhys Jenkins, Ruth Pearson and Gill Seyfang, eds. *Corporate Responsibility and Labour Rights; Codes of Conduct in the Global Economy* (London: Earthscan Publications Limited, 2002), 33.
33 While it may be that the ILO Conventions are meant to be a way to fill the governance gap, it can be argued that it is not a very useful one. ILO Conventions are not properly enforced and are not as effective as domestic law ratifying such Conventions.
34 Rhys Jenkins, Ruth Pearson and Gill Seyfang, eds., *Corporate Responsibility and Labour Rights: Codes of Conduct in the Global Economy* (London: Earthscan Publications Limited, 2002), 1.

35 Rhys Jenkins, Ruth Pearson and Gill Seyfang, eds., *Corporate Responsibility and Labour Rights: Codes of Conduct in the Global Economy* (London: Earthscan Publications Limited, 2002), 3.

36 See Rhys Jenkins, "The Political Economy of Codes of Conduct" in Rhys Jenkins, Ruth Pearson and Gill Seyfang, eds. *Corporate Responsibility and Labour Rights: Codes of Conduct in the Global Economy* (London: Earthscan Publications Limited, 2002), 15: "As in the case of investors, a minority of consumers are also concerned about the ethical dimension of the products which they purchase, as illustrated by the growth in demand for fair-traded coffee and other such products. However, these examples remain niche markets, supplying a predominantly middle class and relatively affluent and educated customer base."

37 Rhys Jenkins, "The Political Economy of Codes of Conduct" in Rhys Jenkins, Ruth Pearson and Gill Seyfang, eds. *Corporate Responsibility and Labour Rights: Codes of Conduct in the Global Economy* (London: Earthscan Publications Limited, 2002), 19.

38 Rhys Jenkins, "The Political Economy of Codes of Conduct" in Rhys Jenkins, Ruth Pearson and Gill Seyfang, eds. *Corporate Responsibility and Labour Rights: Codes of Conduct in the Global Economy* (London: Earthscan Publications Limited, 2002), 28.

39 Stephanie Barrientos, "Mapping Codes through the Value Chain: From Researcher to Detective" in Rhys Jenkins, Ruth Pearson and Gill Seyfang, eds. *Corporate Responsibility and Labour Rights: Codes of Conduct in the Global Economy* (London: Earthscan Publications Limited, 2002), 64.

40 Linda Shaw and Angela Hale, "The Emperor's New Clothes: What Codes Mean for Workers in the Garment Industry" in Rhys Jenkins, Ruth Pearson and Gill Seyfang, eds. *Corporate Responsibility and Labour Rights: Codes of Conduct in the Global Economy* (London: Earthscan Publications Limited, 2002), 109.

41 Brian Holzer, *Moralizing the Corporation: Transnational Activism and Corporate Accountability* (Northampton: Edward Elgar Publishing Limited, 2010), 47.

42 Brian Holzer, *Moralizing the Corporation: Transnational Activism and Corporate Accountability* (Northampton: Edward Elgar Publishing Limited, 2010), 62.

43 Brian Holzer, *Moralizing the Corporation: Transnational Activism and Corporate Accountability* (Northampton: Edward Elgar Publishing Limited, 2010), 72.

44 Richard M. Locke, *The Promise and Limits of Private Power: Promoting Labor Standards in a Global Economy* (New York: Cambridge University Press, 2013), 110.

45 November 3, 2004. The 2004 Sydney Peace Prize Lecture, University of Sydney. Online at: <www.sydney.edu.au>.

46 McKinsey Global Institute, *Independent Work: Choice, Necessity, and the Gig Economy* (McKinsey & Company, October, 2016), 53. Online: https://www.mckinsey.com/featured-insights/employment-and-growth/independent-work-choice-necessity-and-the-gig-economy.

47 Einat Albin and Jeremias Prassl, "Fragmenting Work, Fragmented Regulation: The Contract of Employment as a Driver of Social Exclusion", SSRN Online: <http://ssrn.com/abstract=2709569>, at 13.

48 *Canada Business Corporations Act*, RSC 1985, c. C-44.

49 Stephanie Barrientos, "Mapping Codes through the Value Chain: From Researcher to Detective" in Rhys Jenkins, Ruth Pearson and Gill Seyfang, eds. *Corporate Responsibility and Labour Rights: Codes of Conduct in the Global Economy* (London: Earthscan Publications Limited, 2002), 67.

50 Harry Arthurs, "Profit, Power and Law in the Global Economy" in Wesley Cragg, ed. *Ethics Codes, Corporations, and the Challenge of Globalization* (Northampton: Edward Elgar Publishing Limited, 2003), 55.

51 Harry Arthurs, "Profit, Power and Law in the Global Economy" in Wesley Cragg, ed. *Ethics Codes, Corporations, and the Challenge of Globalization* (Northampton: Edward Elgar Publishing Limited, 2003), 58.

52   Rhys Jenkins, "The Political Economy of Codes of Conduct" in Rhys Jenkins, Ruth Pearson and Gill Seyfang, eds. *Corporate Responsibility and Labour Rights: Codes of Conduct in the Global Economy* (London: Earthscan Publications Limited, 2002), 28.

53   Sometimes those who produce goods and services for a certain company may not be 'employees' of that company but still have rights and obligations that flow from such a relationship, even though it may not be termed an 'employment relationship'.

54   Lance Compa, "Corporate Social Responsibility and Workers' Rights" 4, Online: <http://digitalcommons.ilr.cornell.edu/articles/183>.

55   Lance Compa, "Corporate Social Responsibility and Workers' Rights" 4, Online: <http://digitalcommons.ilr.cornell.edu/articles/183>, at 4.

56   Lance Compa, "Corporate Social Responsibility and Workers' Rights" 4, Online: <http://digitalcommons.ilr.cornell.edu/articles/183>, at 5.

57   Lance Compa, "Corporate Social Responsibility and Workers' Rights" 4, Online: <http://digitalcommons.ilr.cornell.edu/articles/183>, at 5.

58   Krista Bondy, Dirk Matten, and Jeremy Moon, "Codes of Conduct as a Tool for Sustainable Governance in MNCs" in S. Benn and D. Dunphy eds. *Corporate Governance and Sustainability—Challenges for Theory and Practice* (London: Routledge, 2006), 14–15.

59   Andrew Crane, Dirk Matten and Jeremy Moon, *Corporations and Citizenship.* (Cambridge: Cambridge University Press, 2008), 64.

60   Krista Bondy, Dirk Matten, and Jeremy Moon, "Codes of Conduct as a Tool for Sustainable Governance in MNCs" in S. Benn and D. Dunphy eds. *Corporate Governance and Sustainability—Challenges for Theory and Practice* (London: Routledge, 2006), 6.

61   Krista Bondy, Dirk Matten, and Jeremy Moon, "Codes of Conduct as a Tool for Sustainable Governance in MNCs" in S. Benn and D. Dunphy eds. *Corporate Governance and Sustainability—Challenges for Theory and Practice* (London: Routledge, 2006), 9.

62   Krista Bondy, Dirk Matten, and Jeremy Moon, "Codes of Conduct as a Tool for Sustainable Governance in MNCs" in S. Benn and D. Dunphy eds. *Corporate Governance and Sustainability—Challenges for Theory and Practice* (London: Routledge, 2006), 7.

63   Ivanka Mamic, *Implementing Codes of Conduct: How Business Manage Social Performance in Global Supply Chains* (Geneva: Greenleaf Publishing, 2004), 43.

64   Ivanka Mamic, *Implementing Codes of Conduct: How Business Manage Social Performance in Global Supply Chains* (Geneva: Greenleaf Publishing, 2004), 43.

65   Ivanka Mamic, *Implementing Codes of Conduct: How Business Manage Social Performance in Global Supply Chains* (Geneva: Greenleaf Publishing, 2004), 43.

66   See Richard M. Locke, *The Promise and Limits of Private Power: Promoting Labor Standards in a Global Economy* (New York: Cambridge University Press, 2013), 29. "According to Elliott and Freeman, there exists a 'market for standards' in which informed consumers respond with their wallets to activist demands that global brands take responsibility for labor conditions in supplier factories. These purchasing decisions will induce global brands to adopt codes of conduct and exercise their leverage over their suppliers to enforce compliance with these codes."

67   Stephanie Barrientos, "Mapping Codes through the Value Chain: From Researcher to Detective" in Rhys Jenkins, Ruth Pearson and Gill Seyfang, eds. *Corporate Responsibility and Labour Rights; Codes of Conduct in the Global Economy* (London: Earthscan Publications Limited, 2002), 67.

68 Larry Cata Backer blog post on September 21, 2013, Online: <http://lcbackerblog. blogspot.ca/2013/09/changing-corporate-behavior-through.html>.

69 Larry Cata Backer blog post on September 21, 2013, Online: <http://lcbackerblog. blogspot.ca/2013/09/changing-corporate-behavior-through.html>.

70 Wesley Cragg, ed., *Ethics Codes, Corporations, and the Challenge of Globalization* (Northampton: Edward Elgar Publishing Limited, 2003), 2.

71 Jill Murray, *Transnational Labour Regulation: The ILO and EC Compared* (Norwell: Kluwer Law International, 2001), 5.

72 Jill Murray, *Transnational Labour Regulation: The ILO and EC Compared* (Norwell: Kluwer Law International, 2001), 7.

73 Rhys Jenkins, "The Political Economy of Codes of Conduct" in Rhys Jenkins, Ruth Pearson and Gill Seyfang, eds. *Corporate Responsibility and Labour Rights; Codes of Conduct in the Global Economy* (London: Earthscan Publications Limited, 2002), 28.

74 Simon Deakin as quoted in Peer Zumbansen, "The Parallel Worlds of Corporate Governance and Labor Law" *Indiana Journal of Global Legal Studies,* 13(2006), 261–315 at 17.

75 Peer Zumbansen, "The Parallel Worlds of Corporate Governance and Labor Law" *Indiana Journal of Global Legal Studies,* 13(2006), 261–315 at 8.

76 Wesley Cragg, ed., *Ethics Codes, Corporations, and the Challenge of Globalization* (Northampton: Edward Elgar Publishing Limited, 2003), 1.

77 Wesley Cragg, ed., *Ethics Codes, Corporations, and the Challenge of Globalization* (Northampton: Edward Elgar Publishing Limited, 2003), 1.

78 Wesley Cragg, ed., *Ethics Codes, Corporations, and the Challenge of Globalization* (Northampton: Edward Elgar Publishing Limited, 2003), 2.

79 Wesley Cragg, ed., *Ethics Codes, Corporations, and the Challenge of Globalization* (Northampton: Edward Elgar Publishing Limited, 2003), 46.

80 Harry Arthurs, "Profit, Power and Law in the Global Economy" in Wesley Cragg, ed. *Ethics Codes, Corporations, and the Challenge of Globalization* (Northampton: Edward Elgar Publishing Limited, 2003), 55.

81 Harry Arthurs, "Profit, Power and Law in the Global Economy" in Wesley Cragg, ed. *Ethics Codes, Corporations, and the Challenge of Globalization* (Northampton: Edward Elgar Publishing Limited, 2003), 58.

82 Harry Arthurs, "Profit, Power and Law in the Global Economy" in Wesley Cragg, ed. *Ethics Codes, Corporations, and the Challenge of Globalization* (Northampton: Edward Elgar Publishing Limited, 2003), 59.

83 Harry Arthurs, "Corporate Codes of Conduct as a Regime of Labour Market Regulation" in Wesley Cragg, ed. *Ethics Codes, Corporations, and the Challenge of Globalization* (Northampton: Edward Elgar Publishing Limited, 2003), 206.

84 Harry Arthurs, "Corporate Codes of Conduct as a Regime of Labour Market Regulation" in Wesley Cragg, ed. *Ethics Codes, Corporations, and the Challenge of Globalization* (Northampton: Edward Elgar Publishing Limited, 2003), 206.

85 L.M. Montgomery, *After Many Years: Twenty-One 'Long Lost' Stories* (Halifax: Nimbus Publishing Limited, 2017), "Jim's House" at page 204.

Bibliography for Chapter 3

Legislation

Bank Act SC 1991, c 46.

Bankruptcy and Insolvency Act RSC 1985, c B-3, s 13 and s 14,

Canada Business Corporations Act, RSC 1985, c C-44.

Canada Cooperatives Act SC 1998, c 1.
Canada Not-for-profit Corporations Act SC 2009, c 23.
Cooperative Credit Associations Act SC 1991, c 48.
Good Samaritan Act, 2001, S.O. 2001, c. 2.
Insurance Companies Act SC 199, c 47.
Labour Relations Act, 1995 S.O. 1995, c. 1, Sched. A.
Trust and Loan Companies Act SC 1991, c 45.

Caselaw

Communications, Energy and Paperworkers Union of Canada v. Boehmer Box LP (2010) 0474–08-R (OLRB).

Books

Adams, George W. *Canadian Labour Law*, Second Edition (Aurora: Canada Law Book, 1993), Chapter 10.

Bondy, Krista, Dirk Matten, and Jeremy Moon, "Codes of Conduct as a Tool for Sustainable Governance in MNCs" in S. Benn and D. Dunphy eds. *Corporate Governance and Sustainability—Challenges for Theory and Practice* (London: Routledge, 2006).

Cragg, Wesley ed. *Ethics Codes, Corporations, and the Challenge of Globalization* (Northampton, Edward Elgar Publishing Limited, 2003).

Crane, Andrew, Dirk Matten and Jeremy Moon. *Corporations and Citizenship* (Cambridge: Cambridge University Press, 2008).

Holzer, Brian. *Moralizing the Corporation: Transnational Activism and Corporate Accountability* (Northampton: Edward Elgar Publishing Limited, 2010).

Jenkins, Rhys, Ruth Pearson and Gill Seyfang, ed. *Corporate Responsibility and Labour Rights: Codes of Conduct in the Global Economy* (London: Earthscan Publications Limited, 2002).

Locke, Richard M. *The Promise and Limits of Private Power: Promoting Labor Standards in a Global Economy* (New York: Cambridge University Press, 2013).

Mamic, Ivanka. *Implementing Codes of Conduct: How Business Manage Social Performance in Global Supply Chains* (Geneva: Greenleaf Publishing, 2004).

Montgomery, Lucy Maud. *After Many Years: Twenty-One 'Long Lost' Stories* (Halifax: Nimbus Publishing Limited, 2017) "Jim's House".

Murray, Jill. *Transnational Labour Regulation: The ILO and EC Compared* (Norwell: Kluwer Law International, 2001).

Book Chapters

Arthurs, Harry. "Profit, Power and Law in the Global Economy" in Wesley Cragg, ed. *Ethics Codes, Corporations, and the Challenge of Globalization* (Northampton: Edward Elgar Publishing Limited, 2003).

Barrientos, Stephanie "Mapping Codes through the Value Chain: From Researcher to Detective" in Rhys Jenkins, Ruth Pearson and Gill Seyfang, eds. *Corporate Responsibility and Labour Rights: Codes of Conduct in the Global Economy* (London: Earthscan Publications Limited, 2002).

Murray, Jill. "Labour Rights/corporate Responsibilities: The Role of ILO Labour Standards" in Rhys Jenkins, Ruth Pearson and Gill Seyfang, eds. *Corporate Responsibility and Labour Rights; Codes of Conduct in the Global Economy* (London: Earthscan Publications Limited, 2002).

Shaw, Linda, and Angela Hale. "The Emperor's New Clothes: What Codes Mean for Workers in the Garment Industry" in Rhys Jenkins, Ruth Pearson and Gill Seyfang, eds. *Corporate Responsibility and Labour Rights: Codes of Conduct in the Global Economy* (London: Earthscan Publications Limited, 2002).

Articles

Albin, Einat and Jeremias Prassl. "Fragmenting Work, Fragmented Regulation: The Contract of Employment as a Driver of Social Exclusion", SSRN Online: <http://ssrn.com/abstract=2709569>,.

Andrias, Kate E. "A Robust Public Debate: Realizing Free Speech in Workplace Representation Elections" *The Yale Law Journal*, 112 (2003), 2415.

Bradley, Sarah P. "BCE Inc. v. 1976 Debenture-holders: The New Fiduciary Duties of Fair Treatment, Statutory Compliance and Good Corporate Citizenship?" *Ottawa Law Review*, 41 (2009–2010), 325–349.

Compa, Lance. "Corporate Social Responsibility and Workers' Rights" 4, available at: <http://digitalcommons.ilr.cornell.edu/articles/183>.

Corbin, Caroline. "The First Amendment Right Against Compelled Listening" *Boston University Law Review*, 29, 939 at 941.

Flannigan, Robert. "Fiduciary Duties of Shareholders and Directors" *JBL* (May 2004), 277–302.

Johns, Daniel V. "Promises, Promises: Rethinking the NLRB's Decision Between Employer and Union Promises During Representation Campaigns" *University of Pennsylvania Journal of Business and Employment Law*, 10 (Winter 2008), 433 at 434–435.

Richardson, Benjamin J. "Do the Fiduciary Duties of Pension Funds Hinder Socially Responsible Investment?" *BLFR*, 22.2 (2007), 145–201.

Sabel, Charles, Dara O'Rourke and Archon Fung. "Ratcheting Labor Standards: Regulation for Continuous Improvement in the Global Workplace", available at: <http://papers.ssrn.com/sol3/papers.cfm?abstract_id=253833>

Secunda, Paul M. "United States: Towards the Viability of State-based Legislation to Address Workplace Captive Audience Meetings in the United States" *Comparative Labor Law Journal & Policy Journal*, 29 (Winter 2008), 209 at 209–210.

Zumbansen, Peer. "The Parallel Worlds of Corporate Governance and Labor Law" *Indiana Journal of Global Legal Studies*, 13 (2006), 261–315.

Reports

McKinsey Global Institute. *Independent Work: Choice, Necessity, and the Gig Economy* (McKinsey & Company, October, 2016). Online: https://www.mckinsey.com/featured-insights/employment-and-growth/independent-work-choice-necessity-and-the-gig-economy.

Websites

Backer Larry Cata blog post on September 21, 2013. Online: <http://lcbackerblog.blogspot.ca/2013/09/changing-corporate-behavior-through.html>.

November 3, 2004. The 2004 Sydney Peace Prize Lecture, University of Sydney. Online: <www.sydney.edu.au>.

Ogilvy Renault. "Wal-Mart, Unions and Free Speech in Canada" Online: <www.ogilvyrenault.com/files/unionfreespeech01oct04.pdf>, at 1.

4 Transnational Labour Regulation

Creating documents that govern workplace environments that allows for the incorporation of the workers' voices may allow for a more fulsome model of governance—one in which the governed help to develop the terms that govern their working environment.[1] Allowing labour standards to be strengthened outside of state governance is to allow private actors to set the terms of their own relationships. This may lead to a more interactive and fulfilling model of governance between the parties. This allows for workers to have their voices heard and recognized in their own workplaces. The need to be acknowledged and appreciated is fundamental to humans.[2] So, the importance of being heard at one's workplaces where much of one's identity comes from becomes even greater. Society places great emphasis on one's career, and people are judged accordingly. So, it follows that from such importance as self-identity the workplace occupies a huge part of workers' lives. The greatest comfort is probably in the home followed by the workplace. This shifting of workplaces will inevitably lead to unshakiness more widely. Imagine someone who lives in a tiny home and drives Uber for a living. Without placing judgment, that person does not have a comfortable place to relax and unwind. Not that one would ever relax at work but one could feel comfortable.

To truly understand isolation and inequality one must examine Marx's theory of alienation. Marx outlines that workers become alienated from their own work product, from their co-workers, from management and ultimately from themselves. This cannot be solved with superficial increases in workers' rights such as legal tools that help protect workers but goes beyond that to the human interaction within the workplace. How to change human interaction between workers? How to encourage not just civility but beyond that? I term this approach the 'pro-friendly' approach in my classroom where students are encouraged to work together and know each other outside the classroom. Creating those bonds early on in their education allows for greater friendship further along in their studies. The same holds true for workers. Encouraging friendly behaviour early on in the workplace allows for richer relationships in the working environment and greater cohesion. A happy worker is likely a more productive worker. So this is out of enlightened self-interest that management should care about employee morale and making the workplace a pleasant place to be.

Marxism

Karl Marx is a political theorist who stated that society in most states enact laws to further the interests of capital. Workers' rights, which are paramount to him, he claims are downtrodden in most societies. Marx claims that in capitalist societies there are ongoing class conflicts between the 'haves,' the bourgeoisie, and the 'have nots,' the proletariat. Due to 'false consciousness,' the proletariat think that they too can one day become the bourgeoisie, so they internalize the bourgeois ideals in hopes of becoming them one day themselves. "The term false consciousness is used by Marxists narrowly to refer to the adoption of the dominant ideology by the subordinate classes."[3] The proletariat accept the inequalities because they feel that they will one day benefit because they will be on the side that has more power.[4]

> The whole point of the law is to legitimize the assertion of power in the eyes of those who are disenfranchised and dispossessed. By throwing them morsels of legal victories every now and again, they may be mollified by the law's formal equality.[5]

The laws that are enacted in capitalist societies are enacted to protect property rights and capital from those without.

Marx contends that true equality will only be actualized through the rise of the proletariat when they overthrow the bourgeoisie and control the means of production. The concept of equality in capitalist society fails to account for ownership of the means of production being in the hands of few. To Marx, equality is a greater good than even freedom, and freedom should be sacrificed for equality to be achieved. Marx argues that it is unfair to allow for power to be usurped in such a fashion so that the dismantling of an unjust system is just. For Marx, change only seems possible through revolution, not through battles won in courtrooms.

Marxism and the Law

Marxism questions the underlying power structures that exist in most capitalist societies. Marxists argue that capitalist society breeds inequality and masks that inequality through mechanisms that seem neutral, such as the law. Marxism helps people question existing society[6] and opens up discussion for ways that existing societies are beneficial to its citizens and in ways that they are not. Through discussion and evaluation people can consider alternatives to existing society, such as socialism. Marx argues that only through socialism and eventually on to communism, can people be free as capitalist society fosters alienation and excludes some and popularizes others. Systems exist because someone benefits, as those who are in power are able to draft laws that help them to maintain their power. Law can be used as a vehicle for social change; however, for Marxists that change is too gradual and will not bring true equality but instead a form of equality defined by the bourgeoisie.

In a capitalist society, the legal system would reflect the interests of society, or those who are most powerful in society. It seems to follow logic that in a capitalist society, there would be a capitalist legal system. This can be shown in Canada by how welfare fraud is punished more severely than tax evasion, as the system itself is classist. "Judges manipulate the law to suit the interests of the dominant class."[7] This goes against the principles of equality as defined in Canadian society. "Marx accused the liberal state and law of operating in favor of bourgeois property interests: 'your jurisprudence is but the will of your class made into a law for all.'"[8] If the state acts against the interests of workers, then it follows that the legal system that acts within such a state would also act against the interests of workers.

> If the state is an instrument of class oppression, and the legal system is a sector of the state apparatus, then it follows logically that not only is the law also an instrument of class oppression but also once the division of society into classes is terminated under Communism there will no longer be any need for the state and its legal system.[9]

Marxism is the more extreme version of a code for workers' rights. Even within Capitalism, there can be room for increased rights for workers. This will not abolish alienation, but there can be ways to help alleviate the worker from alienation. These methods could be increased worker voice in the workplace as well as greater worker participation through corporate governance mechanisms like works councils.

Not accepting the power of corporations is to deny the truth or the inevitable. Marx wrote in a time of capitalism's infancy because of the industrial revolution. The lasting power of capitalism demonstrates its ability to react to change. Marx himself commented that the bourgeois were revolutionaries as they overthrew feudalism to bring about modern capitalism. By knowing the ability of the revolutionaries the bourgeois are able to combat it. [See Occupy movement and its inability to affect change]. Marx notes that the capitalist system contains the tools for its own destruction. Only through using those tools will change be made. Professor Asher Horowitz notes that even if it is accepted that capitalism can be replaced, its replacement may be worse. This seems to be a 'devil you know' situation. What will be the rally cry in the socialist paradise? 'Bring back capitalism'? As Marx notes in the Manifesto, the bourgeoisie "create a world after their own image." Thus globalization can be termed the Americanization of the world. One in which American products are touted as the mainstream. And consumers are told not to worry about where and who produced the goods that they purchase. If the main concern of corporations is about maintaining the status quo and keeping people unconcerned about the social impact of their purchasing choices, then it seems to be working. Ethical consumption is mostly theory as studies show that while people claim to be concerned about the working conditions, environmental impacts of the good and services that they purchase the actuality does not demonstrate that. Is it is similar to asking people to raise their hand if they are ethical—no one will keep their hand lowered. Now, who cares about stopping child labour? Again, probably the same result. Now, who actually researches where their goods are made? What people say they care about and what results show are two different things. "Marx got the effects of accumulation under capitalism wrong: it can, and often will, raise wages by increasing the demand for labor."[10] The argument between whether lower wages or working standards impedes workers in not quite a difference.

> Consider first, however, whether lower wages (as distinct from lower worker standards) are a magnet for investors. One needs to be careful and not just look at wages; they must be adjusted for labor productivity differences because lower wages may simply reflect lower productivity.[11]

Perhaps looking at capitalism in its various forms would be useful as there are varieties of capitalism. The system of American capitalism is different from German capitalism per se.

> Since the revolutionary writings of Marx and Engels, the term capitalism has been tied to class division, specifically the self-aggrandizement of the capitalist at the expense of the proletariat. The division of society into capitalist and labor has always played a central role in Marxist writings, from examinations of the American Civil War to detailed investigations of pricing, Marxism, and its political derivatives socialism and communism, turn on the dialectic between the capitalists (or bourgeoisie) who own property and the means of production and the labourers (or proletariat) who own no property and are obligated to sell their labor to the bourgeoisie to gain subsistence (Marx and Engels 1847a, 1847b).[12]

The perversion of Adam Smith to stand for the free market running wild needs to be corrected.

> Yet despite the references to 'A. Smith', (never Adam), Schumpeter frequently acknowledged Smith's intellectual powers, concluding that: 'Though *The Wealth of Nations* contained no really novel ideas and though it cannot rank with Newton's *Principia* or Darwin's *Origins* as an intellectual achievement, it is a great performance all the same and fully deserved its success.'[13]

As Smith notes the excess of consumption has no true limit. "The desire of food is limited in every man by the narrow capacity of the human stomach; but the equipage, and household furniture, seems to have no limit or certain boundary."[14] Perhaps the drive of the lumpen proletariat is precisely summed up as follows: "It is better, says the proverb, to play for nothing than to work for nothing."[15] The role of unions is beyond the scope of this dissertation but as Berle and

Means note, "This does not mean that there are not specific situations in which there is labor exploitation or that there would not be labor exploitation in the absence of labor unions."[16]

Marx's Theory of Alienation

Marx's theory of alienation goes deeper than workers achieving mere wage increases and working fewer hours. Alienation, Marx argues, separates workers from other workers, from their manager, from their product and from themselves. Marx argues that in order for the worker to be truly free they must escape alienation.

> The alienation of the worker in his product means not only that his labour becomes an object, an external existence, but that it exists outside him, independently, as something alien to him, and that becomes a power of its own confronting him.[17]

For Marx, because of alienation capitalism will never allow workers to have true freedom, and true freedom would only entail freedom from alienation, nothing less. "Labour produces not only commodities; it produces itself and the worker as a commodity."[18] This means that the worker and their labour becomes a commodity to be bought and sold. "Estranged labour reverses this relationship, so that it is just because man is a conscious being that he makes his life-activity, his essential being, a mere means to his existence."[19] This separation of a person's existence, their need for clothing and food, and their essence, their passion to make and build, is what is at the root of alienation. It forces a person to sell their passion to get food to survive. This is what troubles Marx. The wage contract itself is presented as inevitable and fair.[20] The wage contract is presented as fair and just, thus rebellion is less likely. This is what is hard to struggle against, the fact that everyone or most people are forced to sell their labour and become wage slaves. "This fact expresses merely that the object which labour produces-labour's product-confronts it as something alien, as a power independent of the product."[21]

Wage increases and greater workplace safety legislation alone would not help workers escape from alienation. For Marx, the legal system aids alienation as it sets up employers and employees as opposites when maybe the fact that they are people who should bridge some gap helps to foster alienation because it helps to distance two people in certain relationships. Both the employer and employee suffer as a result. "The more the worker produces, the less he has to consume; the more values he creates, the more valueless, the more unworthy he becomes."[22] The worker due to surplus value of his or her labour is helping the capitalist accumulate more and exploit them even further. The workers themselves are helping to cement their positions of inferiority. "Man's species being, both nature and his spiritual species property, into a being alien to him, into a means to his individual existence."[23] This division of a person's species being and their existence is what

Marx rallies against. He believes that in order for a person to provide for their existence, they should be able to use their passion. Basically, people should work jobs that they care for and enjoy. Not work all day in order to 'put food on the table.' This leads to unhappiness and disdain. "It was inadequate, Marx argued, to demand a 'fair distribution of the proceeds of labour', for such 'legal conceptions' as 'fairness' derive from economic relations inherent to capital."[24]

Beyond Marx

The wage contract sets out that trading one's labour and essence for wages is necessary and inevitable. Without being able to sell your labour you would have no way of providing for everyday needs.

Marx was instrumental in describing why society was the way it was and as he wrote in *Theses on Feuerbach*, "[t]he philosophers have only *interpreted* the world in various ways; the point is, to *change* it."[25] Marx was able to see his vision somewhat realized during his lifetime and see his theories work their way into practice, albeit somewhat distorted from how he intended. Moving from Marx and the specter of Marx onwards to a system that values and appreciates workers' voice is still in the same tone as Marx without the militant aspects. Management can learn to hear workers instead of facing a revolt by workers.

Distancing

What I term 'distancing' is similar to 'othering' as it may explain why we care more for those persons living in our own nations than those living very far away. "David Hume and Adam Smith were both members of the Scottish Enlightenment. Both had written how distance diminished empathy."[26] Perhaps those who live in the developing world are not cared about in North America as those who live close by. Perhaps this is predictable but that is not to say that it is unavoidable. The humanity of workers, consumers, and simply people in other nations should be of concern for nation-states and corporations alike. CSR tells us that the environment must be taken into consideration during corporate decision-making, but this rings hollow without a worldwide view of the world encompassing environments throughout the globe. While there may not be a legal duty towards citizens in other nations, it seems cruel of the corporation to disregard their essential humanity by choosing to pollute their waterways and land simply because they are far away. Subtracting shareholders, bondholders, workers, and consumers the environment is the one thing that connects everyone throughout the world so the corporate duty to the environment is essential.

But what obligation does the state have to protect its citizens from human rights abuses at the hands of the corporation? But even if a duty is established, how far does that duty extend? Does it apply to existing citizens alone? Or does it extend to future generations? And how is that duty satisfied? What is the standard of care once a duty is established?

These are important questions that need to be answered surrounding corporate obligations and how best to act in the best interests of stakeholders and society more broadly.

Compassion Fatigue

Not everything can be quantified to be rarefied, which Professor Bhagwati seems to advocate. Professor Bhagwati outlines how in his opinion, humans are self-interested. "Hume famously argued that 'it is not contrary to reason to prefer the destruction of the whole world to the scratching of my finger' and that 'sympathy with persons remote from us is much fainter than with persons near and contiguous.' "[27] This is useful when considering 'compassion fatigue'[28] in which it is posited that humans become less compassionate when exposed to images of suffering worldwide. This is connected with my theory of distancing. This theory outlines that there is a 'maximum' level of compassion which can be reached and then results in apathy afterwards—compassion is not limitless. So the theory posits that if compassion is not limitless, we should reserve the supply of compassion we have for those closest to us. What the test for closeness would be is not established. Do we care about people in our nation? Do we care about those who share our religion but live in another country? What are the lines that connect and disconnect across borders?

Enlightened Self-Interest

Enlightened self-interest is the notion that by helping someone one day that person may be able to help you another day. By using enlightened self-interest management may be able to coerce workers into being better workers by treating workers more fairly. If one treats workers fairly, and perhaps even kindly, then management would be able to compel workers to give more of themselves to their work—be it time or energy.

Dignity and Respect

Dignity and respect. Even the United Nations notes that we are all born with the right to equal respect and dignity. This extends to workers who deserve to have their humanity recognized within the workplace and work space.

Kindness and Empathy

It may be too much to ask for management to move from dignity and respect towards kindness and empathy, but it is possible. Moving towards greater fulfillment workers can attain such awareness through having management who is more kind in their dealings with workers. And that kindness should flow the opposite way. Empathy is a big concept, but there is room in the workplace for empathy among co-workers and between workers and management.

Pro-Friendly

In my other research in legal education I champion what I term a 'pro-friendly approach,'[29] which means moving beyond simply being civil to one another and adopting a pro-friendly method where students should try to have coffee together and work collectively. This has proven to be effective in the past as students have commented in my teaching evaluations that I create a comfortable space where students feel they can participate actively. This is not just about the classroom—this is an approach that can work in other situations.

Collectivity

Collectivity can be used to express the togetherness that workers can feel when working together to achieve a goal. This may sound idealistic and naïve, but I believe it is attainable. And not that far from reach either. In current times, there is increased activism through social media, while this may be viewed as lazy and actually 'slacktivism,' it may show that people are more caring about social justice currently than ever before. What were gay rights like in the 1950s? What was racism like in the 1950s? Things are getting better, and there is an increased sense of unity and 'oneness' among people of all nations unlike any other time in history.

Globalization is just one aspect as there may be other variables. With increased flow of people across borders the world stage is changing. Not to be trite, but we live in a time of Hamilton (the musical) and Black Panther (the movie) that never existed before. The marginalized are not waiting to be mainstream but are instead changing what it means to be mainstream. This means that cultures that were marginalized and left to be on the sidelines are getting to play on the same playing field as everyone else. This does not negate the inequalities that continue to exist but shows one aspect of unity increasing. Because of the proliferation of social media there is more exchange of culture than ever before. Someone in Mumbai, India, can see what someone in Los Angeles, California, ate for lunch on Instagram and be connected in a way that simply did not exist 20 years ago. Facebook, Twitter, and Instagram have allowed for communities to exist like never before—online. This simple new way of organizing and grouping together individuals has created spaces for those who used to left out to find other who share interests. This also has a downside as cyberbullying is a new invention that morphed from normal bullying to the online realm. As well as other ways that online communities have created damage. This new world can be used to harness the power of workers' voices as there can be new connections made online, as well as the benefits from information being shared online leading to greater protections for workers. This new method of knowledge sharing has advantages for workers in places where they themselves might not have access to this same technology.

The internationalization of the world including the law allows for norms and customs to be worldwide. What was once thought to be exclusively French can be shipped to another nation that same day.

My Model Code of Conduct

While I was one of three law students who drafted the Queen's Code of Conduct, I find that the provisions could be improved. I am suggesting a model code of conduct. Reference to the ILO Conventions can help situate a code of conduct in a broader discussion about workers' rights and can be useful in that regard—to demonstrate that this one particular code of conduct is part of something larger. Professor John Ruggie's work on how states and corporations have a responsibility to protect human rights can also be incorporated in codes with reference to his report. I have indicated by footnote when the language in my model code is borrowed from other codes. While the model code is most situated for a corporation that produces goods and products such as an apparel company it can be amended to suit any corporation's specific needs.

I plan to enact change on the ground by getting corporations to adapt my code as an internal mechanism that guarantees certain fundamental rights to their workers. It is beyond the scope of this book to go into too much detail about my future plans, but I think it is worth showcasing that the model code has practical application. I think that it is important to consider the consequences of one's research and how the practical application of one's research can benefit those who are impacted by the discussion yet not included in the discussion. Workers who produce goods in countries far removed from the corporate headquarters are often left out of the decision-making process that governs their workplace. To combat this distance between worker and workplace, the code of conduct has should have a built-in feedback loop[30] that allows the code to constantly be improved upon rather than stay stagnant once enacted.

In previous research of mine, I have proposed a model code of conduct that is best suited to be implemented in the factory setting and in regards to workers in the retail sector as the elements of the code I devised included such provisions as prohibiting child labour and making sure that there was proper ventilation. The new code I propose for gig workers is different in that the concerns of gig workers is different and divergent from factory workers in the garment industry.

With the rise of precarious labour, there is a more pressing need for workers to be able to control their workplaces and work spaces, see the example of Uber where someone who drives Uber owns the car that is their work space and invites customers into their own private property in order to make a living. This occurrence is so vastly different from past workplaces where people commute to and from work and are not constantly driving their 'workplace' around. Also, note the growth of open space work where workers are no longer able to have offices which are a concern for workers' privacy and confidentiality. Spaces matter and it seems as though workers are becoming more pressured into limiting spaces and management is downloading the work space and space for work to workers. When workers are able to control their working conditions then they will be freer to become a part of the workplace.

My proposed code of conduct outlines such basic rights as the information about maximum working hours, ventilation systems in factories, and remuneration which are typical items to be found in a collective agreement but go beyond a collective agreement by encouraging employers to create an environment in which workers feel appreciated and their voice is acknowledged. This goes beyond legal structures and touches on psychological studies about inclusion in the workplace versus exclusion.[31] By not allowing workers to voice their concerns, management is not able to fully engage with the workers about potential ways to improve the workplace for *everyone*. Workers may see ways to improve productivity, etc. that management may not be able to witness without being on the shop floor. To be able to control the process without having the process control you can be rewarding for workers in a way that simple wage increases would not. The same way that employee stock options can help get employees to become more invested in the company so too can workers who simply feel more appreciated at work help the company to become more productive. It may be argued that an invested worker is a more loyal and devoted worker. This drive could help the worker become more valuable to the organization. In the absence of these improvements the workers may become stagnant and less willing to devote their time and energy to the organization in a way that a respected worker might.

My model of conduct of conduct allows for a company to take a basic outline and build on it to make it work for their particular workplace. I chose the strictest aspects of the four codes I examined (Gap, Reitmans, HBC, and Queen's) to come up with the most rigorous code. This code allows for workers to have their rights protected in an environment that respects their rights and freedoms. While there are other codes or models proposed by various authors my code is detailed and exacting. Other codes may outline what should be included but do not actually detail the language (see Sabel, O'Rouke and Fung 2000). I think that using the code I propose coupled with the model outlined by Kaptein (2008) about constant feedback allows for a code that can change and respond to the needs of the workers. Once a code is in place it should not be stagnant instead it should become stronger and more robust as times goes on—it is malleable. The principles created by Janda et al. (2009) and the one devised by Sethi (2011) set out a framework to show what underlying rules should be included in codes. This leads to a discussion about rules-based versus principles-based regulation. In this example, it is a rules-based code, but there should be acknowledgement that the rules are based on far-reaching principles about respect, dignity, and safety for workers. Also, related to constant improvement is the model created by Locke about workers being able to voice their concerns and have the code respond accordingly.

As noted by Professor Larry Cata Backer codes of conduct do not share the special characteristics of hard law (perhaps a more comprehensive enforcement structure) but they also do not suffer the weakness of law: "They reflect a potentially enforceable private law among the parties consenting thereto, provide a more robust basis in consent legitimacy than that offered by the more remote process of law making."[32] Attaching the governance at the site of the corporation will force that corporation to comply with the code in any jurisdiction as opposed to requiring various laws to become standardized simultaneously.

My proposed model code of conduct would hold corporations to a high standard and includes references to ILO Conventions, which allows the code to be part of a bigger blueprint for socially responsible corporations. To ensure compliance and enforcement of the code of conduct requires a mechanism that monitors the corporation. This is best done by an external monitoring agency such as WRC which when compared to the FLA seems superior due to it conducting factory audits rather than relying on another party to do so. Perhaps the ideal might be to have one code of conduct that is monitored by two monitoring agencies in that they act as check and balance. This may prove to be more expensive than merely having one but would demonstrate a higher level of commitment to the code that is worthy of praise. A rigorous code that is well enforced by an external monitoring agency or two monitoring agencies seems to be the best level of assurance. When a corporation adopts a code of conduct this demonstrates an aspiration to be more socially responsible but only when there is a monitoring scheme will there be true dedication to the code itself. Without a mechanism in place to ensure compliance then the code itself is rather futile.

Codes of conduct allow for greater flexibility as workers could be involved at the initial negotiation stage and on to drafting. Contrasted with a collective agreement the process might be similar in that union members are involved with the negotiation and the drafting of the collective agreement. The difference may be that in the unionized setting where there are collective agreements there is often a template from which a new collective agreement is based upon like when lawyers draft a contract from a precedent document. However, in the environment I envision, it might be that the corporation, with its own group of workers, is starting from first principles in regard to drafting its code of conduct. In the unionized setting the staff from the union in the form of stewards, have expertise that they bring to the table when working with the employer. In the corporate setting, when a code is being implemented this freedom from routine behaviour allows for greater flexibility regarding what can be included in the code or what can be left out. Union contracts can be formulaic, when in contrast, codes can be tailor-made to fit each individual workplace.

There could be the possibility of creating a new monitoring agency that is superior to both the FLA and the WRC. Leaving aside the option of creating a more rigorous code of conduct that may provide greater depth on specific areas or one that is greater in breadth than the original code it could be advantageous to have a stricter compliance mechanism. One way to guarantee compliance may be to develop a new monitoring agency that would be superior to both the WRC and FLA. Such a monitoring agency may conduct more unplanned factory visits, may examine factories in areas that others do not, they may speak to more workers individually about their work experience, etc. Being able to speak with individual workers in a setting off site may allow for workers to speak more openly about their workplace environment than a short chat on site. This new theorized agency could also improve by being cheaper to sign on with than the competing agencies. By making the fees lower this may encourage companies with merely a code of conduct in place to sign on with a monitoring agency as well. It is still important to continue to monitor the monitors to make sure that their reports, findings are accurate and reliable. Without a strong monitoring agency whose reports are dependable the system as a whole will be lacking a crucial element. Without a strong monitoring agency, the code of conduct is left to stand separately and not be examined—this allows for the code to possibly not be complied with or even ignored altogether. For workers to be protected, there must be a safeguard put in place to guarantee that their rights are being protected according to the code, and breaches of the code or non-compliance should be detected and allowed to be remedied before any other action is taken.

The current legal landscape in Canada and the United States does not capture gig workers just like my other research into those who make our clothes in foreign countries are not captured by North American law. How can we act to protect those workers? There are numerous solutions, but the best option I devise is a corporate code of conduct. This allows for flexibility and constant improvement in a way that hard law does not. Codes also allow for worker participation in a way that legislation does not. Gig workers need more protection than currently available to them. They are currently stuck in a place of unclusion because they are not full-time or part-time workers nor are they temporary workers. They fall outside all of the categorization models that exist. As the companies claim to disrupt capitalism the workers must disrupt in their own way to become included in labour and employment law. The codes may be old tools, but they offer an attempt at protection and malleability that hard law lacks.

What are the basic provisions which should be included in all codes? There should be a preamble outlining the purpose of the Code. The following headings and topics were included in my former code:

1   Forced Labour
2   Child Labour
3   Wages and Benefits
4   Overtime
5   Working Hours
6   Working Conditions
7   Health and Safety
8   Harassment
9   Discrimination
10 Environment
11 Freedom of Association, Collective Bargaining
12 Monitoring
13 Access to Facilities

Model Code of Conduct

Corporation X is committed to ensuring that all of its products are produced in an ethical manner, consistent with international labour standards, and all applicable laws and regulations. This Code provides the basic standard for Corporation

X, and all suppliers and sub-suppliers must comply with the provisions outlined in this Code. Violations of this Code may result in the termination of the contract between Corporation X and the supplier/subsupplier found to be in violation.

1. *Forced Labour*

Not needed for gig workers.

2. *Child Labour*

Again, not needed for gig workers.

3. *Wages and Benefits*

Suppliers and their contractors provide wages and benefits in the relevant industry which constitutes a dignified living wage capable of providing for the essential needs of workers and their families.

A living wage shall be defined as a wage which provides for the basic needs (housing, energy, nutrition, clothing, health care, education, potable water, child care, transportation, and savings)[33] of an average family unit of employees in the relevant sector of the country divided by the average number of adult wage earners in the family unit of employees, in the relevant employment sector of the country.[34]

4. *Overtime*

In addition to their compensation for regular hours of work, employees shall be compensated for overtime hours at such a premium rate as is legally required in that country, or as negotiated in a collective agreement, but not less than at a rate equal to their regular hourly compensation rate.[35] Typical overtime rates are 1.5 times regular hourly rates. Also common is twice the hourly rate for workers working on statutory holidays.

5. *Working Hours*

Except in extraordinary circumstances, employees shall (i) not be required to work more than the lesser of (a) 48 hours per week and 12 hours overtime per week, or (b) the limits on regular and overtime hours allowed by the law of the country of manufacture; and (ii) be entitled to at least one day off in every seven-day period, as well as holidays and vacations.[36]

6. *Working Conditions*

Management expected to treat all workers with respect and dignity and provide them with a safe and healthy work environment. Workers must not be subjected to corporal punishment or any other form of physical, psychological, sexual or verbal harassment, or abuse.

- Work spaces must comply with all applicable laws and regulations relating to working conditions, including workers' health and safety.

7. Health and Safety

Employers must provide a safe and healthy work environment in a building that is structurally sound.[37] Management must have a valid building, and where applicable, construction license/certificate for the premises as required by local laws.

8. Harassment

Every worker must be treated with respect and dignity. No worker may be subject to any physical, sexual, psychological or verbal harassment, or abuse including the use of physical punishment. Employers are encouraged to create a collegial working environment.

9. Discrimination

Workers must not be subject to discrimination in employment, including with respect to hiring, salary, benefits, advancement, discipline, termination, or retirement, on the basis of gender, race, religious or personal beliefs, age (other than normal and legally allowed hiring or retirement limitations), disability, sexual orientation, maternity or marital status, nationality, political opinion, union participation, social or ethnic origin, or membership in any legal organization. Employment decisions must be made solely on the basis of knowledge, skill, efficiency, and ability to do the job and meet its requirements.

10. Environment

Not as important for gig workers as their work space moves.

11. Freedom of Association

Licensees and their contractors shall recognize and respect the right of employees to freedom of association and collective bargaining with bargaining representatives of their own choice. No employee shall be subject to harassment, intimidation, or retaliation as a result of his or her efforts to freely associate or bargain collectively. Where not explicitly prohibited by national laws, University licensees and contractors shall ensure compliance with ILO Conventions 87, 98, and 135[38]

12. Monitoring

The company must adhere to monitoring practices that enforce the Code.

13. Access to Facilities

Not needed for gig workers.

Monitoring Agencies

The examination into the efficacy of proposals in shaping corporate behaviour to increase labour standards will be assessed. The assessment of the strengths and weaknesses of various monitoring agencies including: (1) the Worker Rights Consortium, and (2) Fair Labor Association will be conducted. Look at Queen's University as an example of getting a code[39] implemented in 2004 and then signing on with the monitoring agency WRC. The code is the first step. The implementation of the code is the most important piece. Having it be properly enforced is obviously the next most important step. A rule without a remedy is ineffective. There must be a remedy once that rule is breached. Some institutions decide to have two monitoring agencies as York University uses both the WRC[40] and FLA.[41] Looking at the Queen's example section 3 of its code reads:

> The University reserves the right to terminate its relationship with any licensee which continues to conduct its business in violation of the corrective action plan, in accordance with the terms set forth in the licensee agreement. This decision will be rendered by the ad hoc oversight committee responsible for implementation of the Code.[42]

This outlines the various bodies responsible for ensuring compliance with the code. On the internal side Queen's has an oversight committee to monitor compliance with the code and has an external third-party monitoring agency, the WRC. There may be contention if these two entities have a disagreement over the enforcement of the code. The fact that the code is still in force after more than a decade shows how lasting the impact of activists can be on the campus culture. The institutionalization of the anti-sweatshop activism has enduring impacts on the University.

Codes are varied as some are stricter than others. The stricter a code the more difficult it may be to get it implemented. My experience at Queen's getting the University to implement a code was informative. We started Queen's Students Against Sweatshops ('QSAS') with the intention of having the WRC be the monitoring agency and were successful in that, but had to sacrifice certain provisions in order to get the code drafted. The pressures on advocacy groups (QSAS could fall under this umbrella) to conform or accept concessions is strong. What is better—having a weaker code that gets implemented or holding out for a stronger one to possibly be implemented in the future? Concessions have to be accepted and the push for a stronger code in the future must be brought about later. A starting-out point is an important one. None of us viewed our code as one that was compromised compared to other Universities. We were proud to get one implemented and were happy that it did not take very long for this progress to be made. There is not much research on the use of self-monitoring, such as Nike does. "Little research exists on the impacts of codes of conduct and self-monitoring on actual labor conditions. Nike naturally asserts that they respond effectively and sufficiently to labor concerns."[43] The Queen's code references ILO Conventions 138, 182, 155 and Recommendation 164. Also ILO Conventions 87, 98 and 135 are mentioned. As Professor Sethi states an independent external monitoring system builds public trust.[44] Thus a code without a monitoring agency is rather purposeless.

The work of Professor Benjamin Cashore of Yale University builds on the work of Sabel, O'Rourke and Fung who came out with their RLS model in 2000. Cashore notes that governance can start with a limited approach and move to a more comprehensive approach as time goes on (see Figure[45] below). He outlines 'the California effect' which he explains as the notion that businesses in regulated markets act out of self-interest to impose regulations on other companies in less regulated markets. He notes that this can lead to strategic coalitions between businesses and NGOs. This means that slowly the floor level of regulation gets imposed on competitors in the same way that Sabel, O'Rourke, and Fung note in RLS. This increases standards throughout the industry as there is slowly buy-in from other companies.

Worker Rights Consortium

The Worker Rights Consortium is an independent labour rights monitoring agency. The WRC has over 175 college and university affiliates, and its primary focus is on factories that make university-related apparel. It was started in April 2000 by university administrators, students, and labour experts. As noted on their website their "purpose is to combat sweatshops and protect the rights of workers who make apparel and other products."[46] The WRC provides a model Code of Conduct on its website. Monitoring agencies are external organizations that are paid a fee to monitor compliance with a code.

> USAS [United Students Against Sweatshops] and the CCC [Clean Clothes Campaign] have sought to establish a 'foundation' model that centralizes oversight and controls all payments for monitoring. The FLA and SA8000 employ a 'consulting firm' model which allows companies to choose and pay for their own monitors.[47]

The various agencies have different standards, and some are more strict than others. WRC will cancel its contract if there is non-compliance versus FLA will work towards encouraging compliance if there is a breach. "[T]he Worker Rights Consortium (WRC), developed by the United Students Against Sweatshops (USAS) in 1999, employs a different strategy focusing on information forcing, verification systems, and pro-active inspections."[48] What do they do that is different from FLA? They go into warehouses and investigate. FLA is viewed as the less rigorous monitoring agency compared to the WRC.

> It [WRC] puts particular emphasis on developing links with labour organizations and workers in the countries where licensed production is being undertaken. It will develop mechanisms for receiving and verifying workers' complaints regarding violations of the code of conduct. The WRC places considerable emphasis on transparency, requiring full disclosure of plant locations and labour conditions.[49]

The WRC is careful to not be seen as trying to usurp the power and control of unions. The role of monitoring agencies to provide a variation on the auditing system in that the agency will ensure that proper mechanisms are in place in conformity with the code.

> When codes are the result of negotiations involving a number of different stakeholders, they are likely to be more comprehensive and to have stricter monitoring than those which are unilaterally adopted by companies. . . . Thus the WRC code which does not involve any direct corporate participation is more stringent than the FLA code which was rejected by the trade unions.[50]

The divide between which monitoring agencies unions and other advocacy groups choose to align with speaks volumes as to which entities are more corporate driven (and perhaps controlled) than others. A lenient monitoring agency will not provide effective services in that its role is to ensure compliance with the code not merely act as a façade.

Fair Labor Association

The FLA was started in 1999 with the involvement of companies which is in contrast to the WRC which does not include corporate involvement. It may be said that having corporations involved with the founding of the FLA may result in it being viewed as less rigorous as the WRC. "The FLA is a brand accountability system that places the onus on companies to voluntarily achieve the FLA's labor standards in the factories manufacturing their products."[51] This task seems less onerous than the WRC's mandate. "The Fair Labor Association (FLA), convened by the Clinton administration in 1996, is the most advanced and most controversial of current initiatives to establish monitoring and verification systems."[52] The FLA is criticized for being too much aligned with both government and corporate interests. A monitoring agency that appears to demonstrate such biases may be less successful than one where the clear independence has been established since its creation.

> Critics of the FLA argue that the monitoring system is neither sufficiently strong nor independent. The fact that a company can be certified when only 30 per cent of its facilities have been independently monitored, and that it has plenty of time to warn those which are to be inspected, limits the effectiveness of monitoring.[53]

The FLA may also face criticism in the form of its not being independent enough from corporate interest because it lacks a real 'arm's length' distance from its founders.

> Another perverse outcome of this approach is that it may lead the code effort to be captured by the companies with the least amount of commitment to code compliance. This situation is akin to the capture theory of regulation, where the regulators are co-opted by the regulated and thus lose their legitimacy as regulators (Thompson, 2003).[54]

In this instance the monitoring agencies may be said to be occupying the role of regulators by offering services akin to auditing and sometimes drawing attention to delinquent suppliers.

Notes

1 This may be akin to the German model where Boards are often composed of workers to the limit of 50 percent worker representation.
2 See research on bullying.
3 Hugh Collins, *Marxism and Law* (New York: Oxford University Press, 1982), 40.
4 The author would like to note that the term 'more power' is used to allow for the fact the proletariat are not 'powerless' but are instead 'less powerful' in relation to the bourgeoisie.
5 Daniel Cole, "'An Unqualified Human Good': E.P. Thompson and the Rule of Law" *Journal of Law and Society*, 28.2(June 2001), 191.
6 Idea borrowed from Professor Paritosh Kumar, Queen's University, Development Studies from a lecture in October 2005.
7 Hugh Collins, *Marxism and Law* (New York: Oxford University Press, 1982), 63.
8 Brian Tamanaha, *On the Rule of Law: History, Politics, Theory* (New York: Cambridge University Press, 2004), 51.
9 Hugh Collins, *Marxism and Law* (New York: Oxford University Press, 1982), 104.
10 Jagdish Bhagwati, *In Defense of Globalization* (New York: Oxford University Press, 2007), 122.
11 Jagdish Bhagwati, *In Defense of Globalization* (New York: Oxford University Press, 2007), 129.
12 R. Edward Freeman et al., *Stakeholder Theory: The State of the Art* (Cambridge: Cambridge University Press, 2010), 269.
13 Adam Smith, *The Wealth of Nations, Books I–III* (London: Penguin Books Ltd., 1999), 80.

14 Adam Smith, *The Wealth of Nations, Books I–III* (London: Penguin Books Ltd., 1999), 269.

15 Adam Smith, *The Wealth of Nations, Books I–III* (London: Penguin Books Ltd., 1999), 435.

16 Adolf A Berle and Gardiner C Means, *The Modern Corporation & Private Property* (New Jersey: Transaction Publishers, 1991), xlix.

17 Robert Tucker, ed., *The Marx-Engels Reader, 2nd ed.* (New York: W.W. Norton & Co., 1978), 72.

18 Robert Tucker, ed., *The Marx-Engels Reader, 2nd ed.* (New York: W.W. Norton & Co., 1978), 71.

19 Robert Tucker, ed., *The Marx-Engels Reader, 2nd ed.* (New York: W.W. Norton & Co., 1978), 76.

20 Idea borrowed from Professor Asher Horowitz from a lecture to his Introduction to Political Theory class in 2002, York University.

21 Robert Tucker, ed., *The Marx-Engels Reader, 2nd ed.* (New York: W.W. Norton & Co., 1978), 71.

22 Robert Tucker, ed., *The Marx-Engels Reader, 2nd ed.* (New York: W.W. Norton & Co., 1978), 73.

23 Robert Tucker, ed., *The Marx-Engels Reader, 2nd ed.* (New York: W.W. Norton & Co., 1978), 77.

24 Bob Fine, et al. eds., *Capitalism and the Rule of Law: From Deviancy Theory to Marxism* (London: Hutchinson & Co. Publishers Ltd., 1979), 39.

25 Karl Marx, "Theses on Feuerbach" in *Karl Marx: Selected Writings* (Cambridge: Hackett Publishing Company, Inc., 1994), 101.

26 Jagdish Bhagwati, *In Defense of Globalization* (New York: Oxford University Press, 2007), 269.

27 Jagdish Bhagwati, *In Defense of Globalization* (New York: Oxford University Press, 2007), 18.

28 See David Campbell's work, Online: <www.david-campbell.org/>. "Whenever a crisis erupts and photojournalists' document the suffering of those affected, it is commonly suggested that we are no longer affected by such pictures because of the prevalence of a condition known as 'compassion fatigue'. Seeing the same thing time and again, it is argued, has led to an anesthetized and apathetic audience. However, although common and oft repeated, this claim is rarely backed by evidence to support its position."

29 See Vanisha H. Sukdeo blog post for more information:
    "Creating a Pro-Friendly Classroom" posted on the Canadian Association of Law Teachers (CALT) website, August 14, 2014: <www.acpd-calt.org/creating_a_pro_friendly_classroom>.
    "While there is much discussion about anti-bullying in schools I think that the focus needs to go beyond how to combat the menace of bullying and move to the next stage. My idea is to not just alleviate bullying and make the classroom a neutral setting but to create a pro-friendly classroom, one in which the focus is not just on being civil but being friendly. Also, I am very interested in exploring how to make classrooms a 'safe space' for the exchange of ideas and tolerance but also 'friendly spaces' in that creating a warm, happy environment for students might help to foster learning. This may be a tall order at a law school but I have hope. The idea that I am working on is something akin to anti-bullying but more along the lines of 'pro-friendly'."

30 See Ivanka Mamic, *Implementing Codes of Conduct: How Business Manage Social Performance in Global Supply Chains* (Geneva: Greenleaf Publishing, 2004), 68.

31 Jane O'Reilly, "Is Negative Attention Better Than No Attention? The Comparative Effects of Ostracism and Harassment at Work" Online: <http://pubsonline.informs.org/doi/abs/10.1287/orsc.2014.0900>.

32 Larry Cata Backer blog post on September 21, 2013, Online: <http://lcbacker-blog.blogspot.ca/2013/09/changing-corporate-behavior-through.html>.
33 This is similar to the definition of 'living wage' offered by Mamic.
34 From the Queen's Code
35 From the Queen's Code. The Queen's Code is the only one that includes overtime as a separate heading. The other codes that include the word only include it with working hours.
36 From the Queen's Code. The Queen's Code is the most detailed as other codes state things like the company must adhere to the law.
37 This is especially important in light of Rana Plaza.
38 From the Queen's Code
39 Queen's Code of Conduct, Online: <www.queensu.ca/studentaffairs/trademarklicensing/codeofconduct.html>.
40 WRC, Affiliate schools, Online: <www.workersrights.org/about/as.asp>.
41 FLA, Affiliate schools, Online: <www.fairlabor.org/fla/go.asp?u=/pub/mp&Page=CollegesUniversities>.
42 Queen's Code of Conduct, Online: <www.queensu.ca/studentaffairs/trademarklicensing/codeofconduct.html>.
43 Charles Sabel, Dara O'Rourke and Archon Fung, "Ratcheting Labor Standards: Regulation for Continuous Improvement in the Global Workplace", Online: <http://papers.ssrn.com/sol3/papers.cfm?abstract_id=253833> at 22.
44 S. Prakash Sethi ed., *Globalization and Self-Regulation: The Crucial Role that Corporate Codes of Conduct Play in Global Business* (New York: Palgrave Macmillan, 2011), 13: "There must be an independent external monitoring and compliance verification system to engender public trust and credibility in the industry's claims of performance. Performance with code compliance on the part of member companies or groups must be subjected to independent external monitoring and compliance verification. It is in this area that companies and industries offer the most resistance. It is argued that external monitoring would create an environment of distrust and policing."
45 Benjamin Cashore, et al., "Can Non-state Governance 'Ratchet Up' Global Environmental Standards? Lessons from the Forest Sector" *Reciel*, 16.2(2007), 158–172 at 170.
46 WRC, 'Mission', Online: <www.workersrights.org/about/>.
47 Charles Sabel, Dara O'Rourke and Archon Fung, "Ratcheting Labor Standards: Regulation for Continuous Improvement in the Global Workplace", Online: <http://papers.ssrn.com/sol3/papers.cfm?abstract_id=253833> at 24.
48 Charles Sabel, Dara O'Rourke and Archon Fung, "Ratcheting Labor Standards: Regulation for Continuous Improvement in the Global Workplace", Online: <http://papers.ssrn.com/sol3/papers.cfm?abstract_id=253833> at 23.
49 Rhys Jenkins, "The Political Economy of Codes of Conduct" in Rhys Jenkins, Ruth Pearson and Gill Seyfang, eds. *Corporate Responsibility and Labour Rights; Codes of Conduct in the Global Economy* (London: Earthscan Publications Limited, 2002), 27.
50 Rhys Jenkins, "The Political Economy of Codes of Conduct" in Rhys Jenkins, Ruth Pearson and Gill Seyfang eds. *Corporate Responsibility and Labour Rights; Codes of Conduct in the Global Economy* (London: Earthscan Publications Limited, 2002), 28.
51 FLA, "About Us", Online: <www.fairlabor.org/fla/go.asp?u=/pub/mp&Page=About_Menu>.
52 Charles Sabel, Dara O'Rourke and Archon Fung, "Ratcheting Labor Standards: Regulation for Continuous Improvement in the Global Workplace", Online: <http://papers.ssrn.com/sol3/papers.cfm?abstract_id=253833> at 23.

53 Rhys Jenkins, "The Political Economy of Codes of Conduct" in Rhys Jenkins, Ruth Pearson and Gill Seyfang, eds. *Corporate Responsibility and Labour Rights; Codes of Conduct in the Global Economy* (London: Earthscan Publications Limited, 2002), 26.
54 S. Prakash Sethi ed., *Globalization and Self-Regulation: The Crucial Role that Corporate Codes of Conduct Play in Global Business* (New York: Palgrave Macmillan, 2011), 11.

Bibliography for Chapter 4

Books

Berle, Adolf and Gardiner C Means. *The Modern Corporation & Private Property* (New Jersey: Transaction Publishers, 1991).

Bhagwati, Jagdish. *In Defense of Globalization* (New York: Oxford University Press, 2007)

Collins, Hugh. *Marxism and Law* (New York: Oxford University Press, 1982).

Fine, Bob, et al., ed. *Capitalism and the Rule of Law: From Deviancy Theory to Marxism* (London: Hutchinson & Co. Publishers Ltd., 1979).

Freeman, Edward et al. *Stakeholder Theory: The State of the Art* (Cambridge: Cambridge University Press, 2010).

Jenkins, Rhys, Ruth Pearson and Gill Seyfang, eds. *Corporate Responsibility and Labour Rights; Codes of Conduct in the Global Economy* (London: Earthscan Publications Limited, 2002).

Mamic, Ivanka. *Implementing Codes of Conduct: How Business Manage Social Performance in Global Supply Chains* (Geneva: Greenleaf Publishing, 2004).

Marx, Karl. "Theses on Feuerbach" in *Karl Marx: Selected Writings* (Cambridge: Hackett Publishing Company, Inc., 1994).

Sethi, S. Prakash ed. *Globalization and Self-Regulation: The Crucial Role that Corporate Codes of Conduct Play in Global Business* (New York: Palgrave Macmillan, 2011).

Smith, Adam. *The Wealth of Nations, Books I–III* (London: Penguin Books Ltd., 1999).

Tamanaha, Brian. *On the Rule of Law: History, Politics, Theory* (New York: Cambridge University Press, 2004).

Tucker, Robert. ed. *The Marx-Engels Reader, 2nd ed.* (New York: W.W. Norton & Co., 1978).

Articles

Cashore, Benjamin. et al. "Can Non-state Governance 'Ratchet Up' Global Environmental Standards? Lessons from the Forest Sector" *Reciel*, 16.2 (2007), 158–172.

Cole, Daniel. "'An Unqualified Human Good': E.P. Thompson and the Rule of Law" *Journal of Law and Society*, 28.2., June 2001.

O'Reilly, Jane. "Is Negative Attention Better Than No Attention? The Comparative Effects of Ostracism and Harassment at Work" Online: <http://pubsonline.informs.org/doi/abs/10.1287/orsc.2014.0900>.

Sabel, Charles, Dara O'Rourke and Archon Fung. "Ratcheting Labor Standards: Regulation for Continuous Improvement in the Global Workplace" Online: <http://papers.ssrn.com/sol3/papers.cfm?abstract_id=253833>.

Websites

David Campbell's Work. Online: <www.david-campbell.org/>.

FLA, Affiliate Schools. Online: <www.fairlabor.org/fla/go.asp?u=/pub/mp&Page=CollegesUniversities>.

Larry Cata Backer blog post on September 21, 2013. Online: <http://lcbackerblog.blogspot.ca/2013/09/changing-corporate-behavior-through.html>.

Queen's Code of Conduct. Online: <www.queensu.ca/studentaffairs/trademarklicensing/codeofconduct.html>.

Sukdeo, Vanisha H. "Creating a Pro-Friendly Classroom" posted on the Canadian Association of Law Teachers (CALT) website, August 14, 2014. Online: <www.acpd-calt.org/creating_a_pro_friendly_classroom>.

WRC, Affiliate Schools. Online: <www.workersrights.org/about/as.asp>.

5 Conclusion

The conclusion will show how workers can have an increased voice by using tools outside of the typical legal ones. Without state protection the rights can be viewed as less stringent but working outside the system allows for greater malleability and flexibility to be able to cater to individual workers in individual workplaces. Workers' rights is about better working conditions, hourly wages, and benefits, but it is also about being treated in a more civilized manner where one's humanity is recognized. Only through all of these parts working together will a true version of workers' rights emerge—one where workers are not viewed as mere tools but within and of the system itself.

The capitalist system exploits workers by presenting the wage contract as fair and unavoidable. Workers are forced to sell their labour to make money to afford food and shelter. Gig workers are only different from the average worker because their work is more precarious and piecemeal. The work of a gig worker is also less predictable and stable than the average worker. Workers can distinguish themselves based on income or education as a lawyer may shun the label of 'wage slave' because they live in a large house and drive a nice car. But if they lose their job tomorrow, they are in a similar situation as that retail worker or barista as their favourite coffee shop. If you are not independently wealthy or living off passive income, then the likelihood of you being a wage slave is very high. Rather than shun the label and continue to split hairs about which worker is more exploited, it is better to embrace the label and work on how to fix the system. How to allow someone who works as a barista but makes music on the side be able to focus more time and energy on their music? How to encourage the engineer who wants to paint to be able to do so? These are not idealistic options, but rather ones that exist in another world. These ideas can become actualized in a world that does not place such an emphasis on being overworked and over-tired constantly because of the demands of the workaday world. A different world, where workers are encouraged to explore what they want to do for a living rather than simply focus and be defined by what they currently do for a living, is possible. People are so defined and confined by their jobs as though the job one does is that person's complete existence which is problematic. Maybe that janitor volunteers in his spare time? While that mean old scientist is mean to everyone he meets. Why laud someone simply for the job they do rather than the role they occupy in the world outside of simply their job? A world exists where people are defined beyond their labour role and instead by their complete existence. Where labour and the value of one's labour does not define the worker. This is the escape from isolation and inequality. This is the movement towards workers have their voices acknowledged and included in decision-making in a way that allows for them to have input in their working environment. This will help shift the workplace from being exclusionary for workers towards becoming more inclusionary. This new workplace world would allow workers to have more autonomy and control over their workplace and within their workplace. This new workplace world is possible. Another world is possible.

Gig workers are simply another product of changes in the very nature of work. From the Industrial Revolution onwards workers have merely been carried along, while changes occurred with capital being able to steer the ship with workers as mere passengers. Workers in the gig economy can turn the disruption of platform capitalism around to become a time of disruption in the labour and employment realm and re-capture the ship to be controlled by workers. To be able to use both hard law and soft law instruments to strengthen their rights workers may be able to gain more than lost. If workers are able to increase the strength and volume of their voices then they may be able to be heard from a growing audience—an audience that both cares enough to hear those voices and will do something to help. Hearing the voices and failing to act is ineffectual and pointless. Being to raise awareness to labour issues and get consumers to either start caring about product sourcing or continue to care about the same will result in better working conditions for workers. Consumers can boycott or buycott products and their purchasing decisions can bring about change. Also, being able to tap into ethical investment can help workers as those who invest in corporations may be swayed to care about the corporations they choose to invest in. If investors view certain corporations as being risky investments because they may face a boycott or gain media attention about corporate misbehaviour then those investors may choose to invest elsewhere. Those are simply two examples from the bottom up with consumers forcing change to top to bottom with investors creating change.

The 'Seattle Solution' is one way forward where Uber drivers can band together to exert collective action. The London approach of changing the regulations about Uber is another approach. The Unifor method in Canada is yet another approach. It is up to Uber drivers as individuals to figure out what works for them as well as for Uber drivers in blocks to decide if an entire city's Uber fleet should band together. This method of collective organizing can help workers who feel isolated due to the sheer loneliness of working such a job.

Codes of Conduct

While I argue that codes of conduct are the best way forward for workers critics of CSR may argue that codes may not be the best way to secure or increase the rights of workers. With the rise of capitalism and what may be termed 'corpo-ratism' workers must be willing to acknowledge that power and the ability to gain strength in their collective ability allows for speaking truth to power. Only through engaging with corporations will workers be able to forge ahead. The labour movement in many forms has accepted this new mode and has adapted as a result. For workers to have a seat at the table like in the German model may be just one option, and other options may prove useful to other workplaces; no one solution will work in every single workplace. If workers are given increased autonomy and voice about their workplaces then they would be able to choose which model works for their individual workplace.

No workplaces are identical, and workers are best positioned to know what changes would work in their own workplaces. Including that Uber driver into decision-making processes may allow for those higher up know how to make changes to the corporate that better suits the needs of those who get money from the company. That word choice is deliberate in that those are not necessarily Uber workers in the way that someone works for their direct employer. The gig economy has broken down, such basic structures with the promise of disrupting, while it may result in too much damage. What is to exist in the former place before the disruption? What should exist there versus what does exist there? The space created has allowed for workers to face even lower wages than previously and more cruel and inhumane working conditions than before. At least in the former model there was structure of being trained, having a manager to assign duties, co-workers to chat with, and a steady income and perhaps even benefits. While that model seemed confining and restrictive the alternative is worse. The workers who fight for greater work–life balance may have gotten swept up in the fight and their life is now their work.

Disruptor and Disruption

Many new enterprises in the gig economy such as Uber see themselves to be disruptors within the capitalist mainstream economy. They envision themselves to be revolutionary and able to bring about change that helps workers gain control of their own work. In so doing the opposite has been actualized—gone are stable jobs with a boss to oversee concerns to be replaced with piecemeal work where the direct consumer is the boss. This new boss has no training or ability to be a boss.

Disruption can lead to disorder. Instead we should consider returning to order and maintaining stability for workers. These new disruptions of standard employment have allowed for precarity to thrive. Disruption does not have to be paired with precarity. There must be a better model where the two are not intertwined and interconnected.

Reserve Army of Labour

Marx coined the term 'reserve army of labour' to describe how Capitalism needs a certain percentage of workers to be unemployed to keep wages down. If there is always a reserve army of labour waiting to work for lower wages then the market is able to flourish. If everyone was employed then maybe workers could argue that they should be better paid for providing labour but if that same worker sees someone over their shoulder waiting to work that job for less money than that keeps workers happy to have a job while also keeping their compliant.

Individuals who are members of the reserve army of labour clamour for a job, any job, a low level job, a job for which they are overqualified, etc. This creates animousity among workers who view other workers as the enemy rather than a potential ally. Jealousy and anger are directed at the person who has a job or even got that job you applied for when the anger should be kept for the system as a whole not the individual participants who 'won' within the system.

Emotional Labour

The phrase 'emotional labour' is used to describe the burden on workers to constantly be viewed by customers as in good mood, or having a positive disposition. It is not enough to be doing a good job but one must be sublimely happy while completing one's work. A 'whistle while you work' approach to work. This is part of a bigger problem within the system that says that workers should be thankful for having a job, so of course it follows that one should be perceived as happy while at work. Again, the point is that the perception is important—how the worker actually feels is irrelevant. I imagine it is hard to smile if one is being exploited at work.

What is the problem with forcing people to be perceived as happy while at work? It creates an illusion that everyone is happy to serve. That everyone is enthusiastically happy to find you pants in your size. While workers should not be grumpy or sullen while performing their tasks perhaps neutral is the better standard to hold workers to rather than grinning like fools. I do not imagine that they are extraordinarily happy to be at work so why force them to pretend to be? For the customer experience? It makes me as a customer cringe when workers are forced to be happy.

Organizational Justice

Organizational justice offers an explanation of how when workers feel more included they perform better in the workplace. As explained by Bies and Moag, interactional justice shows that the fairness of interpersonal justice in the workplace is important in regards to workers feeling included and the belief in fairness of outcomes.[1] When workers feel included and that they have a voice in the workplace, then there is greater buy in to the workplace governance mechanisms such as codes of conduct. "When we internalize a belief or value we are more likely to behave in accordance with it (Rokeach, 973)."[2] This sense of justice and fairness is important in the workplace in order to fulfill one's sense of self because many people feel that their jobs are a very large part of their lives. People are often asked what they do for a living and are judged by the answer. In a world where social status is valued,[3] then what one does for a living allows others to decide how much importance to place on that person as an individual.[4] Employees in various workplaces are similar in that greater control over the workplace governance mechanisms allows for greater worker output and satisfaction. "Disputants preferred procedures that afforded them process control, and eschewed those that did not."[5] This ability to control one's workplace governance and have input in devising the system itself may lead to greater acceptance and increased compliance.

> Process control allows individuals a chance to express their feelings. Even when the rationally economic outcomes do not go the way individuals might like, having the opportunity to speak conveys to people that they are respected and valued by the group.[6]

Worker voice is valuable because the more workers feel included and respected, the greater they will work for the organization. The ability to have one's voice heard is important in and of itself, having that input actually acted on is separate. "As Tyler (1984) demonstrated nearly two decades ago, the beneficial effects of voice are more likely to occur when an individual perceives that their views were given reasonable consideration."[7] Building morale in the workplace leads to greater output from workers. "Once a relational contract is established, these workers possess a broader set of obligations. They are more likely to remain with the firm and exert extra effort on its behalf."[8]

There Are Limits to the Law

Law has limits and there are certain behaviours that law cannot regulate. CSR is about being more socially responsible, but also about empathy and caring for others, or at least treating them in a more humane way. This will change the very foundation of corporate law if human empathy and caring starts to seep its way into the rather cold exterior of the corporation. There are also limits to empathy and caring as explored in compassion fatigue and distancing. There is not enough 'care' for everyone. Those who oppose CSR would argue that corporations are not meant to be caring and empathetic, but the rules of the game have changed. With the increased use of cooperatives, and the creation of Benefit Corporations, CICs, and CCCs, the realm of corporate law has changed and the past is unlikely to return. Perhaps increased caring and a more moral corporation is not disastrous to corporations in general as if all corporations become more socially responsible then the playing field is level, and there may no longer be room for the heartless and cold corporation. As that form of the corporation may be one that has expired. That form of corporate model may be too antiquated to last and with the rise of CSR and the movement from millennials for the desire for social justice jobs the corporation may have to fall in line with CSR principles to attract the best and brightest talent. Some MBA graduates are willing to take a cut in salary to work at a socially responsible corporation over an unethical one. This will lead to changes in the way corporations recruit and to care about their brand in relation to their ability to attract talent.

The evolution of the ethical consumer also raises issues about ethical versus unethical corporations and the market share occupied by each. These issues are all interconnected with the principles decided in recent court cases and how the corporation functions in Canadian society. These broad rather disconnected issues and theories come together in *Peoples* and *BCE* as it heralds in a new corporate era—one in which the shareholder no longer occupies a pedestal without falling off. The move towards stakeholder theory actualized means that while the pedestal may still exist, it has been lowered and is on shaky ground. The shareholder as a protected and honoured person in the realm of the corporation is no longer the ideal held to be continued, but the fall from grace is rather a short trip to a less-honoured position, but one still being adored. Shareholders in *BCE* were relegated to just another stakeholder group, but one that gets to vote to approve arrangements, and other such powers that they hold exclusively. As noted elsewhere, rather than say that Canada has accepted stakeholder theory as actualization, it is better to say that Canada is transitioning to stakeholder theory so shareholder-focused theory is more apt.

The shareholder-focused model will allow for the details to be ironed out about how expansive the duty owed to the corporation is and where it ends. There is no point in trying to argue that all corporations have duties to society as a whole. There must be clear demarcations as to how far the duty extends (the breadth) and how far the duty goes (the depth). This will allow for clearer and better defined duties so that the fulfillment of those duties will be more readily completed.

My idea about transportable law is not that different from the laws that punish returning citizens who have committed crimes abroad. It is in recognition that behaviour that is not condoned domestically should not be tolerated when committed on foreign soil. This runs against the notion of sovereignty but also allows a country to control its own citizens without bending to differing jurisdictions. So the issue is not so much about sovereignty and one nation having lax laws pertaining to its own citizens, but it considers the actions of its citizens when abroad.

Expansion of Fiduciary Duties

Expanding the fiduciary duties of a corporation would allow those fighting for rights in regards to corporate behaviour to have a greater claim to such rights as they would be statutory mechanisms rather than unclear ideals. Codifying such language gives greater strength and shows society that these are the principles or values that we expect corporations to comply with. Codification signals to the corporation, those who commit wrongs, and society at large that there is certain importance to be given to all stakeholders and not just shareholders. When the phrase 'the best interests of the corporation' becomes expanded beyond merely shareholders then corporations will be able to align their aspirations about being socially responsible with actualizing those aspirations into reality. This is the movement from stakeholder theory to stakeholder theory being actualized. Only then will the interests of stakeholders matter beyond being a talking point and on to becoming the lived reality of the corporation.

Common law jurisdictions progress by developments in the law. These changes can be incremental or drastic. The change in Canadian laws to include same-sex marriage was rather drastic and changed the law for individuals and society. The change in the law from *BC Health Services* to hold that government employees have the right to collectively bargain is rather drastic.[9] The change in the laws from *BCE* did not seem as impactful on the same level as such fundamental rights as marriage equality and the right to associate, but it is pervasive in ways that the average citizen does not stop to consider. Whether your investments are tied up in a corporation that cares about being socially responsible is important. Whether your pension plan is invested in progressive corporations is important. Whether those who hold top positions within corporations believe in CSR is important. These varying layers of importance need to be examined by those who invest in certain corporations. Where your pension dollars go is less malleable.

Not OK Computer: Automization and the Worker

This section examines how work is becoming more automized and how this may lead to job loss for workers. Instead of hiring many workers who need rest and may face illness, etc., the replacement of workers with robots allows for management to hire workers who are not able to unionize, who do not need sleep or to lunch breaks, and allows for a one-time investment in the purchase and then costs for maintenance. Workers being replaced with machines is not new as the rise of Luddism will be discussed.

Also, the skills that were once needed are now obsolete. So rather than embrace technological advances, perhaps the average worker should fight against.

Luddism

The question of whether technology actually helps the modern worker needs to be explored. Many jobs are lost to mechanization. The Luddite Revolution in England in the nineteent century was an effort by workers to destroy machines that were thought to be taking away jobs. Also, it was believed that goods produced by machines were inferior to those which were 'handmade' or produced by true artisans.

> But today, in most commodities and activities, technology matters and has diffused greatly, both because many have access to similar pools of knowledge and because multinationals can take scarce knowledge almost everywhere if they choose, as they often do, and they do produce globally.[10]

The increase in globalization has helped to undercut the artisan. Also the skills that were once needed are now obsolete. "The *piece up* (yarn tying), *doffing* (removing full bobbins), and *draw in* (starting the warp threads) jobs are all gone now, the victims not of competition from China but of technological progress and mechanization."[11] China is not to be blamed for job losses due to the increased mechanization. "While production, revenues, and exports are growing, employment is shrinking because of rapid advances in technology and labor productivity. In short, textile jobs are not going to China, textile jobs are just going, period."[12] The increased development of machines has led to job losses. So rather than embrace technological advances perhaps the average worker should fight against.

> The first jenny contained eight spindles, immediately multiplying by eight the yarn that could be produced by a single worker. . . . By 1832, the price of cotton yarn in Britain had fallen to one-twentieth the price it had sold for in the 1780s. The race to the bottom had begun.[13]

The Luddites may have sensed to impending doom, but not to the extent possible in modern times.

> Early cotton mill workers were pushed into the mills not by preference but by desperation and a lack of alternatives. Little skill was required for most jobs in the textile factories, so many workers were children from the 'poorhouses' who were sent by the parishes to earn their keep. Work in the cotton mills meant that children could be economically self-sufficient from the age of five.[14]

Not Just Numbers, They Are Men (and Women)

What amplifies the wrongs committed along the supply chain would be the cruel conditions and dehumanizing conditions that workers face. It is an indignity to be subjected to cruel workplaces where one is controlled minutely and without input in the working process. It is the difference between being acted upon and acting within. This is my take on Foucault's model of power and how one can be active in the power-making process. This is the move from the worker as automaton to an autonomous worker with some input about the work. This is a move from dehumanizing towards a more humane workplace. 'Acting within' the system I use to mean that one is part of the system but the system is not controlling you; instead you are a part of it and able to move within it. This difference is important for workers who feel silenced in the workplace as though their voices do not matter and only the voice of the employer gets heard. Workers' rights is about better working conditions, hourly wages, and benefits, but it is also about being treated in a more civilized manner where one's humanity is recognized. Only through all of these parts working together will a true version of workers' rights emerge—one where workers are not viewed as mere tools, but within and of the system itself.

Notes

1 Russell Cropanzano, Deborah E Rupp, and Marshall Schminke, "Three Roads to Organizational Justice" at 5.
2 Russell Cropanzano, Deborah E Rupp, and Marshall Schminke, "Three Roads to Organizational Justice" at 8.
3 Russell Cropanzano, Deborah E Rupp, and Marshall Schminke, "Three Roads to Organizational Justice".
4 Whether this assignment of power is fair or just is another topic.
5 Russell Cropanzano, Deborah E Rupp, and Marshall Schminke, "Three Roads to Organizational Justice" at 18.
6 Russell Cropanzano, Deborah E Rupp, and Marshall Schminke, "Three Roads to Organizational Justice" at 21.
7 Russell Cropanzano, Deborah E Rupp, and Marshall Schminke, "Three Roads to Organizational Justice" at 22.
8 Russell Cropanzano, Deborah E Rupp, and Marshall Schminke, "Three Roads to Organizational Justice" at 54.
9 *Health Services and Support—Facilities Subsector Bargaining Association v British Columbia* [2007] SCJ No 27; 2007 SCC 27; [2007] 2 SCR 391 at para 19: "We conclude that s. 2(*d*) of the *Charter* protects the capacity of members of labour unions to engage, in association, in collective bargaining on fundamental workplace issues. This protection does not cover all aspects of 'collective bargaining', as that term is understood in the statutory labour relations regimes that are in place across the country."
10 Jagdish Bhagwati, *In Defense of Globalization* (New York: Oxford University Press, 2007), 12.
11 Pietra Rivoli, *The Travels of a T-shirt in the Global Economy Second Edition: An Economist Examines the Markets, Power, and Politics of World Trade* (Hoboken: John Wiley & Sons, Inc., 2009), 172.
12 Pietra Rivoli, *The Travels of a T-shirt in the Global Economy Second Edition: An Economist Examines the Markets, Power, and Politics of World Trade* (Hoboken: John Wiley & Sons, Inc., 2009), 173.
13 Pietra Rivoli, *The Travels of a T-shirt in the Global Economy Second Edition: An Economist Examines the Markets, Power, and Politics of World Trade* (Hoboken: John Wiley & Sons, Inc., 2009), 94.
14 Pietra Rivoli, *The Travels of a T-shirt in the Global Economy Second Edition: An Economist Examines the Markets, Power, and Politics of World Trade* (Hoboken: John Wiley & Sons, Inc., 2009), 95.

Bibliography for Chapter 5

Caselaw

Health Services and Support—Facilities Subsector Bargaining Association v British Columbia [2007] SCJ No 27; 2007 SCC 27; [2007] 2 SCR 391.

Books

Bhagwati, Jagdish. *In Defense of Globalization* (New York: Oxford University Press, 2007).
Rivoli, Pietra. *The Travels of a T-shirt in the Global Economy Second Edition: An Economist Examines the Markets, Power, and Politics of World Trade* (Hoboken: John Wiley & Sons, Inc., 2009).

Articles

Cropanzano, Russell, Deborah E. Rupp, and Marshall Schminke. "Three Roads to Organizational Justice" *Human Resources Management*, 20 (2001). Online: <http://researchgate.net/publciation/241700240>.

Index

agency theory 3
AirBnB 15, 53, 60, 61, 62, 65, 69
alienation 13, 15, 27, 120, 121,
    123–124
Andrias, Kate 93
Arthurs, Harry 109

Backer, Larry Cata 83, 105, 128
BCE 4, 83, 85, 87, 102, 146, 147
BC Health Services 43–44, 46, 147
benefit corporation 88, 145
Berle and Means 122–123
Bernard, Elaine 44
Bhagwati, Jagdish 125
board of directors (board) 3
bourgeoisie 120
Bradley, Sarah 84
business ethics 24

Cameron, Jamie 45
Canada Business Corporations Act
    1–2, 99
*Canadian Charter of Rights and
    Freedoms* 42, 43, 44, 45
capitalism 7, 16, 27, 62, 69, 101, 121,
    122, 123, 130, 142, 143
capitalist 16, 62, 120, 121, 143
Cashore, Benjamin 134
CAW 46–51
Clean Clothes Campaign 21, 25, 103
Code(s) of conduct 17, 20, 25, 26,
    46, 82, 83, 86, 99, 100, 101, 102,
    104, 105, 106, 107, 108, 127, 129,
    130, 142
collective agreement(s) 25, 41, 46, 47,
    50, 86, 96, 107, 109, 128, 129
collective bargaining 13, 44, 45, 68
collectivity 126
Compa, Lance 100

compassion fatigue 125, 145
corporate philanthropy 3, 87
Corporate Social Responsibility (CSR)
    4, 20, 21, 24, 51, 85, 88, 97, 100,
    102, 124, 142, 145
corporate veil 1
Cragg, Wes 108
Crane, Andrew 86

Deakin, Simon 107
directors and officers 1, 4, 15, 84,
    99, 103
distancing 124–125, 145
Dodge 3

emotional labour 144
employer free speech 89–93
Employment Standards Act 41
Etherington, Brian 46
ethical consumer 94, 97, 146
ethical consumption 103, 121

Fair Labor Association (FLA) 83, 101,
    129, 133–136
false consciousness 120
fiduciary duties 2, 83, 84, 146
fissured work 55, 56
Flannigan, Robert 2
Foucault 148
framework of fairness 42, 46–51
Frisch, Max xiv
Fudge, Judy 46

Gandhi, Indira 15
gap 21, 128
Garden, Charlotte 68
gig economy 5, 14, 15, 17, 18, 21, 22,
    52, 53, 54, 55, 57, 58, 59, 60, 64,
    65, 66, 68, 69, 110

Gindin, Sam 49
Glasbeek, Harry 28
good corporate citizen 86, 87, 102
Good Samaritan Corporation 87, 88
Guevara, Che 64

Horowitz, Asher 121
Hudson's Bay Company 2, 128
Human Rights Watch 21

independent worker 53, 54, 55, 56, 57,
    58, 59, 61, 66
International Labor Organiation (ILO)
    30, 41, 93–94, 104, 106, 107, 127,
    129, 134
isolation and inequality 5, 13, 17, 18,
    26, 27, 62, 110, 119, 142

Janda, Richard 128
Jenkins, Rhys 94

Labour Relations Act 41
Labour Trilogy 41, 43, 46
Langille, Brian 44
Locke, Richard 25, 104, 128
Luddism 147–148
Lupa, Patrick 3
Lyft 58

Mamic, Ivanka 104
Maquila Solidarity Network 21
Marx, Karl 9, 13, 14, 15, 16, 27,
    110, 119
Marxism 120–123
Marxist 8, 18, 120
Master and Servant Act 1
Matten, Dirk 86
McDonald's 22
McGaughey, Ewan 2, 51
Mechanical Turk 63, 70
Model code of conduct 127–133
monitoring agency 83, 99, 105, 129,
    130, 133–136
Moon, Jeremy 86
Murray, Jill 93, 94

nexus of contracts 1, 3
Nike 20, 21, 23–25, 104, 134

One Big Union 9
Oxfam 25

partnership 3
Peoples 4, 83, 84, 85, 87, 146
Prassl, Jeremias 22, 56, 58

precariat 62
precarious work 17, 18, 53
private regulation 25
pro-friendly 119, 126
proletariat 58, 120, 122

Queen's Code of Conduct 127,
    128, 133

Rana Plaza 13, 17
Red Scare 7, 8
Reitmans 128
Reserve army of labour 16, 143
Richardson, Benjamin 84
Roy, Arundhati 98
Ruggie, John 21, 127
Ryan, Sid 50

Salomon v Salomon 1
sedition 10–11
Sethi, S Prakash 128, 134
shareholder(s) 1, 3, 4, 46, 82, 85, 86,
    88, 97, 99, 100, 102, 103, 124,
    146, 147
sharing economy 53
Smith, Adam 122
stakeholder(s) 4, 16, 52, 84, 88, 89, 95,
    100, 103, 105, 146, 147
Stanford, Jim 48
Starbucks 4, 22
Steinbeck, John xiii
Stewart, Fenner 2
Students Against Sweatshops 20
supply chain(s) 15, 20, 21, 24, 25

Trade Union Act 1
Trudeau, Pierre Elliott 29
Tucker, Eric 50

Uber 14, 15, 18, 22, 26, 52, 53, 56, 57,
    58, 60, 61, 62, 63, 64, 65, 66, 67,
    68, 69, 71, 72, 97, 111, 119, 127,
    142, 143
Unfair labour practice (ULP) 31, 41
Unifor 68, 97, 142; *see also* CAW
    (former name of Unifor)

voice(s) 4, 13, 18, 27, 42, 46, 62, 63,
    86, 94, 98, 102, 106, 119, 121, 124,
    126, 128, 141, 144, 145, 148

wavering work 60, 63–64
Weil, David 55
Winnipeg General Strike 4–13
Witte, John 25

worker(s) 4, 13, 14, 15, 16, 17, 19, 20, 22, 24, 26, 29, 31, 41, 42, 46, 52, 53, 58, 59, 60, 62, 63, 82, 85, 86, 88, 89, 91, 94, 95, 98, 101, 102, 105, 106, 107, 108, 110, 119, 121, 123, 124, 126, 127, 128, 129, 130, 141, 142, 144, 145, 147, 148

worker exhaustion 13
Worker Rights Consortium 21, 83, 129, 133–136
works council 48, 51, 121

zero hour contract 58
Zumbansen, Peer 107

For Product Safety Concerns and Information please contact our EU
representative GPSR@taylorandfrancis.com Taylor & Francis Verlag GmbH,
Kaufingerstraße 24, 80331 München, Germany

Printed and bound by CPI Group (UK) Ltd, Croydon, CR0 4YY
01/05/2025
01858438-0007